The Unholy Three:
Screen Villains and English Gentlemen

The Unholy Three:
Screen Villains and English Gentlemen

by John Hamilton

Midnight Marquee Press, Inc.
Baltimore, Maryland, USA

Copyright © 2009 by John Hamilton
Interior layout and cover design by Susan Svehla
Copy Editing by Bill Littman

Without limiting the rights under copyright reserved above, no part of this publication may be reproduced, stored in or introduced into a retrieval system, or transmitted, in any form, or by any means (electronic, mechanical, photocopying, recording or otherwise), without the prior written permission of the copyright owner or the publishers of the book.

ISBN 13: 978-1-887664-95-0
ISBN 10: 1-887664-95-5
Library of Congress Catalog Card Number 2009932869
Manufactured in the United States of America

First Printing by Midnight Marquee Press, Inc., Oct., 2009

Dedication

This book is a small and wholly inadequate tribute
to my mum and dad.

TABLE OF CONTENTS

Preface by Richard Gordon   8

Acknowledgements   10

Introduction   11

George Coulouris:
Shout at the Devil   14

André Morell:
Flesh and Blood   105

Dennis Price:
The Naked Truth   196

Preface

For anyone of my generation, the title of this book will immediately conjure up images of those three great master villains of the screen, Boris Karloff, Bela Lugosi and Lionel Atwill. They were the awesome stars of the first big wave of horror film classics in the early days of sound. Count Dracula, the Frankenstein Monster and a variety of mad scientists became responsible for frightening us as children and, at the same time, making us fans of screen horror for a lifetime. The protagonists in this book are among their worthy successors and the author has told their stories in fascinating detail.

I had the privilege of knowing both Dennis Price and George Coulouris when they appeared in films of mine, and I enjoyed a brief association with Andre Morell via 'six degrees of separation' when I distributed one of his most disturbing pictures called *The Man and The Snake*. By then they had somewhat exhausted their talents in worthier directions; Coulouris had been a stage star on Broadway as well as appearing in such Hollywood film classics as *Citizen*

Dennis Price, Lisa Danielly and Richard Gordon pose together on the set of *Curse of Voodoo*.

Kane and *Watch on the Rhine* for which he will always be remembered. Dennis Price had come to the end of a long and notable career as a leading man on stage and screen in diverse vehicles ranging from Ivor Novello's *The Dancing Years* and *The Bad Lord Byron*, and the role for which he will perhaps always be remembered, opposite Alec Guinness in *Kind Hearts and Coronets*. Andre Morell had achieved greater importance in innumerable stage classics than in his occasional film roles.

I always favoured casting such distinguished names in my films whenever it was possible, partly because I considered them 'good value for money' and also for the pleasure of meeting them. When Messrs Morell, Price and Courlouris took up residence in the world of horror and science fiction thrillers, they added a considerable touch of class to the genre.

Regrettably I did not make the acquaintance of Andre Morell in person although I saw him often on the stage and screen but Dennis Price had personality and charm to spare, even when his career was slipping, and I have not forgotten the pleasure of those times or his gratitude to me. I first encountered George Coulouris when he played a gangster in a film I was co-producing but really did not get to know him properly until he made a cameo appearance in *Tower of Evil*, and he regaled me in between takes with fascinating stories of his New York and Hollywood career, particularly when he was a member of the Mercury Theatre Company that was formed by Orson Welles and John Houseman.

This book has brought it all back to me for which I am grateful. You are about to enter that world of bygone days briefly in the pages of John Hamilton's superlative book.
—Richard Gordon
August 2008

Acknowledgements

I am particularly grateful to the Coulouris family— Elizabeth, George and Mary Louise— and to Jason Morell for sharing their time and enthusiasm for this project.

I'd also like to thank the friends and colleagues of Messrs Price, Coulouris and Morell who were only too pleased to share their memories; sadly too many have passed on since the start of this journey but their contribution made my work possible: Michael Armstrong, Robin Askwith, Hazel Court, Vera Day, Brian Dean, Julie Ege, Freddie Francis, Robert Fuest, Jess Franco, Liz Frazer, Tudor Gates, Renee Glynne, John Hough, David Jackson, Euan Lloyd, Christopher Neame, Kate O'Mara, Jimmy Sangster, Peter Graham Scott, Madeline Smith, Damien Thomas, Brook Williams and the much missed Tony Tenser.

Also my thanks to Alison— for all her unflinching support, scepticism and belief.

Finally it goes without saying I am deeply indebted to Richard Gordon; my appreciation is matched only by my admiration.

Introduction

By way of introduction let me pose three trivia questions. Which British actor at the height of his fame was receiving more fan mail than Humphrey Bogart and went on to play Dracula, Frankenstein and Van Helsing? Name the actor whose films earned Oscar nominations for Best Film three years in a row in the Forties and then in the Fifties repeated the feat with three successive British Academy Award nominations? Which actor can claim to have worked with Alfred Hitchcock, David Lean, Stanley Kubrick and John Gilling? By the time you finish this book you will find out the answers to these questions and by reading about the careers and lives of Dennis Price, George Coulouris and Andre Morell, I hope you will learn a lot more besides.

One question you probably won't get a definitive answer on is what Dennis Price, George Coulouris and Andre Morell have in common—partly because I don't know myself. There is some superficial common ground, all three made films for Hammer for example but interestingly none of them appeared in the studio's 'classic' monster movies. All three could be classed as British actors but then Coulouris was not often given the opportunity to play a Brit, something which irked the actor greatly. Dennis Price on the other hand seldom played anything but Englishman—even when cast as a foreigner there was always a decidedly English quality about him. In the case of Andre Morell, he switched easily from swarthy foreigners to English gentlemen. All three appeared in the stage as well as the screen. Dennis Price was an accomplished film actor who worked on stage reluctantly and then seldom strayed beyond his well-observed public persona. George Coulouris always thought himself a theatre actor and, although he gave some remarkable performances on screen, was never really happy

there, he accepted it as a necessary evil. Andre Morell by contrast was adept at both disciplines, as well as television and moved easily and successfully between them throughout his career.

All three appeared in huge movies both in their native Britain and in Hollywood, titles like *Kind Hearts and Coronets*, *Citizen Kane* and *The Bridge on the River Kwai* are regarded amongst the finest films ever made. And of course all three made low-budget films, mainly in Britain but in the case of Price and Coulouris the odd — sometimes very odd — venture to the twilight world of European exploitation and horror. You generally will not find titles like *Vampiros lesbos* or *L'anticristo* appearing in the critics' Top Ten Lists. Andre Morell was less inclined to travel as he slipped through middle age and was spared that particular treat; instead he turned out largely lamentable British 'B's, *The Vengeance of She* springs to mind.

If you dig deeper there are more threads loosely connecting the trio; Morell and Price appeared in the same television show; Coulouris and Price appeared in the same film; Price's most famous co-star was Morell's wife Joan Greenwood...and so it goes on. But even the most obvious connection is pretty tenuous; they all worked with the director Terence Fisher; Price in the science fiction thriller *The Earth Dies Screaming* and Coulouris in *Mask of Dust* and *Kill Me Tomorrow* and Morell most famously in *The Hound of the Baskervilles*.

The three men do have at least one other thing in common and it is one reason they have been assembled here; they all essayed very different but quite remarkable screen villains.

Dennis Price flitted easily from the elegant and witty charm of mass murderer Louis Mazzini in *Kind Hearts and Coronets*, to the cold-blooded psychotic, Hardwick in *Holiday Camp*. After a brief career as a leading man, he specialized in English gentlemen on the make, con men and ne'er do wells in films like *Privates Progress* and *I'm Alright Jack*. His roles were usually played for laughs, although black-hearted villainy was never far from the surface in films such as *The Earth Dies Screaming* where, stripped of his usual mannerisms and quips, Price presents a truly dangerous foe, self-serving, ruthless and a far more complex character than the film otherwise deserves.

George Coulouris created the archetype for duplicitous Nazis such as Teck de Brancovis in *Watch on the Rhine*; a role so successful it became his calling card in Hollywood for many years. But Coulouris was much more than a one trick pony and he showed there were many shades of grey to his villainy. In *None But the Lonely Heart* he essayed thuggish brutality in the East End of London; then in *California* he was the racist megalomaniac Capt. Pharaoh Coffin. In *The Womaneater*, easily one of his most entertaining screen creations, he gave us sweaty dementia with Dr. James Moran, the maddest of mad professors.

Andre Morell created one of televisions most calculating and chilling heavies with O'Brien in the seminal *1984*, the scenes where he tortured Peter Cushing were so horrifying it provoked censure from the British Government and outcry in the national press. Morell, bemused by the reaction, repeated the formula on the big screen with *Cash on Demand*, adding a roguish charm to his portrayal of Hepburn, a bank robber heaping mental anguish on Cushing's hapless bank manager. Morell showed another brand of murderous villainy as Walter Venable in John Gilling's taut thriller *Shadow of the Cat,* showing no remorse as he plots and schemes his way to a hidden fortune.

There was much more to all three men that their screen villains of course and over the course of long careers, in large and small roles, lavish and modest budgets, they offered comedy, musicals, drama and tragedy. Whatever they appeared in, whatever the quality of the material they were given, they were never less than watchable and that truly is the main thing they have in common. They belonged to a generation that is now gone, a generation that loved to shudder at their carefully chosen words, that cowered or hissed when they appeared; and the screen is a poorer place with their passing.

George Coulouris between scenes with Marguerite Chapman during the filming of *Mr. District Attorney*.

George Coulouris: Shout at the Devil

At the turn of the last century the industrial heartland of England was more famous for its shipping canals than its culture, and the urban sprawls of Liverpool and Manchester were more likely to spawn tradesmen than actors. It wasn't all "dark satanic mills," however, and Salford, on the outskirts of Manchester, can lay claim to at least one bona fide Hollywood star. His reputation stretches from California via Broadway all the way to Hammer's Bray studios on the banks of the Thames. George Coulouris is perhaps best known as a leading player in Orson Welles' legendary Mercury Players, but he is also recognized as one of the most distinctive actors to grace the stages of London and Broadway. Always thinking of himself as a "theatre actor," Coulouris would have hated to be remembered as a screen star but in the mid-1940s he was seen regularly supporting the likes of Ingrid Bergman, Cary Grant and Bette Davis. In just a few short years he managed to carve a lucrative niche as Hollywood's most intelligent and physically threatening villain.

Turning his back on Hollywood, Coulouris chose to spend the remainder of his screen career working in low-budget British B pictures. During the evenings he trod the boards to full houses as he reveled in the works of Shakespeare, Ibsen and Shaw. His days were spent on the soundstages of *The Woman Eater* or *Bluebeard's Ten Honeymoons*. Although he was dismissive of cinema in general and fantasy movies in particular, Coulouris was never less than professional and committed about his work, even when the role or film barely merited the effort. His reputation as a screen actor rests on one film—*Citizen Kane*—but many a poor movie has been saved from obscurity by his presence. George Coulouris may just have been one of the finest and most formidable screen heavies of the 20th century.

Though he wasn't always comfortable with the fact, George Alexander Coulouris came from proud and independent Greek stock; his father Nicholas Koulouris had been born into grinding poverty close to Sparta in 1873. He would frequently invoke this heritage as his inspiration to climb the social ladder, one rung at a time. The memory of his early struggle had a profound effect on Nicholas; he was a hard and uncompromising man and would not tolerate weakness in himself or in his family. His son would later describe him as a "gutsy little Greek who was not satisfied to starve in a little mountain village." As a young man Nicholas watched the tramp steamers heading to the ports of England and America and when the opportunity came for a one way passage to Liverpool he climbed aboard.

If the streets weren't exactly paved with gold they did at least offer almost limitless possibilities to someone like Nicholas Koulouris. At the end of the 19th century, Liverpool was at the hub of the sprawling British Empire and its seven-and-a-half miles of docks would serve passenger liners and merchant ships from the most exotic and obscure ports in the world. Although he spoke only a smattering of English, Nicholas found work as a manual laborer toiling long hours for low pay. This job allowed him the opportunity to study not only the language, but the character of his adopted countrymen. Nicholas' seemingly inexhaustible energy and his hunger to learn and seek out new opportunities would soon lead him out of the docks. However, throughout his life the memories of those early lean years would haunt him.

Around the same time, a young lady called Abigail Redfern, nine years older than Nicholas, was working as a maid in a large manor house in Lancashire for the princely sum of £12 per year. Abigail came from a respectable but working class English family living in Sutton in the North of England; she was the middle of three children born to William and Louisa. In the days of limited employment options for women, domestic service was considered an acceptable career and Abigail counted herself lucky to have escaped factory work. She would in time leave in search of a more rewarding position but by then Abigail had learned the practical side of serving demanding customers and keeping a tidy house and, perhaps most significant of all, Abigail had learned the value of being seen and not heard. Abigail and Nicholas' paths crossed in the seaside resort of Blackpool, a few miles north of Liverpool on the Irish Sea. By then Nicholas' indomitable spirit had taken him out of the docks in the unexpected direction of the plush Palatine Hotel where he talked his way into a job in the kitchens. Despite a lack of formal catering experience, Nicholas impressed his new employers as much with his charm as his skill in the kitchen and he was offered the job of head chef. Soon afterwards Abigail started at the Palatine as a chambermaid, by which time Nicholas' reputation as a chef was the talk of the resort.

How or when the couple met hasn't been recorded but Nicholas was considered something of a catch in the town and the two soon embarked on a romance that would lead to marriage. Despite his success, Nicholas was tired of working for others; he and Abigail took their savings and went into business for themselves with their own café, the King's Restaurant, close to the same docks where he started out. The signs outside read, "oxtail soup for 2d" and "homemade steak pudding for 6d" and the cafe soon became popular with both the dock workers as well as casual passersby. As his own lord and master Nicholas was in his element and the café gave him the chance to use his opportunistic nature; once during a dock strike he contracted to supply meals for the 300 extra police officers who had been drafted in, and while the policemen were filing through the front door to collect their steak puddings, the strikers were at the back door collecting soup from a huge galvanized bath tub!

The couple's only child George, named after one of Nicholas' brothers, was born on the 1st of October 1903 when the family was still living in a relatively modest house in Hulton Street in Salford. By then Nicholas had outgrown the restaurant business and had branched out into salvage. He realized quickly that the endless flow of ships in and out of the docks represented massive potential for those who could see the value in discarded metal, abandoned equipment and assorted debris. Nicholas would strike up a conversation with ship's captains from all over the Mediterranean, particularly the Greeks who were only too pleased to hear a friendly voice, share a glass of ouzo—and of course come to some mutually beneficial arrangement! Leaving Abigail to run the restaurant, Nicholas bought anything that was for sale whether he had a market for it or not. George, just a child at the time, later recorded:

> Dad started buying things without waiting to see how things were. He bought a thousand pounds worth of assorted screws. I spent a long day repackaging them from their rust-stained paper containers into new packages.

Of course the family was expected to pitch in and even George was put to work, "scrubbing rusty corned beef tins till they were shiny enough to pass the food inspector." Expanding his horizons further, Nicholas negotiated the purchase of a consignment of hawsers, the thick mooring ropes which after constant use would fray and unravel and would end up thrown into the sea. George was given the task of unthreading them into hemp which could be sold to local papermakers—quite literally money for old rope! George hated being cheap labor for his father, in particular "hanging up strands of hemp which seemed abominable and looked like the hair of long drowned blondes." The hawsers contract was enough for Nicholas to set up "Nicholas Coulouris General Merchants" and open a small yard a few hundred yards from the restaurant.

The outbreak of the Great War in 1914 presented Nicholas with the opportunity of a lifetime. With the merchant fleets of Britain and her allies being ravaged by the Kaiser's U-boats, all manner of damaged, soiled or simply abandoned merchandise found its way to the ramshackle yard to be refurbished, reupholstered and re-used. Young George marveled at his father's industry:

> Selling cuttlefish, olive oil, painter's dustsheets, Hessians, textiles, everything that took dad's fancy at the damaged goods sales he haunted every few weeks and could see a profit to be turned from. One time he got a bargain of four barge loads of coal. The demurrage of 80 pounds sterling a day ran away with the profit but he took a gamble because he thought he knew where he could sell it within a couple of days. And he did.

Nicholas reveled in his new found status as a successful business man and moved his family out of Hulton Street into the far more desirable New Park Road, still in Salford. For Nicholas success was important for its own sake but for his son it was just as important to be seen to be successful. The family's growing affluence did not make George the same as the other boys, despite his efforts he remained at the most impressionable age, an outsider. "I was called a dirty dago," he wrote, "a greasy Greek and asked why I didn't go back home where I came from." By the end of the war the family was considered well off, middle class even, and George had moved to the impressive Manchester Grammar school but the taunting continued. Childhood evoked few if any happy memories for the boy:

> I played happily together with a set of semi-hooligans who all looked down on me as a greasy Greek, suffering cruel jokes such as a tub of water being poured over me because they'd realized I was wearing a new suit. I put up with it for the sake of companionship...

It wasn't just his Mediterranean complexion that was getting George noticed; the boy was developing a powerful physique, a large chest and broad shoulders and muscular arms. In later years commentators would suggest he could have been a boxer or a wrestler but whatever the appearance given by his size George's tastes were more refined. He cultivated a passion for that most gentlemanly of sports, cricket, an obsession that would last his whole life. Away from the sports fields George was discovering the versatility of his voice and a natural gift for mimicry; his impersonations of the celebrated Shakespearean actor Sir Frank Benson reduced his class mates to fits of giggles which in turn encouraged the boy to show off shamelessly for their entertainment:

> Everybody thought it was marvelous, and one time when the master asked the boys, what are you going to be? When it was my turn the other boys yelled out: "an actor, an actor!" And that sort of made me feel good and I thought, well probably I should be an actor if they feel as enthusiastically as that about it. But it was a very strange ambition in my environment at the time.

As the "strange ambition" took root, George began to find out more and more about acting and that in turn developed into a deep love of the stage:

> By the time I left my very good English grammar school I was deeply and romantically attached to England culturally

> and spiritually. I learnt the greatness of Shakespeare. His verse drove me wild, so much so that I pranced around the streets of Manchester howling out parts of *Othello*, to shut up abruptly when I felt someone had noticed something about the innocent-looking young man who just passed by.

Nicholas' business acumen didn't extend to forward planning; he failed to make provision for the post-war slump and the recession of 1920 almost wiped him out. To make matters worse he had fallen for the flattery of another Greek businessman who convinced him there was a fortune to be made importing leather goods from Spain. Nicholas provided the capital to set up the business, only to have his partner abscond back to Greece with the goods and the money. Enraged, Nicholas would spend the next few years scouring the Mediterranean looking for revenge and/or compensation. Up until then it was taken for granted that George would follow in his father's footsteps into business but while Nicholas was away the boy discovered the delights of music, particularly Schubert, Schumann and Brahms. George, who had a fine voice, practiced to recordings of the Russian Feodor Ivanovich Chaliapin, then a huge draw in the opera houses of Europe and America. Pursuing his fascination with the stage George poured over biographies of the great 19th century actors Edmund Kean and Henry Irving with their classic portrayals of Shakespeare's tragic figures Shylock, Lear, Othello and Macbeth.

By the time Nicholas returned to take his place as head of the household it was clear that George had no inclination to learn the family trade. Nicholas was having none of it and in 1923 he started the serious work of indoctrinating his son into the world of commerce. Nicholas had opened a shop in Greece hoping it would restore his fortunes and stocked it with quality textiles and other goods from England. Despite his protests George was dispatched to the "old country" to work in the new venture. Far from a spiritual home, George saw Greece as a foreign country; he didn't understand the language or the people and once again considered himself an outsider. Mixing with Greek boys of his own age George was made aware for the first time just how inhibited his life in Salford had been:

> They didn't realize how completely messed up I was because of my upbringing in puritanical England. On one hand we had it drummed into us that masturbation inevitably led to insanity; on the other that sex led to VD, insanity and death. We choose the lesser evil and masturbated only. I kept finding little notes I'd left myself cursing myself for doing it again and swearing never to do it any more.

George always maintained he had little in common with his father and throughout his writings there is no sense of affection; he describes Nicholas' temper and intolerance and even when he talks about his father's generosity he makes it clear that he despises his lack of culture and sees him as an opportunist and a cultural philistine. The two men also had marked differences in their attitudes to sex, highlighted when George recalled an early attempt to visit a local brothel:

> When I asked my father for half a crown spending money, he cross-examined me. I blushed violently and gave the game away. Later on, in London after spending the day with him doing business, I asked for a pound—same rigmarole before he handed the money over. I spent the night with a plump prostitute in Clapham somewhere without anything really happening.

At the time George was only too aware of his father's philandering, which was an open secret on the streets of Salford. He was also aware of the affect it had on his mother who had to endure the gossiping and snide remarks from neighbors, as well as the sympathy of well-intentioned friends. When writing over 50 years later the bitterness was still very much in evidence:

> In the eyes of Salford, my father was a criminal because of his sexual behavior, chasing women openly, being seen in the street with them and so on. He left behind him a string of illegitimate children. After his death, the grandfather of one of his offspring wrote to me a pathetic letter asking me to take care of his granddaughter "as a gentleman." I ignored it.

Predictably there was never any possibility of Nicholas supporting George's ambitions on the stage. Returning to England, the boy found the courage to face down his father but the reaction was as expected:

> He started pacing up and down till he almost wore out the carpet. "We spend a fortune on his education (not true, the fees were very low), send him to the Grammar School for six years and now he wants to be an actra, an actra!" As an alternative, I suggested journalism which meant going to university—same rigmarole about the cost of education plus. "Now the bloody bishop wants to waste four years at university...what then? How are you going to earn a living, from journalism?" The case for journalism was closed.

The long-suffering Abigail, on the other hand, was quietly ambitious for her son and quite taken with the idea of George being a famous actor. Throughout her married life she played the role of loyal and supportive wife and perhaps this was her own subtle rebellion. Secretly she started to save a little money from her housekeeping each week and when George could stand the frustration no more and resolved to run away, she volunteered to send what she could to help support him. Leaving a note that simply said, "You force me to go to London to try and become an actor because you wouldn't hear of it," George Coulouris set out to face the world.

Arriving in London with high expectations George met his first disappointment when the YMCA was full and he was forced to expend his meager finances renting a room. From there things got worse; the tedious chore of writing to theatre managers, actors and directors produced nothing of value except an offer as a stagehand/understudy for a third-rate company but George was too proud to accept their 30 shillings per week. When he did get a chance to audition, the youngster would launch into a full-blooded recital of Anthony's oration from Shakespeare's *Julius Caesar*: "oh, pardon me thou bleeding piece of earth that I am meek and gentle with these butchers." It wasn't until he met Robert Atkins at the famous Old Vic theatre that Coulouris learned he was practically unemployable. Realizing that there was no room for diplomacy in art, Atkins told George that his thick Northern accent and rapid-fire delivery made the Bard incomprehensible. There was no place, Atkins cautioned, for Coulouris on the English stage—not with that voice! A dejected Coulouris wrote to Sybil Thorndyke, who was in the middle of her celebrated run as Saint Joan, a part created for her by George Bernard Shaw. In full body armor, the formidable Ms. Thorndyke received George in her dressing room and advised a scholarship at the Central School of Speech and Drama. Unfortunately the auditions for the next term were months away and with no prospect of acting work Coulouris took the only job available.

Sybil Thorndyke as St. Joan

Using nothing but charm—perhaps he had more in common with his father than he thought—he landed a job as a waiter on the *Majestic*, the world's largest passenger liner and the pride of the North Atlantic route. For the next two and half weeks he spent his days scrubbing the floors and the evenings at the mercy of the tyrannical maitre d' and the beck and call of the first class passengers. At least it got him to New York, an experience he would never forget:

> I had seen Fritz Lang's *Metropolis* in London and here I was in it; the shabby streets, the woebegone passers-by, the rectangular charm-less intersection of 42nd Street and Sixth Avenue and the El thundering over my head. I felt absolutely alien. The aridity repelled me. To me New York was like a dream...I paid what I thought was a high price for a movie ticket, to see Douglas Fairbanks in *The Thief of Baghdad*—something to boast about back in London when it would turn up some time later.

Coulouris' career as a waiter was over almost as soon as it began; inexperience shone through and arriving back in Southampton he was summarily sacked. Left again without an income he took a job with the Berlitz language school as an English teacher in their agency at Lucerne in Switzerland. It was a pleasant enough assignment for Coulouris, and the young girls at Berlitz were so taken with his baritone voice and hearty renditions of the "Volga Boat Song" that they convinced him he should head for Italy and pursue a career as an opera singer. That turned out to be a short-lived pipe dream; singing lessons in Milan convinced him of its futility and he returned to London more determined than ever to succeed as an actor.

Coulouris struck it lucky for once and won a scholarship to the Elsie Fogerty School of Speech and Drama, one of the better regarded London stage schools, boasting Laurence Olivier amongst its previous graduates. Predictably Coulouris was frustrated by the endless exercises in enunciation and technique; he wanted to start proper acting, not "practice" emotions. Coulouris also disliked the smug superiority of his fellow pupils, all from well-to-do homes in the south of England. Once again he felt like an interloper, excluded by the middle class etiquette of his tutors and peers. After a year he felt he had learned everything he needed to know about the mechanics of stage acting and more importantly, he had smoothed out those tortured vowels that had so offended Robert Atkins.

By now Nicholas recognized that George was as stubborn as he was and grudgingly offered financial help—at least until the boy saw the error of his ways—but it wasn't the reconciliation it could have been. In 1926 Abigail died, effectively ending any emotional ties George might have had with Salford. George returned to the North East to attend the funeral and stayed only to make his professional debut at the Rusham Repertory playing a clergyman in *Outward Bound*. The failure of the play didn't dampen the debutante's enthusiasm; if anything it sped his return to London where the West End beckoned. Coulouris accepted the role of a stretcher bearer in the Royal Shakespeare Company's production of *Richard III*, staying on to play minor roles in *Macbeth* and *The Tempest*. Frustrated by the low salary he demanded an increase only to be told if he felt that strongly he should ply his trade elsewhere—which he promptly did!

Coulouris shrugged off this disappointment by appearing opposite Ivor Novello, the hottest star on the London stage, in *Sirocco* written by no less a luminary than Noel Coward. The latter's fortunes had dipped in recent months but the actor-director-songwriter, following his success with *The Vortex* and *Hay Fever*, was still regarded as the toast of sophisticated society. The impresario's relationship with the press was never an easy one and they were desperate to see him fall on his face. In the lead-up to the opening night, the newspapers worked their readers into something of a lather by suggesting that *Sirocco*, the most sedate of farces, was a "sordid tale of free love amongst the upper classes."

Noel Coward

Director and producer Basil Dean went into the opening night unaware or unconcerned that the audience's expectations and reality were on wildly diverging paths. Coulouris later wrote:

> The first night was a catastrophe. I was dressed as an Italian woman in a festival scene, naked to the waist with all kinds of beads all over my chest. And at the curtain I was standing next to Coward and the people were howling for his blood because he had just attacked the Church of England in *Home Chat* or something, I don't know. And Coward, with absolute aplomb, bent down, picked up the bead, bowed low to me and handed it to me while the populace were howling for his blood.

The vitriolic abuse that greeted the cast on the opening night of December 17, 1927, continued as the play staggered through a mere 28 performances be-

Noel Coward Play Tosses Wrench Into British Calm

By MILTON BRONNER
NEA Service Writer

London, Dec. 16—It used to be said that it was only Paris which got excited over the drama, so much so that often the police and the troops have to be called out to curb the too ebullient emotions of the crowd. But sober, staid, phlegmatic old London the other day gave a singular exhibition which shows that the Briton is not as calm and unemotional as he loves to picture himself.

Noel Coward's new play "Sirocco" was produced at Daly's, which for years had been the home of musical comedy. The gallery and part of the pit kept up a disturbance all during the performance. They giggled in the wrong places. They made audible comments. And when the thing was over, they booed loud and long.

The next day most of the so-called dramatic critics imitated the gallery and pit. They sneered. They giggled. They booed.

Take Vengeance

It was as if, being sore at themselves, they took it out of the hide of the dramatist. For when Coward first presented plays, they had slopped over. Some of them had called the young man a genius.

Having gone the limit in superlatives, they then had that morning-after feeling when "Sirocco" was produced and went to the other extreme. The man they once praised to the skies, they now damned. Because in some of his lighter plays he had displayed a certain wit and epigrammatic talent, they now denounced this new play for lack of it.

They were not discriminating enough to see that basically "Sirocco" was a serious play on a serious theme and that cheap wit and epigram would have been out of place. Several of these so-called critics wrote with a spite that was fiendish.

Only two writers on the drama—St. John Ervine and Gordon Beckles—seemed to have kept their heads and their sense of proportion. If they did not burst into superlatives, neither did they sink to vituperation. They gave a sane appraisal of the play. The truth is, of course, that Coward is not a genius; never has been. He is simply a very competent purveyor of an evening's amusement. And he is so young—only 25—that he is still growing and may go very far. "Sirocco" is a sign of growing pains.

Then the Applause

And here is an ironic comment on what weight the critics have and also a display of the British sense of fair play:

On Thursday night a considerable part of the gallery and pit booed the play.

On Friday morning most of the critics wrought themselves up into a display of bad temper and bad manners.

On Saturday night a crowded house saw the play, and gallery, pit and stalls united in quite general applause.

It's not the first time that most of the British press has given such a deplorable exhibition. When our famous film "The Big Parade" was shown in London practically every British film critic exhausted his ink-pot writing vituperative stuff. But the film went on and on, being shown to packed houses. The British public has learned to take its critics with a ton of salt.

fore it was put out of its misery. Despite his *sang froid* on the night, the stress was too much for Coward who had a nervous breakdown soon after. Wisely perhaps, Coulouris hid low and moved out of London into rep at the Cambridge Festival Theatre where he played Yank in Eugene O'Neill's *The Hairy Ape* and Mercutio in *Romeo and Juliet*. Professionally it was his first taste of success, with audiences and critics at last showing appreciation of his craft. On a personal level it was to change his life.

Louise Franklin, a Philadelphia-born art student, had been engaged by the company to paint scenery and play the odd bit part; this came at the end of her tour of Europe and she was already planning her return to the U.S. George and Louise hit it off immediately and she convinced him that all you needed to succeed in America was talent and ambition. Coulouris believed he had both in abundance and, despondent at what he saw as the moribund and class-ridden state of theatre in England, set out across the Atlantic.

In 1929 George and Louise arrived in New York and the actor immediately launched into the tried and trusted pattern he had established in London. With less than $250 Coulouris moved into the YMCA and began to bombard agents and managers with letters exaggerating his experience in the West End and Oxford. Coulouris found himself handicapped by the American Actors Association, which, deeply jealous of its English equivalent, had ruled that English actors had to remain idle for six months following every role regardless of its longevity. For someone in Coulouris' precarious financial position this could be ruinous and he was forced into seeking out non-union companies. One such offer came from a manager in Boston who offered him a role in *The Novice and the Duke*, an un-credited version of Shakespeare's *Measure for Measure*. The whole production seemed so slapdash that Coulouris wrote to the Actors Association about it; the grateful union—negating the English actor rule—then offered him membership!

By the time George and Louise were married in 1930, the American dream had become somewhat tarnished. By playing small roles Coulouris managed to keep the wolf from the door and assemble a small pot of savings but it was hardly the success he had expected. Once again Coulouris' restless ambition clicked in and he decided to return to London for one last attempt to conquer the West End stage. It was a depressing experience for the young couple; London proved an unwelcoming place and Coulouris' Broadway experience cut no ice with the superior attitude of the theatre managers. Even while staying with friends and scrimping on all but necessities, they watched their money dwindle and after a year of frustration and disappointment, they cashed in their remaining savings and bought two one-way steerage tickets to New York.

Soon after returning to the East Coast, Coulouris talked his way into a job at the Stockbridge Theatre, again exaggerating his still limited experience. In addition to a number of roles in their forthcoming season, Coulouris was engaged to pass on his wisdom to the theatre's students. Amongst the young hopefuls was Katherine Hepburn, already displaying the headstrong nature that would make her a legend on the stage and screen. Coulouris' association with the actress got off to a bad start when he suggested that she had only "negligible talent" but could be a fine actress if she was "prepared to work at it." The outspoken redhead retorted, "I'll never come back to this theatre unless there's a star on my dressing room door!" The relationship recovered enough for Coulouris to engage in some playful teasing. "I sent her squealing to her room," he remembered, "by turning off the lights, hunching up my shoulders and holding a red electric torch under my hideously distorted face." They did meet again in London many years later when Hepburn was appearing at the Playhouse. Coulouris called backstage but she had only the vaguest memory of their earlier encounter.

A few minor parts followed on Broadway but it wasn't until he played Tallent in the comedy of manners *The Late Christopher Bean* that he made a significant impact with a run of over 200 performances in 1932 and 1933. MGM was impressed enough to pick up the rights and, engaging Sam Wood to adapt the play for the screen, summoned Coulouris to California to recreate his role in what was now called *Christopher Bean*. The studio insisted on star names and hired Lionel Barrymore and Marie Dressler to supplement the Broadway talent which also included Beulah Bondi. The money was good; Coulouris could earn as much in a few weeks in Hollywood as he did during an extended run in New York but it wasn't a wholly pleasurable experience for the actor:

> It was very early, 1932, the beginning of the talkies. They had no idea how to do talkies because it was as new to them as it was to us going there. I was quite sort of overcome by the responsibility of being in a big studio and feeling all this overhead was going on all the time—it was rather frightening.

Wood was one of those rare directors who managed to match quantity with quality and he would go on to direct four Oscar-nominated movies. From the start of shooting he was keen to recreate the spirit of the original production and use his Broadway actors to show the way:

> One day Bondi, who had been advising them as to the way it was done on the stage, wasn't there, so the director sent for me early in the morning. He said would you come over and do me a favor. I want you to tell Lionel Barrymore and Marie Dressler where the laughs came and how this scene was played in the theatre. And I felt this was a terrible ordeal, to go to these people who had been working for 40 years and become

world famous and I was a relative beginner, to have to tell them what to do in a scene. But they were very nice about it and it passed off very well.

Christopher Bean wasn't a box-office success and Coulouris found the laborious process of constructing a film totally uninspiring; it would be seven years before he was lured before the cameras again. Returning to New York, he enjoyed runs in *Saint Joan* and as Lord Darnley opposite Helen Hayes in *Mary of Scotland*. Then in October 1936 he opened at the St James Theatre in the anti-war play *Ten Million Ghosts* written and directed by Sidney Kingsley, then a prominent member of the Group Theatre, a collection of leftist intellectuals including Elia Kazan and Lee J. Cobb. In the 1930s socialism (or communism) had a fashionable aura for the East Coast intelligentsia who saw it as the only real counter to fascism. Coulouris, who was never a member of the Group Theatre, nevertheless enjoyed the company of many of its prominent figures and would remain in close contact with them over the next decade.

> ### 'SAINT JOAN' TO OPEN LAST WEEK OF RUN
>
> Katharine Cornell will begin the last week of her San Francisco engagement in Bernard Shaw's "Saint Joan" at the Curran tonight, with Arthur Byron, Maurice Evans, Charles Waldron, Eduardo Ciannelli and George Coulouris in the leading roles. There will be matinees on Wednesday, Friday and Saturday, Miss Cornell ending her visit here with the Saturday matinee. Playgoers have been urged to note that the curtain rises at 8:15 o'clock sharp at night and 2:15 o'clock sharp at the matinee. No one is seated during the first scene, which lasts 18 minutes.
>
> Joan is the fourth Shavian role Miss Cornell has acted. When she was in boarding school she played Napoleon in Shaw's "The Man of Destiny," and in her stock days she was seen as Dora in "Fanny's First Play."
>
> San Francisco saw her in "Candida" three years ago. Shaw has asked her to act "Candida," "Heartbreak House" and "Saint Joan" in London, and some day she may play the first and last of these plays there.

During rehearsals for *Ten Million Ghosts*, Coulouris, who had only a minor part, shared a dressing room with a 22-year-old actor who was even further down the bill: Orson Welles. Having carved a reputation as an *enfant terrible* with a much publicized all black version of *Macbeth*, Welles was simply slumming to pay the bills until he could establish his own company. Welles may have electrified the critics but Coulouris wasn't overawed and he remembered challenging the younger man's pretensions:

> Why did you just do this *Macbeth* with an all-colored cast? Just to be different, wasn't it? And what about the time *Macbeth* got ill, in Indianapolis, and you had to rush there and black up all over to play a Scotsman—didn't you feel rather silly?

NO SUPERABUNDANCE OF COMPETENT YOUNG ACTORS ON BROADWAY JUST NOW

Writer Asserts That Unknown Actor Who Really Impressed Last Season Was Orson Welles

BY MARK BARRON

New York, July 24.—While this is not an invitation for an avalanche of would-be young actors and actresses to storm Broadway, a check-up at this interlude before the new season reveals there isn't an overabundance of promising new actors and actresses to take the leading roles of new plays.

Last season the theatre discovered only about a dozen new players of star or semi-star calibre, while there was a time when four or five dozen unknown players would bob up with a definite bid for stardom.

The unknown actor who really impressed was Orson Welles, a youth of 22 who, at first glance, is a bit stout and considerably unromantic. But the lad knows how to act. In the WPA production of "Dr. Faustus" he attracted cheers, a triumph he won after playing a very indifferent juvenile in "Ten Million Ghosts" earlier in the season. Previously he had played bits in a couple of Katharine Cornell shows.

Welles' success is encouraging to actors unsuited to romantic roles. It also suggests to managers that it is possible to give character leads to the younger actors, which not only varies the dramatic fare, but perhaps would protect these same managers from the raids of Hollywood. Yet for all his failure to conform to the Robert Taylor requirements of the films, Welles is eagerly sought by the west coast. It is his present plan, however, to remain on Broadway, probably as the youngest of the actor-managers.

The Mohammedans believe that to be fat is to be beautiful.

Kingsley's play lasted only 11 performances which left Welles free to join John Houseman at the old Comedy Theatre, now vacant, and transform it into the base for their newly launched Mercury Theatre company. With a predilection for Shakespeare in particular and British theatre in general, Welles, taken with Coulouris' experience and knowledge, offered him $40 per week and a choice of roles in the first production of the inaugural season, *Julius Caesar*. As well as adapting and directing, Welles had already earmarked the role of Brutus for himself but that didn't worry Coulouris. After a decade of waiting he jumped at the chance to finally play Marc Anthony on the stage.

In an attempt to save money, Welles staged the production in modern dress with minimalist sets but turned the poverty to his advantage by stressing the analogy of contemporary fascism and by presenting Caesar as a Mussolini figure. Fascist symbols and imagery, including a spectacular recreation of the infamous "Cathedral of Light" effects of the Nuremberg rallies, were worked into the production design. Setting aside the gimmick of modern dress and the fascist regalia, both of which had been seen before, Welles' gift to the production was his tremendous energy and enthusiasm, which seemed limitless. There was also his legendary spontaneity, largely created by his eccentric rehearsal methods. Coulouris, a more conventional actor than he would probably have admitted, was unimpressed by this anarchic approach. Simon Callow, Welles' biographer, describes Coulouris as the "licensed melancholic within the group" and records how he would openly contest Welles' directions:

> Moody, sardonic Coulouris…during breaks from rehearsals would throw tennis balls against the wall, muttering, "Be a singer! Don't be an actor! Acting's horrible."

Seventeen years after Coulouris' death, his son, also called George, gave his own take on Callow's rather one-sided dismissal of his father:

Rare shot of Courlous on stage at the Alvin Theatre in Maxwell Anderson's *Mary of Scotland* (193?), in a scene with Ernes Cessart and Helen Menken.

> Dad wasn't afraid to speak out, he would always welcome criticism from others and was forward in giving it himself — sometimes a little too forward. He would focus on the important things or the things that he thought were important and sometimes lost sight of other people's sensitivities. But he always managed to maintain relationships; he worked with Welles numerous times so he couldn't have caused that much disruption.

Whatever the shortcomings of Welles' methods, the play captured the imagination of both critics and the public, and from the moment it opened on November 11, 1937, *Julius Caesar* was a huge hit. Coulouris' performance in particular was singled out in most reviews, including the *New York Post* which noted, "even 'Friends, Romans, countrymen" sounds on his tongue as if it were a rabble-rousing harangue he is uttering for the first time." The *New York Times* offered:

> George Coulouris has the one passage of declamatory eloquence in the performance; in the funeral oration, which is imaginatively staged, he dominates the multitude with sound.

Coulouris, ever his own worst critic, was less than satisfied:

> It was acceptable; my voice sounded good; my diction was clear; my delivery of the verse correct. And yet I miss almost everything in the part including the hypocrisy of the big speech, with its slow build-up in the crowd of hatred for Caesar's killers. So it was with most acclaimed performances.

Variety, not noted for its subtlety, predicted a hit and summed up the box-office potential with "BARD BOFFOLA!" True to expectations the play was a huge success and ran to full houses until June 11, 1938. *Julius Caesar* only closed to make way for the next in the season—much to the chagrin of the theatre manager who pleaded with Welles to extend the run. A re-cast version without Coulouris was then dispatched on a tour of the East Coast and Canada. Meanwhile Coulouris played "The King" in Thomas Dekker's long-neglected Elizabethan dramatic comedy *The Shoemaker's Holiday* which spins together three interlocking stories about shoemakers in "ye olde world England." Dekker's central story focuses on the meteoric rise of Simon Eyre from humble cobbler to Lord Mayor of London while the two supporting stories are straightforward romances. The King only appears in the first of these as a supporting character creating the impetus for the two star-crossed lovers to find happiness. Hardly a demanding role but it at least gave a working class lad the chance to convince as royalty—English royalty at that!

> George Coulouris, well known in Greek American circles, has been portraying the role of Mark Antony in the New York production of Shakespeare's "Julius Caesar." Coulouris first came into prominence in "The Late Christopher Bean" with Pauline Lord. The critics lifted him to that very small list of capable character actors. Since then he has appeared in some of the Theatre Guild plays and was starred in "Blind Alley," the successful psychological melodrama. His impersonation of Basil Zaharoff in Sidney Kingsley's play, which failed earlier this season, won high praise.

Rehearsals for *The Shoemaker's Holiday* started while *Julius Caesar* was still playing, so the company had to fit around Coulouris' demanding schedule of eight performances per week, which was soon augmented with radio commitments. The cast also had to cope with Welles' erratic time-keeping; he would start a rehearsal at 10:30 a.m., then disappear for long periods only to re-appear and announce he was breaking for lunch! It wasn't unusual for the cast to be kept hanging around until the small hours of the morning awaiting the "eminent" return of the prodigy. Welles was equally inconsistent with his treatment of the company, a policy that annoyed Coulouris greatly. The stated intention of Mercury from the outset was to establish a close-knit group of versatile actors but the success of *Julius Caesar* started to dilute that vision when a whole new company was formed for the tour. Much to Coulouris' disgust, new actors were then brought in to the resident company including a young Vincent Price fresh from his triumph as Prince Albert in the Broadway and West End productions of *Victoria Regina*. Despite (or because of) Welles' unpredictable methods, *The Shoemaker's Holiday* delighted theatergoers and the Mercury Group had another huge hit on its hands.

The third and last play in the inaugural season was an adaptation of George Bernard Shaw's black comedy *Heartbreak House* with Welles as Captain Shotover, the ancient patriarch of a once grand English family now hopelessly in decline. Coulouris played the working class Boss Mangan whose arrival at the Shotover retreat triggers the worst in the family's snobbery and prejudices. Despite the quality of the writing and the size of the role it wasn't altogether a happy experience for Coulouris. The myth that Mercury was a collaboration of equals fell in tatters with Welles' prima donna antics, particularly during the irregular rehearsals which were once again scheduled around his anti-social hours, latest seductions and endless self-promotion. But if Coulouris was annoyed by Welles, he was driven to distraction by the arrival of fiery Irish actress Geraldine Fitzgerald, who was assigned the leading role by a doting Welles. Callow reports:

> Rehearsals were dominated by the neverending feud between Coulouris and Welles. To this was added a new one between Coulouris and Geraldine Fitzgerald, who proved able to give as good as she got, and better; at one point during the run, exasperated beyond endurance, she kicked him in the shins.

This time Welles' production was not well received. The critics, sharpening their pencils for the golden boy's first stumble, waxed vitriolic about his performance and lukewarm about the staging and cast—except for Coulouris who got good reviews. Unfazed by such a public failure, Welles basked in a position of national celebrity thanks mainly to Mercury's success on radio. *Mercury Theatre on the Air* was yet another offshoot of the theatre company and assembled as a largely independent group with a handful of key actors, including Coulouris and Joseph Cotton. Well-known faces now associated with Welles, such as Agnes Moorhead, came from this radio company with the director naturally an omnipresent figure. To launch the venture Welles adapted Bram Stoker's *Dracula,* **a** novel with a narrative well suited to the medium. Thanks to the huge success of Bela Lugosi in the 1931 Universal film, the Count now enjoyed a household name.

Coulouris played a scholarly Jonathan Harker. Demonstrating his mastery of technique, he managed to transform Stoker's rather dull creation into an intelligent and vulnerable character. Agnes Moorhead played Mina opposite Welles as an urbane and threatening Count. There was effective use of sound effects such as barking dogs and creaking doors and a wonderful score by Bernard Herrmann, responsible for so much memorable work before the piercing *Psycho* score came to dominate his career. Of course the show was all about Orson Welles who also played Dr. Seward and spoke the opening and closing narration. In fact Welles' name is mentioned no fewer than nine times in the opening three minutes! The play was well received by listeners but a long way short of the massive hit that Welles later liked to suggest, and it wasn't until the infamous *War of the Worlds* broadcast that Mercury's radio arm really established itself. Nevertheless Welles identified the production as one of his favorites from the Mercury era and for a long time considered mounting a filmed version. He later told biographer Peter Bogdanovich:

> [N]obody has ever made it; they've never paid any attention to the book, which is the most hair-raising marvelous book in the world. It's told by four people, and must be done with four narrations, as we did on the radio... All the movies are based on the play, not the book. Nobody has ever gone back to the book.

The relationship with Welles remained a difficult one but by now Coulouris needed the security of a regular income. In 1937 Louise gave birth to a baby boy, christened George, and then in 1939 a little girl, Mary. Despite (or perhaps because of) posing such a challenge, Welles insisted on casting Coulouris again and again for his radio company, soon renamed *The Campbell Playhouse* after attracting sponsorship from the soup giant. Coulouris was featured in productions of *Treasure Island*, *The Count of Monte Cristo* and *Heart of Darkness,* but he was less impressed by the theatrical options coming from Mercury. Ignoring Welles' pleas, Coulouris declined to play Robespierre in Mercury's version of *Danton's Death* and opted to join Eddie Dowling's lavish production of *Madame Capet* at the Cort Theatre on West 48th Street. That show wasn't popular and ran for only seven performances but Coulouris stayed on with Dowling for a successful run of *The White Steed*, a turgid drama set in contemporary Ireland with the actor rendering an "Oyrish" priest by the name of Shaughnessy.

Meanwhile the Mercury Theatre staggered through its chaotic second season with an increasingly bored Welles already looking for a new challenge. The final nail in the company's coffin came not from the critics or public but from Hollywood or more specifically RKO. Welles' reputation had been growing for some time but the fact that he achieved national notoriety after *War of the Worlds* defined the power of radio for a whole generation. The great man ensured that his was the only name associated with the broadcast, and the uproar

Louise and George pose with their children Mary and George, Jr. at Spuyten Duyvil house in 1939.

and subsequent front-page headlines carried Welles all the way to California. RKO executives, desperate to be associated with that sort of high profile success, offered the most extravagant contract in movie history, and Welles duly abandoned New York for the glamour and luxury of Los Angeles. Effectively Welles had been given *carte blanche* to film whatever he liked, whenever he liked with whomever he liked. Digging out the old Mercury radio script *Heart of Darkness,* he announced that Joseph Conrad's story of the deranged and deluded Kurtz and his reign over a forgotten corner of Africa would be his first movie. Breaking up the theatre and radio companies Welles selected those he saw as the cream and offered them a five week contract to join him in Hollywood. Joseph Cotton, Agnes Moorhead, Everett Sloane and George Coulouris were among those who accepted.

Given his past experience with movies and his obvious love of the stage it is unlikely that Coulouris saw Hollywood as anything other than a sojourn in the sunshine—albeit a well paid one. Welles was scheduled to start principal photography in October 1939 and his troupe started to gather in California from the early autumn onwards. Coulouris, taking a short term lease on a house on Hobart Boulevard, was confident he would be back in New York for the start of the 1940 theatre season but as always Welles was working on his own agenda. Billed by RKO as "the hottest director in town," the writer-director-star was expected to produce something special. He was also under pressure to do it himself: the scripts were all credited to "Mercury" with Welles given undue credit. Herman J. Mankiewicz was kept discretely in the background working on the script while Welles gabbed enthusiastically about the scope of his great project. Amongst the innovations planned for *Heart of Darkness* were a torrid love interest and the morphing of Kurtz into a fascist dictator.

Welles assured the Mercury players they would all get challenging roles, while handing around copies of his elaborate production sketches and revealing he would be playing both leading characters as well as directing. Marlowe's view and the camera's would be one and the same.

The outbreak of war in Europe and the subsequent shrinking of the world market effectively put paid to the project. The accountants at RKO, faced with interminable re-writes and prevarication from Welles, viewed the projected $1 million budget with growing unease. To make matters worse, Welles had vastly underestimated the amount of specific effects needed to sustain a "point of view" for a whole film as well as the impact on the shooting schedule. Under some pressure from his paymasters Welles agreed to put the project on the back burner and move quickly on to something simpler. Coulouris recalls being summoned to a cast meeting, expecting a script only to hear Welles announce Conrad was now out:

> He's a dead duck; we're not taking his option. Ambler's the man, and *The Smiler with a Knife* is the book. We haven't started on the script yet, but don't worry boys, you're all on the RKO payroll until the script's ready, and at your present salaries.

By then Louise and the children had joined Coulouris on Hobart Boulevard for what was looking increasingly like a paid vacation but the holiday spirit wasn't long-lived. RKO balked at the continued extravagance and a week later the contracts of all the Mercury actors—with the exception of Welles—were terminated. Coulouris, Cotton and others were left high and dry in Hollywood. The problem was confounded by Welles' attitude; he wanted his actors to be available at a moment's notice and had instructed their agents not to find them alternate work. He also insisted that his big screen debut was made with a cast of "unknowns."

Throughout this whole period Welles continued his weekly radio broadcasts with Coulouris appearing on an irregular basis; he was amongst the red herrings in Agatha Christie's *The Murder of Roger Ackroyd* (with Welles as both detective and prime suspect) and popped up in the festive offering of *A Christmas Carol* featuring guest star Lionel Barrymore. Radio was clearly no substitute for the stage nor could it offer enough money for Coulouris to support his young family. Risking the wrath of Welles, Coulouris signed on at Warner Bros. in February 1940 to take the inconsequential role of a valet in the turgid $1 million melodrama *All This and Heaven Too* starring Bette Davis and Charles Boyer. Meanwhile RKO's interest in *The Smiler with a Knife* started to wane when the executives realized, despite all the proclamations about their "boy wonder" (one newspaper even referred to Welles as the "Christ child"), the much touted debut feature would be nothing more than a routine thriller. Welles, already bored with that script, seized the opportunity to start what would finally become *Citizen Kane*.

By then Coulouris was working regularly in films; he followed *All This and Heaven Too* with the muddled comedy drama *The Lady in Question* for Columbia, playing an earnest defense lawyer who spends the opening scenes trying to get Rita Hayworth acquitted of murder. By the time *All This and Heaven Too* opened, *Citizen Kane* had been shooting for nearly a month. (In his press releases for *Kane,* Welles still insisted on taking credit for discovering all of the Mercury actors, claiming they were all new to films except for Dorothy Comingore who had done some extra work.)

Coulouris with *enfant terrible* Orson Welles in *Citizen Kane*

Welles' sprawling epic tells the story of the fictitious tycoon Charles Foster Kane, charting his rise from childhood poverty to untold wealth and power through a complex series of flashbacks and pseudo-newsreel footage. The film had greatness stamped all over it, from its epic scope to the daring camerawork and experimental narrative structure. The authorship of the remarkable screenplay (credited jointly to Welles and Herman J. Mankiewicz) has been hotly debated for over 60 years while the unending attention given to the production process, as well as the final cut, have made *Citizen Kane* perhaps the most analyzed film ever made.

Certainly the film was everything RKO wanted from its protégé, a startlingly confident debut, enhanced considerably by Gregg Toland's stunning cinematography and an outstanding Bernard Herrmann score. Naturally, Welles played the titular character, with Coulouris as Walter Parks Thatcher, a terse Wall Street banker appointed as trustee and guardian of the young Kane; the mutual antagonism and grudging respect between the characters mirrored the real-life relationship of the actors. Thatcher's aloofness was established from his initial introduction via an enormous stone statue (actually a cleverly shot scale model which earned Coulouris a modest bonus payment for accommodating the sculptor). Acting the part proved more demanding not least because of Welles' insistence on authenticity: to create a snowstorm, he used cornflakes painted white, an uncomfortable experience for all the actors. Coulouris recalled that Welles also struggled to communicate with his actors:

> I remember one scene we had, it went to 50 takes. And he said to me after one of them: "What's the matter with you; you're giving a terrible performance, like vaudeville? Why don't you do it properly?"

Coulouris thought at the time (and he never wavered from the view) that the "boy genius" was hopelessly out of his depth. Forty years later he confided with his friend the BBC producer Brian Dean:

> George told me that the cast were convinced that Welles didn't know what he was doing and he was simply filming every scene from every possible angle in the hope that he could sort it out in the editing suite.

Word of mouth spread around Hollywood that Welles was creating something special but Coulouris seemed oblivious to anything magical in the air at RKO. He wrote:

> I get $1,000 a week...I have now been on salary for 17 days and have worked one and a half. The movie is going to be terrible, as Welles is a ham and is in practically every scene. I have been unable to restrain my opinion of him so have passed it on to all the stupid, idiotic sheep-like make-up men, cameramen etc. who regard him as a genius. Oh this is an irritating place. Why the hell can't they stick to their business of entertaining morons and not gabble about art is beyond me.

Coulouris' view of the production may well have been influenced by his first experience of heavy screen makeup. Like many of the other characters in the movie, Thatcher is shown both as a young man and during his later years: to create the aging effect the actor had to arrive at the studio at 5:00 each morning and subject himself to the rigors of makeup man Maurice Siderman:

> I got into the chair and I would have some kind of mask made of clay over my face with straws through the nostrils...then the rubber would be put on and then he put a silk stocking over my head and on the top of the silk stocking a bald rubber plate. It took about four hours and then we would start.

Harry Shannon, George Coulouris, Agnes Moorhead, Buddy Swann in *Citizen Kane*

RKO's investment of over $800,000 was significant but by no means the gigantic sum often suggested. *Casablanca* cost over $900,000 and was considered modest, while Welles' next film, *The Magnificent Ambersons*, clocked in at over $1 million. But the "Christ child" honored his side of the bargain and RKO was handed a genuine masterpiece, going on to earn 11 Academy Award nominations. Unfortunately, even before it was released, Welles also handed the studio a major headache. Newspaper tycoon William Randolph Hearst interpreted the film as a thinly veiled pastiche of his life, particularly his relationship with actress Marion Davies. When he failed to persuade RKO to bury the project he mobilized his empire, comprising some 28 major newspapers and 18 magazines, including the *New York Daily News* and *Cosmopolitan*, to destroy the film. RKO executives prevaricated on the film's release hoping to win Hearst round, leaving Welles and his actors wondering if their film careers had fallen at the first hurdle.

Coulouris remonstrated to Welles soon after shooting wrapped, hoping to persuade him to return to New York and the Mercury. Welles, well and truly consumed by Hollywood, retorted, "I can do anything, out-Barnum Barnum, out-Hitchcock Hitchcock!" Welles in fact did go back on the stage in March 1941 and, while the wrangling over *Citizen Kane* raged, he escaped to the relative sanity of the St. James Theatre, directing a successful run of *Native Son*.

By then Coulouris had already opened and closed in *Cue for Passion* at the Royale Theatre for Richard Aldrich; it ran for only 12 performances, closing on December 28, 1940.

Citizen Kane was finally released nationwide in May 1941 by which time Welles had abandoned the theatre completely and returned to Hollywood. Unfortunately the initial release wasn't the box-office success RKO needed but history has been kinder and the film has since acquired an almost mythical reputation, not least for the strength of the acting, all the more remarkable given the relative inexperience of the cast. Chief amongst them was Coulouris, not a natural cinema actor but successful enough to win the Board of Review "Best Actor" award and for an ebullient Welles to christen him "a grand actor." Coulouris, dismissive of his film work, was also causing some ripples of his own in the Broadway production of Lillian Hellman's *Watch on the Rhine* directed by Herman Shumlin.

Left-wing sympathizer Hellman, horrified by the rise of the Nazis and the war in Europe, was determined to shake America out of its complacency. Having already enjoyed success on Broadway with *The Children's Hour* and *The Little Foxes*—both directed by Shumlin—she intended *Watch on the Rhine* to be that wake up call. The story centers on a young couple, the Mullers, members of the German resistance movement who flee Europe to the presumed safety of Washington D.C., only to find the fascists blackmailing and murdering their way through the nation's capital. Hungarian-born Paul Lukas and Mady Christians, who had appeared in Mercury's *Heartbreak House,* played the leads. Coulouris was cast as Count Teck de Brancovis, a Romanian exile who exploits the Muller's vulnerability for personal advantage. The smoothly duplicitous Count is a desperate man, living off his wits and whatever money he can extort from friends and enemies alike. It was a peach of a part with Coulouris flicking effortlessly from charming host to amoral opportunist in the blink of an eye, and when the play opened on the April 1, 1941, the actor electrified critics and audiences alike.

Watch on the Rhine proved an instant hit on Broadway and subsequently on national tour. Coulouris, reveling in de Brancovis' shades of gray, was particularly popular with critics who observed for the first time the powerful physique and hooded eyes that made him a natural for villainous roles. *The New York Times*' review was typical, drawing readers' attention to a "lucid and subtly repelling performance." Coulouris, never an actor prone to over-analyzing his craft, documented some of his thoughts about the role shortly before his death. Talking specifically about the scene where the Count confronts his prey, he said:

> In the play I am a fascist, he is a communist. Therefore the bastard thinks he is superior to me. I deny this. I know I'm

his superior. I like Beethoven and Bach. He's probably never heard of them. I take as big risks as he in my work so finally knowing all this I am able to say exactly in the right intonation, "Your hands are shaking, Herr Muller." I almost whisper it, meaning: Why are you're hands shaking and mine not if you are such a goddamn hero?

In a stand out season on Broadway, which also included Boris Karloff in *Arsenic and Old Lace*, *Watch on the Rhine* was *the* hit, garnering amongst its awards the New York Drama Critic's Circle award for "Best Play."

Shortly afterwards, cast and crew were shipped off to Washington to recreate the play for President Roosevelt. Coulouris was later told that every sixth seat in the stalls was occupied by secret serviceman, and, much to his amusement, his prop gun was replaced by a rather obvious wooden replica. The meal the cast enjoyed with Roosevelt and his wife afterwards was a moment of lightness in what was becoming an increasingly dark world situation.

The Japanese attack on Pearl Harbor on December 7, 1941, and the subsequent declaration of war by Germany brought a new resonance to *Watch on the Rhine*. Hollywood executives launched into their patriotic duty and suddenly flag-flying, morale boosting movies were the order of the day. Hellman, who once slaved as a $40-per-week script reader for Sam Goldwyn, overcame her inherent resistance to Hollywood and sold the film rights to Warner Bros. Hal Wallis was assigned to produce, with Hellman and her long-term lover Dashiell Hammett, author of *The Maltese Falcon,* hired to adapt the play for the big screen. Warner's contract star Bette Davis took the role of Frau Muller, a curiously passive part for the actress, while suave Englishman George Sanders was penciled in to play Count de Brancovis. Herman Shumlin, who also made the move to Hollywood, insisted on Paul Lukas as his lead and when Sanders passed on de Brancovis was permitted to engage George Coulouris. For the third time in his career Coulouris moved into a temporary rental in Hollywood. Lucile Watson, who had played the matriarch figure on stage, was also retained for the film and would go on to earn a Best Supporting Actress nomination. Beulah Bondi and Henry Daniell also appeared, as did Coulouris' old sparring partner Geraldine Fitzgerald, now under contract at Warners and hired to play Marthe de Brancovis. The outspoken actress, perhaps still harboring some jealously, told *The New York Times*:

> The public loves monsters…I would much rather have Coulouris' part. That would really be tiptop, to be a double-dyed 100% monster and gnash my teeth in front of the camera.

Paul Lukas, Bette Davis and Coulouris in *Watch on the Rhine*

Behind the cameras the celebrated Max Steiner did the score; costumes were by Australian Orry-Kelly who would go on to win three Oscars during his career; photography was by Hal Mohr who also had an Academy Award under his belt and would win another for *The Phantom of the Opera* (1943).

With America now at war, *Watch on the Rhine* played much more as an exercise in "rally round the flag" than a forewarning but if you overlook the drum banging the film has much to offer. Shumlin does a competent job and the cat and mouse antics propel the narrative but the real appeal remains in the acting department. Bette Davis is subdued in a role far beneath her ability but Lukas is very good, offering a dignified and noble performance, matched by a powerful turn from Coulouris. As on the stage, de Brancovis steals the show, displaying just enough ingratiating charm to conceal his reptilian nature and provides the perfect foil for Muller's uncompromising moral righteousness. While the later can declare unequivocally, "I fight fascism; that is my trade," de Brancovis holds a much more ambiguous position; he isn't a fanatic or a loyalist but merely an opportunist. "I do not do it without some shame," he says curtly, "and I must therefore sink my shame in large money." Interestingly the film survived its encounters with the guardians of the nation's morals relatively unscathed: the

infamous Production Code Administration objected only to the murder scene, not because Coulouris is throttled to death but because Muller doesn't show enough remorse.

With all the patriotic fervor, it was of course Lukas who received all the plaudits, including an Oscar. *Watch on the Rhine* also picked up nominations for Best Screenplay, Best Supporting Actress and Best Picture, as well as recognition from the Golden Globes and the New York Film Critics Circle, who awarded their Best Picture award. Nazis could hardly win awards but Coulouris could content himself with a performance that lingers in the mind long after the end credits have rolled. (While he was never recognized by the Academy, Coulouris' work did feature in *All This and Heaven Too* and *Citizen Kane,* which had both been nominated for Best Picture in 1941 and 1942 respectively. In 1944 *For Whom the Bell Tolls,* in which he had a cameo role, was also nominated).

Coulouris stayed on at Warner Bros. to make another film, again starring Bette Davis, this time with the actress given a more demanding role. *Mr. Skeffington* is a silly, melodramatic story of a vain woman who marries for money and after many, many hardships finds true love. Claude Rains, the object and victim of Davis' flighty passion, plays the luckless title role. Coulouris features briefly in a fine supporting cast including Jerome Cowan and Walter Abel. *Mr. Skeffington* would prove a box-office hit but had little to satisfy a demanding actor like Coulouris.

In late 1942, soon after his bit role in *For Whom the Bell Tolls*— a favor for *Christopher Bean* director Sam Wood—Coulouris reflected on his Hollywood status. *Watch on the Rhine* had not yet opened but Coulouris had acquired a reputation as a solid and reliable character actor. The financial security was very appealing but professionally it was far from satisfying. Coulouris decided to return to New York to find a part that would stretch him as an actor: Shakespeare's most black-hearted villain Richard III. Coulouris mounted his own production, sinking nearly all of his savings—some $25,000—into the financing and, borrowing a touch from Orson Welles, announced he would produce, direct and take the leading role. The Forrest Theatre in Philadelphia was booked with an opening date of March 24, 1943. It is tempting to think Coulouris would have been better served waiting for the national release of *Watch on the Rhine* but the actor as always was determined to succeed or fail on his own terms. Opening night proved a sobering experience; *The New York Times*' theatre critic Lewis Nichols noted:

> Mr. Coulouris is a good actor, in whose record is a long list of saints and sinners, and presumably he should be able to do well by the evil Richard, who lived by the dagger and thereby perished. But in his own revival he does not make Gloucester a full figure, and he can send across the footlights little of the fear and horror, which are essential reactions to the role when perfectly stressed. Further, and it is most unlike Mr. Coulouris he often speaks indistinctly.

Few, if any, of the reviewers had anything kind to say about the production, though the influential George Jean Nathan at least recognized a great screen villain in embryo and described Coulouris' performance as "a screen Bela Lugosi crossed with a grand opera Quasimodo." Unlike Welles, Coulouris could recognize failure when it stared him in the face and accepted defeat graciously:

> I unfortunately in doing the play had so much to do that I devoted no time at all to my performance, and finally on the first night realizing that I didn't know how to play the part, was faced with a big theatre, a fashionable audience—my wife in the front row. So I gabbled through as fast as I could, the curtain hour came down, and I sort of came to my senses. Afterwards I said to my wife, as we were crossing the stage, "This is a flop, isn't it?" She said, "Yes, I'm afraid it is."

Richard III ran only 11 performances and lost the actor nearly all the money he had invested. Stung by the financial failure more than the critical one, Coulouris resolved to return to Hollywood "to make some money" but despite his earlier work in the film capital, he struggled to convince producers that he wasn't just a theatre actor. It was a further six months before the success of *Watch in the Rhine* started to pay off and Coulouris was elevated to Hollywood's resident villain.

In June 1944 the actor was back at RKO, once again in jackboots, to shoot *The Master Race*. Written and directed by Herbert J. Biberman, the film, which started shooting soon after D-Day, envisaged a Nazi regime in its death throes with the top ranking officials abandoning the sinking ship. Coulouris was given top billing as Colonel Von Beck, a nasty piece of work who launches a team of agents to undermine the Allied democracies from within, even offering to sacrifice the Fuhrer as a decoy exercise! With ice in his veins, Von Beck casually assumes the identity of a murdered Belgian resistance fighter and hides out in the dead man's village, even blackmailing the widow and daughter into helping with the charade. A happy ending is ensured when a "decent" German exposes Von Beck, who is executed by the Americans. Dramatic stuff but Biberman

misses out on the gripping possibilities offered by a German resistance while getting bogged down in a "how will we ever learn to trust each other again" sentiment. Rape, blackmail, murder and racism all feature in the narrative and are dealt with in the same over-earnest way that manages to defuse much of the excitement. That said, the film is worth the price of the ticket just to see Coulouris hamming it up as the fanatical Von Beck, the definitive ruthless Nazi who even pre-empts the Bond villains by having a purring cat as a permanent attachment.

RKO then featured Coulouris out of uniform but still playing the heavy for their slice of life soap opera *None but the Lonely Heart* directed by Clifford Odets, another veteran of the Group Theatre. (*Variety* earlier had announced that Alfred Hitchcock had been signed.) Cary Grant played against type as Ernie Mott, a chirpy cockney given to clicking his heels in the air and spouting trite little homilies about life. After years of aimless wandering and staying just within the law, Mott returns home to a dreary London backstreet to look after his dear old ma, played by Ethel Barrymore who would pick up an Oscar for her trouble.

Coulouris played a small time hood, Jim Mordinoy, who forms one side of a love triangle with Mott and his cockney girlfriend, Ada. It is a good part for the actor who happily chomps on raisins and displays an unsettling air of good humor while threatening the lives and welfare of the locals. The close-up after a pawnbroker is beaten up is particularly chilling with Coulouris nonchalantly purring, "Open your mouth about this and I'll fix you right. And your families too, see." This was classic Coulouris villainy; totally understated, almost casual, he never raises his voice but with his powerful physique and unblinking eyes, demonstrates that he is capable of very bad things. Later, when Ada asks what he believes in, Mordinoy shrugs and says, "Nothing. Simple ain't it? Nothing in the whole wide world." It is a remarkable performance in a film that was clearly a vehicle for Grant to prove (or, as it happened, disprove) his dramatic range. Coulouris so totally dominates his scenes that it is a stretch to believe that Mott has either the physical strength or intelligence to take him on. For once Hollywood defied expectations; eschewing any sort of inspirational ending, the film closes on Grant, unfulfilled and alone, and Barrymore dying of cancer in a prison cell. Not a dry eye in the house, with Mordinoy providing a nice counterpoint to all this slush and for once getting the girl—albeit by force. Odets' sedate direction and the beautiful black and white cinematography make the film watch-able, and there is a nice recreation of grim London backstreets only let down in the chase sequence which has a decidedly Californian look.

For an actor who earlier had complained to the press that he was "used to villains, I've played so many," Coulouris seemed reconciled to his screen image. In London, *The Times* saw in Coulouris "the very essence of cultivated wickedness" and Hollywood producers were now tapping into this quality. Inevitably he was now being considered for horror movies, then a genre very much in decline. Coulouris came very close to making his genre debut for no less a luminary than Val Lewton and his justly famous B unit at RKO. After a decade and a half of Universal's lumbering monsters, Lewton was redefining the rules for horror cinema, introducing subtlety and nuance to a series of compelling and unstated thrillers—a reputation for atmospheric and dark chillers that remains undiminished. Lewton had identified Coulouris as his preferred choice for the role of Toddy MacFarlane, the pompous anatomy lecturer based loosely on Robert Knox, for *The Body Snatcher*. It was a fascinating proposal that would have starred Coulouris opposite Boris Karloff in the title role and Bela Lugosi in a supporting part. It wasn't to be; by the mid 1940s Coulouris was regularly sharing a bill with Hollywood heavyweights like Gary Cooper, Bette Davis and Claudette Colbert, and simply was out of Lewton's budget range. The role instead went to Henry Daniell who had appeared with Coulouris in *All This and Heaven Too* and *Watch on the Rhine*.

In early 1945 Coulouris again was hired to play a Nazi in *Hotel Berlin*. This Vicki Baum story, depicting the now fashionable last days of Hitler's Germany, first appeared in *Colliers* magazine in late 1943 when the theme had a strong element of wishful thinking. Warner Bros. snapped up the rights for $50,000 and engaged Baum to write the script, following the same format of her previous success *Grand Hotel*. By the time the film was ready to roll, the end of the Nazis was in sight and to protect his investment, Jack Warner had to galvanize the full resources of the studio to get the film version into cinemas before Russian tanks entered Berlin. Sound technicians worked around the clock, as did the three orchestras recording the soundtrack. Two separate teams of editors poured over the footage to assemble the final print in an unprecedented five days. English director Peter Godfrey, better known for his B movies, helmed the potboiler which intermingles the diverse stories of several characters at one particular time and location. Included in the mix is a German aristocrat (Raymond Massey) involved in a plot to kill Hitler, a freedom fighter on the run from the Gestapo, a scheming actress, and a socialite with a sick mother. The plot devices include the usual mix of love and betrayal, death and betrayal, and betrayal and betrayal. Coulouris plays the hotel's head of security, Gestapo Commissioner Joachim Helm, steadfastly holding the party line and ignoring the reality all around him. It wasn't that different from his earlier work, something which the actor recognized:

> I decided I'd played several Nazis so I'd better do something about changing my appearance a bit. So I had my hair, what was left of it, blonded for this…I don't suppose it made much difference to the performance.

That other great Hollywood villain Peter Lorre costars, in a sympathetic role for once, as an anti-Nazi scientist who seems to spend the duration of the film in an alcoholic daze. Raymond Massey and Henry Daniell added support, the latter as a Nazi on the run determined to start the Fourth Reich in North America. Baum continued the revisionist view of good Germans and bad Nazis, ending predictably with the baddies getting their just desserts amidst general optimism about the future of Europe. Rushed into cinemas a month before the fall of Berlin, the film was still ringing cash registers as Germany signed the official surrender on the May 7, 1945.

It is a measure of Coulouris' success that he was now being cast in major pictures and while he wasn't by any stretch of the imagination a box-office star, he was supporting A-list actors and fine directors. On these somewhat narrow terms, the next few years could be said to represent the absolute pinnacle of his screen career. *A Song to Remember* is a lush (and highly inaccurate) biopic of Polish composer Frederic Chopin with matinee idol Cornel Wilde winning an unlikely Oscar nomination for the title role. Shot in Technicolor by Charles Vidor, this romantic tosh looks gorgeous and has the scope of a major film; sadly it also has the vacuous performances and limp screenplay that are all too common in this genre. Coulouris plays music publisher Louis Pleyel with suitable gravity but is largely wasted in all the excess.

Lady on a Train was slightly more mundane but no more credible. Deanna Durbin, Universal's lightweight singer star, witnesses a murder on a train and when the police don't believe her, she sets out to catch the perpetrator herself. The usual suspects wander through the sub-Agatha Christie narrative directed without flair by Durbin's future husband Charles David. Coulouris enlivens things briefly as Sanders, the decidedly sinister manager of the famous jazz emporium "The Cotton Club" who, for his own reasons, attempts to thwart Durbin's investigation.

Marginally more interesting was *Confidential Agent* with Herman Shumlin again adopting an anti-fascist stance, this time using California to stand in for Civil War Spain. Peter Lorre was amongst the heavies out to prevent Charles Boyer securing the English coal he needs for the Republicans to fight the good fight. Lauren Bacall, then being touted by the studio as their latest sex symbol, provided the glamour but even with author Graham Green supplying the source material and James Wong Howe the elegant photography, *Confidential Agent* never rises above the routine. Coulouris is in henchman mode and given little to do but look menacing while Lorre's sneering villainy steals the show.

Interestingly both Humphrey Bogart and William Holden had previously been announced for the lead, either of whom would have been preferable to Boyer's limp hero.

Nobody Lives Forever offered Coulouris more of a challenge as sleazy, duplicitous gangster Doc Gangson in a film noir directed by Jean Negulesco. The story centers on small time hustler Nick (John Garfield), who does his bit for Uncle Sam and then returns home to resume his old trade. He is persuaded to take part in an elaborate confidence trick run by local hood Gangson. The target is wealthy and attractive widow Gladys Halvorsen (Geraldine Fitzgerald). Predictably Nick falls in love with Gladys, resolves to do the right thing by her and save her from the bad guys. Equally predictably Doc sniffs a double-cross and to prevent Nick swindling him out of his ill-gotten gains, kidnaps Gladys and forces a showdown. Coulouris pulls out all the stops and Gangson isn't a merely a ruthless opportunist but a dangerous psychotic; it's a mesmerizing performance which creates arguably the most brutal and menacing character in the actor's already extensive repertoire of dark villains. Coulouris is so good that he easily could have overbalanced the film if not for the much-underrated John Garfield who, in a role originally intended for Humphrey Bogart—seemingly first choice for all tough guy roles in the 1940s—manages to match not only Coulouris' physical strength and guile but also a strong sense of vulnerability. If you can ignore the odd weakness of plotting then the acting of the principals and solid direction from Negulesco make *Nobody Lives Forever* an entertaining movie and certainly deserving of more attention than it now receives.

Coulouris may have missed out on working with Bogart (again) but in *The Verdict* he managed to appear with the great man's erstwhile co-stars Sydney Greenstreet and Peter Lorre, who had been launched as a sort of double act following their success in *The Maltese Falcon*. Set in 19th Century London, *The Verdict* marked the directorial debut of Don Siegel, a name more associated with gritty contemporary thrillers than fog-bound whodunits but the director made sure he evoked every cliché of the genre in this tale of betrayal, ambition and murder. The rotund Greenstreet plays a disgraced police chief forced into early retirement after overseeing the execution of an innocent man. When a close acquaintance is stabbed to death he turns amateur detective and along with his faithful lackey, a decidedly eccentric and generally inebriated artist (Lorre), he sets out to solve the crime. Coulouris is Buckley, Greenstreet's successor at Scotland Yard and the archetypal petty bureaucrat, as officious as he is inefficient. The otherwise stock character has one extra twist however; we learn that he withheld the evidence that would have saved his boss' career—and the condemned man.

As one might expect the acting from the leads is full-bodied, with Lorre and Greenstreet making likeable hams but curiously (this was their fifth and last film together) there is surprisingly little chemistry between them. Coulouris on

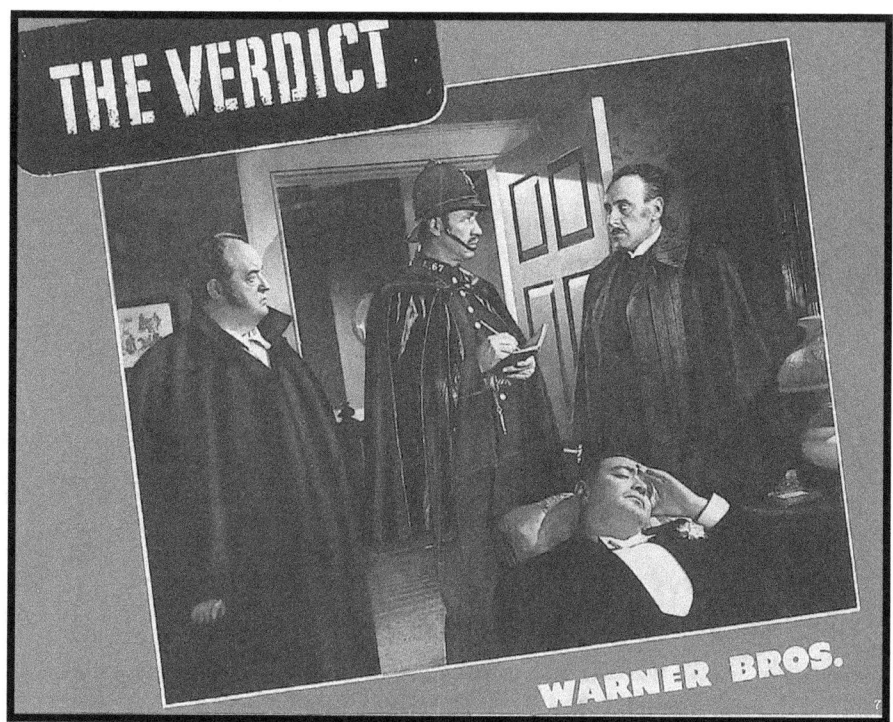

THE VERDICT

the other hand gets to rein in the temptation to overact and offers a diverting portrayal of a petty but dangerous man. Buckley defines the expression "the banality of evil" and he is an odious and self-serving pen-pusher driven out of ambition and envy rather than inherent badness. The friction between Coulouris and heavyweight — in every sense — Greenstreet adds considerably to the tension and is a nice counterpoint to the altogether too flippant banter between Greenstreet and Lorre. It wasn't a leading role but this was a big budget movie from a major studio, Warner Bros., with London recreated on the back lot and across some 25 studio sets all expertly photographed by Ernest Haller. There is the cozy familiarity of Victorian London, as seen by Hollywood, complete with impenetrable fogs, top hats and capes and cheeky wenches, but Siegel's competent direction is defeated by a script that requires practically everyone to act in an overtly suspicious manner. The creaky plot devices and drawing room manners don't hold up to close inspection but the acting makes the film entertaining enough.

Coulouris' next assignment was something quite different, as the Paramount publicity handouts confirmed: "Your eyes, your ears, your heart never had a greater thrill..." The film was the ambitious *California,* a lavish remake of the silent epic *The Covered Wagon* set during the mass migrations westward of the 1840s. Army deserter Jonathan Trumbo (Ray Milland) leads a wagon train of assorted homesteaders across the prairies while bickering with Lilly Bishop

Coulouris and Barbara Stanwyck in *California*

(Barbara Stanwyck), a "tart with a heart" who has been run out of town by the moral majority. Lilly joins the train over Trumbo's objections and the sniping between the two leads drives the early part of the movie but it really isn't until the arrival of Coulouris' outrageous Captain Pharaoh Coffin that things start to get interesting. *California* is a film that Coulouris would often site as his personal favorite of all his Hollywood films and it is easy to see why. Coffin is exactly the sort of larger than life character that allowed Coulouris to shine and director John Farrow, clearly aware of what he was getting, allows Coulouris a free rein. An unconscionable swine of the first order, Coffin is never happier than when he is bleeding the miners dry or hatching his own madcap schemes for self-advancement. Amongst his less appealing qualities, Coffin exhibits a vile racist streak, most evident when Trumbo challenges him on the mistreatment of former slaves. After listening to Trumbo's condemnation, he snorts:

> Bilge, Mr. Trumbo, bilge! Most men love the chains they wear. They need a master the way they need their mothers. I've heard such talk from pulpits, "the meek shall inherit the earth." No, Mr. Trumbo, the earth belongs to the men who make the law, and the law belongs to the men who can lay it down.

Farrow retains the gritty realism needed to add credibility but doesn't let it get in the way of a rattling good yarn and creates an entertaining spectacle well-deserving of its box-office success.

West Coast life suited Coulouris' young family and although the actor shunned the more glamorous aspects of Hollywood life he wasn't above indulging in some of the trappings of success. In 1942 Coulouris moved from Hobart Boulevard and purchased Farley Grainger's old house at 608 North Roxbury Drive in Beverly Hills. Coulouris could be seen there on weekends thumping a tennis ball against a wall and when he wasn't working, which was seldom, he would play tennis with close friends like John Garfield whom he knew from the Group Theatre in New York. And of course there was cricket. Coulouris put nets up in the yard so he could practice with the children and every Sunday the family would gather under the Union Jack in Griffith Park where the Hollywood Cricket Club staged their matches. This little part of the British Empire counted amongst its most prominent members the likes of Laurence Olivier, David Niven and of course the legendary C. Aubrey Smith, founder and president. However appealing the lifestyle, Coulouris found that it couldn't compensate for the lack of professional challenge and he was becoming increasingly disenchanted with the films offered to him.

Pharaoh Coffin would be the last great character that Coulouris would create in Hollywood but he would continue to appear in American movies almost continuously for the next two years. The roles included A melodramas such as *Mr. District Attorney* and Douglas Sirk's thriller *Sleep My Love;* these films were successful enough in their own right but lacked what the actor considered quality and were barely worth his effort. Even a return visit to John Farrow on the Alan Ladd action film *Beyond Glory* recreated little of the spark of *California*. Attempts to extend his range into comedy met with mixed success; the limp Bob Hope vehicle *Where There's Life* for Paramount, which also features George Zucco, was a waste of everybody's time; while Red Skelton's *A Southern Yankee* for MGM offered some low-brow humor and little else.

Radio provided diversity for Coulouris and he featured on a regular basis on thriller shows like *Suspense* as well as providing narration for "The Cavalcade of America" production of *The Story of Penicillin*. As was common at the time, Coulouris recreated some of his more famous screen roles and appeared in networked productions of *Watch on the Rhine* which also featured Paul Lukas and Bette Davis, as well as a version of *The Master Race*. One of the last films Coulouris made in Hollywood was an adaptation of an earlier stage production *Joan of Arc* with the incomparable Ingrid Bergman, looking all of her 33 years, playing the teenage virgin martyr. RKO made the film and engaged Coulouris for the small role of Sir Robert de Baudricourt, Governor of Vaucoulers and one of Joan's prominent English tormentors. An impressive cast, which also

includes the great heavies George Zucco and J. Carrol Naish, is largely wasted in a straight-faced and stagy adaptation of the Maxwell Anderson play.

Joan of Arc's release was largely overshadowed by the row over Bergman's affair with married director Roberto Rosselini which became public soon afterwards. The press and public deemed that the actress' private life made a mockery of one of history's purest saints and the backlash drove Bergman out of Hollywood and very nearly destroyed her career. It also completely swamped any public or critical perception of the movie; so much so that the film is generally regarded as a box-office failure despite returning some $4 million on what was a relative modest investment— proof that there really is no such thing as bad publicity! By then Coulouris' dissatisfaction with Hollywood had crystallized and, determined to return to the stage, he had moved his family back to the East Coast, to Port Chester, Connecticut, within easy striking distance of Broadway. Despite so much success in Hollywood, the actor expressed only disappointment with the way his career had developed:

> I want to do some proper acting. I started out to be an actor...
> I wanted to do Shakespeare and I've been sidetracked, I've been in America doing modern plays, I went to Hollywood and did all these things, and I've still not done what I really set out to do.

Coulouris' return to the stage was certainly a change of pace, although true to form he was still playing the villain. The lyricists Betty Comden and Adolph Green, who had written the hit *On the Town* in 1944 and would later count the likes of *Singing in the Rain* on their resumes, offered him a major role in their new musical *Bonanza Bound*. Coulouris played Waldo, a would-be prospector who contrives to start a bogus gold rush in the fictional town of Cruickshank. It would mark not only Coulouris' comeback to legitimate theatre but the opportunity to sing for the first time to a paying audience.

> **Voice of Broadway**
> By DOROTHY KILGALLEN
> **Gossip in Gotham**
> Raymond Massey is a flu victim . . . "Bonanza Bound" backers talk hopefully of opening it again in eight weeks with a new rewrite job. The eight weeks' lapse is necessary to get rid of certain run-of-the-play contracts . . Actor Murvyn Vye and his wife are together again—at least in the bistros .. Lana Turner's friends are worried about the possibility of an alienation of affections suit.

The actor reasoned a success in a musical could open up a whole new career direction for him; one very much removed from Hollywood's pantomime Nazis. One can certainly understand the attraction for Coulouris; Waldo gently ribs his screen image and includes one operatic number, "Misunderstood," where the character bemoans his villainous stereotyping. Comden and Green pulled out all the stops; choreography was by jazz legend Jack Cole, music by Saul Chapin whose work would feature in *An American in Paris* and *Kiss Me Kate*, and the cast included Allyn Ann McClerie, wife of Green who also appeared himself. The show opened out of town in Philadelphia on December 26, 1947, with the promise, all being well, of a Broadway run in the New Year. But the reviews were scathing and *Bonanza Bound* lasted barely a week before closing.

Coulouris was on more familiar ground when he accepted an offer from Jose Ferrer to appear in the summer season at the New York City Centre Theatre. Starting in May 1948, Coulouris starred in Ben Johnson's satire *The Alchemist* and followed on with Eugene O'Neill's one act drama *The Moon of the Caribees* and then *The Insect Comedy* by Josef and Karel Capek. The productions were respectfully received but Coulouris was still unsettled; he looked enviously to England where actors like Laurence Olivier and Ralph Richardson were reaching the height of their powers and pushing theatre in general, and the Bard in particular, in new and challenging directions. Coulouris had been corresponding with Anthony Quayle about joining the 1950 season at the Royal Shakespeare Company in Stratford but much to his disappointment, it didn't come off. Still the prospect of a return to the British stage was very tempting and whatever resistance he felt about uprooting the family yet again was dispelled by events unfolding back in California.

> NEW YORK CITY CENTER
> OF MUSIC AND DRAMA
> Spring Season 1948
> *presents*
> **THE NEW YORK CITY THEATRE COMPANY**
> JOSÉ FERRER, *General Director*
> *in*
> ## THE INSECT COMEDY
> *by*
> JOSEF and KAREL CAPEK
> A Play in Three Acts with Prologue and Epilogue
> Originally produced in New York by William A. Brady under the title
> "The World We Live In"
> Dramatized and Adapted by OWEN DAVIS
> *with*
> GEORGE COULOURIS
> *and*
>
> | | | |
> |---|---|---|
> | Ted Allegretti | Rita Gam | Alexander Scourby |
> | Tom Avera | Claire Hale | Mildred Joanne Smith |
> | Bobby Busch | Joyce Hill | Robinson Stone |
> | Mack Busch | Phyllis Hill | Charles Summers |
> | Stanley Carlson | Paula Laurence | Ray Walston |
> | Robert Carroll | Betty Low | Sidney Walters |
> | Leonardo Cimino | Annabelle Lyons | Jane White |
> | Chevi Colton | Nan McFarland | Bert Whitley |
> | José Ferrer | Arthur Newman | Howard Wierum |
> | | Thomas Poston | |
>
> Directed by Mr. FERRER   Choreography by HANYA HOLM
> Settings and Lighting by HERBERT BRODKIN
> Costume Direction by EMELINE ROCHE
>
> *(Program continued on next page)*

As the 1930s rolled into the 1940s, the concept of socialism as an acceptable alternative to fascism was quickly dispelled. Many of the East Coast intellectuals who had espoused the Communist Party line before the war had migrated to California where they enjoyed the lifestyle of the affluent middle classes. Despite their new-found wealth some of them continued to promote the Soviet Union as the idealized political model but by 1948 the climate had changed and the Russians were seen as the main threat to the American Dream. When the infamous House Committee on Un-American Activities (HUAC) launched its crusade against the "Hollywood Communists," studio executives, stars and public figures joined the clamor to expose the "red menace in the backyard." The result was the notorious "Hollywood Blacklist" which contained the names of actors, directors, writers and producers thought to be either communist themselves or sufficiently sympathetic to the party to make them dangerous. Their political views, or in many cases perceived political views, ensured that these men and women were to all intents and purposes banned from working in mainstream American movies.

Coulouris was by upbringing and inclination left of centre; as early as 1939 *The New York Times* described him as a "liberal" and would later associate him with the left-wing factions of the actor's union Equity. During the early days of the witch-hunt, Coulouris saw many of his friends and colleagues pilloried by their own countrymen; amongst the first to be named on the blacklist was Herbert J. Biberman, writer and director of *The Master Race*. Also singled out was Lillian Hellman who was added to the "List" after she refused to name acquaintances with Communist Party affiliations, as was Dashiell Hammett. They were joined by Sidney Kingsley, writer of *10 Million Ghosts*, Alvah Bessie who worked on *Hotel Berlin* and Coulouris' tennis buddy John Garfield. Clifford Odets, director of *None but the Lonely Heart*, found himself singled out by the committee when Lela E. Rogers, Ginger Rogers' mother, testified that the film was the "perfect example of the propaganda that communists like to inject." Coulouris' name never featured on the Hollywood blacklist though he was to be associated generally with the McCarthy witchhunts. His son George explained:

> Dad wasn't a communist; he never called himself that nor was he ever a member of the Communist Party. He did have a lot of friends who were either communists or socialists, the likes of Sam Wannamaker and Dalton Trumbo, and he would admit to strong left-wing sympathies. I know he attended a few fund raising events for the Soviet Union during the war, so it may be safe to describe him as a "fellow traveler" but whether he was at risk from McCarthy is a question I can't really answer. He certainly didn't leave America because of the threat of the blacklists but he did feel a sense of disgust about what was going on.

Coulouris found himself increasingly at odds with his adopted countrymen. His daughter Mary Louise remembers one incident in particular:

> Dad picked me up at school once in Connecticut, it was a private school. He wasn't a communist but he could be very outspoken and he didn't like the way that his friends were being treated and somehow got into a debate with some teenagers about the whole thing. It ended up with him saying something critical of the American Government; they shouted at him, "If you feel that way why you don't you get out?" I think it shocked him.

Although he had successfully applied for American citizenship—more a tax move than a sign of patriotism—Coulouris had retained dual nationality. Red tape around repatriating Louise and the children back to England wasn't a problem but the final decision to move the family could not have been an easy one. George, Jr. remembers:

> We had a family meeting to talk about what it was like, the schools, the social environment and so on. Dad wasn't negative about the U.S. at all but I think he saw Britain as a better society both for his career and also to bring up a family.

With a noisy party of friends and well-wishers gathering at the docks in New York to see them off, the family took their leave of the United States and embarked on the *Queen Mary* for the long voyage back to England. George

Coulouris would work in America again but he would never make another film there.

England in 1949 was a very different country than the one George and Louise had left nearly two decades before. The enormous debts run up during World War II had virtually bankrupt the country and rationing, first brought in as a wartime measure, was re-introduced by the socialist Labour Government struggling to get a grip on a balance of payments crisis. The government took the view that to enforce a cure, the economy needed to be brought under tight fiscal control and amongst the stringent measures introduced were restrictions on overseas travel and thresholds applied to currency taken out of the country. For Coulouris' children, who were raised as Californians, this was something of a shock, as George then age 12, remembered:

> England took a lot of getting used to. I remember sweets were still rationed, which was a shock, and Dad was annoyed because he couldn't get a decent restaurant! Dad had to spend a lot of time teaching us things like Latin and algebra, which we hadn't done in America but were required for English schools. Then there was the weather of course...

The Coulouris' new home was in Putney, close to the Thames in South West London, a far cry from their relatively luxurious West Coast home. With the English winter setting in the Coulouris household had to make do with one coal fired stove in the kitchen and old fashioned electric radiators spread throughout the house.

If the social adjustment offered a challenge, Coulouris also had to face re-establishing himself professionally. British theatre was notoriously shy of Hollywood actors — even those with a Broadway pedigree — and outside the West End and a few well established companies in the provinces, theatres faced an uncertain future in the austere economic climate. The film business was in an even worse state; cinemas still offered a buoyant market for Hollywood movies but the indigenous industry was in deep recession. The near collapse of the Rank Organization in 1949 had sent shock waves through the industry; studios laid off technicians; actors were struggling for work and more and more production companies were either closing down or moving over to the limited opportunities offered by the fledgling television industry. Coulouris resolved to get by taking whatever work he could to make ends meet.

Only weeks after arriving in England, Coulouris found some temporary respite from the English winter when he bundled the family into the back of a car and drove them to Portugal where he had been engaged to play the heavy in a tepid thriller called *Kill or Be Killed*. He played the murderous Sloma who tangles with Lawrence Tierney's weary hero and ends up feeding the fish, literally. The publicity department promised cinemagoers they would:

> See Lawrence Tierney fighting by the only law he knew! See the relentless danger-infested manhunt! See the most fiendish murder ever conceived—the terrible death of the man-eating Piranhas!

Sloma contributed the latter, perhaps the most unlikely demise the actor had yet experienced. Sadly even that treat wasn't enough to entice audiences and the most notable thing about the film was the jungle setting, which was to become almost a second home to Coulouris over the next few years!

Coulouris could afford to shrug off the disappointment of *Kill or Be Killed*; soon after returning from Portugal he was engaged by one of the most respected theatres outside of London. The Bristol Old Vic, closely affiliated to its London equivalent, was one of the few British provincial theatres to establish an international reputation and the quality of their productions ensured that the company

just managed to stay afloat. The actor appeared in Shakespeare's *As You Like It*, followed by title roles in *Tartuffe* and *The Admirable Crichton*, Brutus in *Julius Caesar* and Sir John in *The Provok'd Wife*. Coulouris would later reprise *Tartuffe* at the Lyric in London in a run that attracted both critical and box-office success. J.C. Trewin noted in *The Observer*:

> If during the course of a play, I am fired by a desire to rush up to the stage, through the pass door, and to throttle the villain,

then I suggest that the actor is doing his work well...George Coulouris has indeed some of the awful grandeur of Tartuffe.

Talking about the actor's stage presence, Trewin went on to coin the marvelous expression, "he darkens the Parisian sun." Stephen Williams, in the *Evening News*, reminded his readers again of the great villain in their midst:

> That broad face, loathsomely benevolent, as white as a lump of underdone fat and scored with lines of reproachful piety, the unctuous voice and the ready stoop of the born timeserver. What a hypocrite is here. Note also the masterly repose when other people are speaking of him. Mr. Coulouris commands one of the most difficult arts of the stage: to do nothing.

The same critic drew attention to "the kind of horrible greatness that Milton's Satan might have had." It was a splendid personal triumph and over the next decade the provincial theatre scene was to prove a happy hunting ground for Coulouris, including highlights such as *King Lear* in Glasgow, *Enemy of the People* in Cambridge, and touring with Sam Wannamaker's company. His uneasy relationship with the London theatre establishment kept him for the most part out of the West End but he did feature in *Hamlet* as Claudius and Malvolio in *Twelfth Night,* both at the Embassy in North London. Soon the family could afford to move out of that dreary house in Putney into a striking but somewhat dilapidated cottage in the Vale of Health in Hampstead, a 200-year old artisan's house in a secluded lane, now a highly desirable suburb of London. The cottage could best be described as basic; there was no central heating, it had an outside toilet and was badly in need of repair. The actor and his wife fell in love with the place even if they couldn't afford to have it modernized immediately. Over the next few years, whenever he wasn't working, Coulouris turned his hand to a number of building projects around the family home. Predictably building materials were on ration so he needed to be discrete about his renovations.

Coulouris on a day out, photo from the 1950s

While his theatre work may have been to his satisfaction, Coulouris' film career was slow to take off. In 1951 he had something of a breakthrough with *Appointment with Venus*, appearing third on a bill featuring David Niven and Glynis Johns. In this moderately budgeted Rank film the "Venus" of the title is a prize pedigree cow left behind on the German occupied Channel Islands and now the subject of a top secret mission to restore her to her rightful owner. Hollywood's favorite Nazi was cast with one eye on the North American market as Captain Weiss, the straight-faced German commandant determined to evacuate the prize bovine to the Fatherland, only to be outwitted by the heroics of Niven and Johns. Every bit as lightweight and whimsical as it sounds, the film did receive a release in the U.S. under the less inspiring title of *Island Rescue* but failed to match the success it enjoyed in Britain.

Apart from reintroducing audiences to the actor's underplayed gravitas, *Appointment with Venus* was also significant for Coulouris because it was his first with the producer-director team of Betty Box and Ralph Thomas. The former was the sister of erstwhile Gainsborough boss Sidney Box and could claim to be not only one of the few women producers active in England but one of the most astute. Ralph Thomas (brother of Gerald Thomas, producer of the inane *Carry On* comedies) was a competent if unpretentious director who would go on to helm a number of successful British films. Thomas' affable personality made him popular with the cast and crew and his propensity to shoot quickly without losing quality made him a favorite of studio bosses. His nickname for many years, "Five Minutes" Thomas, was testament to the amount of footage he could produce in one day. The Box and Thomas partnership prospered with a number of comedies and thrillers none of which could be described as cutting edge but nearly all of which proved popular at the box-office. More importantly for Coulouris, they liked the comfort of familiar faces in both cast and crew and they would ensure regular employment for the actor through the 1950s.

On the whole Coulouris' British films offered little in the way of acting challenges but his next movie was an exception. With a tagline that screamed

"The Soul of a SAVAGE... in the Soft, Beautiful body of a WOMAN!" casual patrons of *Outcast of the Islands* might be forgiven for thinking they were about to see an exploitation potboiler. In fact the 1952 London Films production was a prestigious adaptation of Joseph Conrad's novel of the same name, directed by Carol Reed whose previous work included *Odd Man Out* and *The Third Man*. Alexander Korda's company may have lost some of its luster since the days of Charles Laughton in *The Private Life of Henry VIII* but it was still considered important enough to attract a heavyweight cast including Ralph Richardson, Trevor Howard and Robert Morley. The setting is the jungle (again!) with exteriors in Ceylon and studio work in the more mundane surroundings of Shepperton. The Malaysia of the British Empire is beautifully recreated right down to the drawing room bigotry and stiff upper lip snobbishness. The natives by contrast are all seething passions and dark mutterings, a volatile mix, which leads to the inevitable revolt and brutality.

Howard stole all the plaudits as the flawed anti-hero Willems, betraying everything he values with his obsession with the beautiful dark-eyed Aissa. Coulouris was made up as the swarthy Babalatchi and, looking fetching in a sarong, managed to convey both wisdom and an earthy cunning without resorting to clichés. This was a more or less faithful adaptation of Conrad's novel with some excellent performances, even if one can imagine Coulouris bristling at playing yet another "greasy foreigner." Noted critic Pauline Kael called it a "marvelous film." The British Academy agreed and gave it a nomination for "Best Film" in a strong year that also included *The African Queen* and *A Streetcar Named Desire*. *The Sound Barrier* was declared the winner. Unfortunately *Outcast of the Islands*' overwhelming pessimism was too much for the British public and the film was met with little enthusiasm in its home market. In the U.S., despite the best efforts of the distributor to lighten the tone, eight minutes were pruned, and the film suffered the same fate.

Coulouris was then seen to less effect in a far more popular film, Muriel Box's lighthearted thriller *The Venetian Bird* (aka *The Assassin*), which starred diminutive action star Richard Todd and was shot in Rome. Frustrated by studio interference, Box and Thomas had developed a penchant for shooting abroad which gave their films a refreshing quality not found in the lanes and forests around Pinewood! Cast again as a foreigner, Coulouris played an Italian policeman in a minor supporting role, which the actor surely justified by the opportunity to revisit the Italy of his youth. Box later recalled that the actor seemed a little too intent on soaking up the local atmosphere:

> He tended to stay out late talking and drinking with friends who would walk him back to his hotel in the early hours and stand outside, laughing and holding noisy conversations, usually ending up waking most of the technicians. As they had to be up and at work at dawn, the technicians didn't take kindly at all to the frequent nocturnal disturbances... The next night several chamber pots were filled with murky "Canal No. 5" and God knows what else and, as soon as the babble started up below and wakened them, the technicians got going and a malodorous deluge descended onto the noisy gathering. There was no more trouble with George and his mates after that.

Coulouris stayed on with Box and Thomas for his next two films neither of which merit more than a glance. *The Dog and the Diamonds* is 60 minutes worth of kiddy matinee fodder with some annoying children outwitting jewel thieves in an old house, with Coulouris predictably counting amongst the villains. It was shelved for almost 10 years before a fleeting U.S. release proved it wasn't worth the wait. *A Day to Remember* didn't promise much more and turned out to be a dreary little comedy about a pub darts team on a day trip to Bologne in France.

More ambitious work beckoned in 1953 with an adaptation of Graham Greene's *The Heart of the Matter,* set but not filmed in West Africa. Trevor Howard, who had been so memorable in *Outcast of the Islands,* leant his considerable presence to what turned out to be a tepid little movie with none of the style of previous Greene adaptations. Coulouris appeared in another pointless cameo but he and Howard did cause some consternation on set when they were in a car accident. Howard, a notorious tippler, was speeding to the local pub after a hard day at the studio when he lost control of the car; luckily no-one was hurt and no permanent damage was done. The film was hardly worth their efforts despite the British Academy's continued loyalty to Greene with the obligatory Best Film nomination. Next up for Coulouris was the inane *Duel in the Jungle,* set in another far flung outpost of England's dwindling Empire, this time Rhodesia. Imported Hollywood star Dana Andrews plays a tough insurance investigator who, together with Jeanne Crain, "through screeching jungle haunts, across the veldt of violence, past lion fang and boa coil... they shadowed the 'Dead man of the Transvaal' they had to bring back alive!" Coulouris and that reliable scene-stealer Wilfred Hyde-White added some fun but their efforts are undermined by George Marshall's leaden direction. The forgettable movie briefly made the headlines for the wrong reasons when second unit director Tom Kelly was killed when his boat over turned on the Zambesi River.

While his film career was mired very much in B movies, Coulouris started to explore the opportunities offered by television. His early experiences with the BBC and their haphazard approach to live broadcasts did little to endear the medium to the actor, though he did volunteer to turn out for the BBC's cricket team!

By the mid-1950s the television production standards had improved considerably and Coulouris was persuaded to appear in one of the more interesting series to come out of England. *Colonel March of Scotland Yard,* which starred Boris Karloff, was a sort of 1950s version of the *X Files,* which proved popular on both sides of the Atlantic. Karloff played the title role, a grizzled investigator from the Yard's "Department of Queer Affairs" with Coulouris guest starring in an episode called *The Deadly Gift.* The show was shot in late 1954 at the tiny Southall Studios in South London and sedately helmed by former Gainsborough director Bernard Knowles, director of the ghost story *A Place of One's Own.* Despite the improved quality, Coulouris had little time for the small screen and saw it purely as a means to supplement his income, rather than an art form in its own right. The actor would continue to appear on the small screen throughout the next two decades, acting in televised plays, guest starring in peak time series like *Danger Man* and even taking a recurring role in the science fiction series *Pathfinders to Venus.* Despite this he never overcame his contempt for the medium; in an interview in 1971 with the *Sunday Telegraph* he said:

> Television has wrecked acting... If somebody had told me 30 years ago that by this point in my career I'd be spending a lot of my time in some cheerless, dusty rehearsal room preparing for a single performance in something not very important I would have said it could never happen.

Coulouris, center, playing it for laughs in *Doctor at Sea*.

In the same interview he summed up the contrast between the stage and the small screen:

> I can go all over England and my face will be recognized more easily than some of these big shots, who spend most of their time on the London stage, like old Larry and Scofield and Gielgud, but that's no good to me. I get barrow boys saying to me: "You must be hard up, mate. I haven't seen you on the telly for a bit."

Betty Box saved Coulouris from further television work with a role in her landmark comedy *Doctor in the House*, adapted from the enormously popular series of books. The actor got to ham it up as a particularly grumpy patient stuck against his will in a hospital ward tended by the hapless Dr. Sparrow. The slapstick bumbling and comic misunderstandings tickled the nation's funny bone to the tune of a staggering 17 million tickets sold—nearly half of the adult population of Britain! The film stars Dirk Bogarde in the leading role and its success made him the preeminent star of post-war British cinema but the series, like its successors the *Carry On* films, proved that humor is one genre that doesn't cross the national boundaries. *Doctor in the House* was also nominated for a British Academy award, giving Coulouris' films three consecutive British nominations to match his American achievement. Coulouris went on to appear in the equally popular sequels *Doctor at Sea* (1955) and *Doctor at Large* (1957).

After an appearance in the tedious detective yarn *The Teckman Mystery*, Coulouris reported to Hammer Films, temporarily relocated from their base in Bray to Sidney Box's old studio at Riverside, for the low-budget thriller *Mask of Dust*. With their Technicolor horror movies still in the future, Hammer's astute head James Carreras concentrated his modest resources on a stream of thrillers and comedies largely adapted from recognized sources at the BBC, initially radio and later television. By staying close to the BBC, Carreras kept Hammer afloat while the industry around him crumbled and, by exploiting modest tax incentives offered to overseas filmmakers, he persuaded U.S. companies to invest in what would otherwise be strictly domestic fare. The link to the BBC ensured Hammer had brand recognition with audiences now more inclined to watch or listen to their favorite stars in the comfort of their own homes. Carreras' alliances with U.S. film companies and distributors ensured these Hammer films had distribution on both sides of the Atlantic.

Mask of Dust was a fairly typical Hammer production. The BBC had adapted the pulp novel, by John Manchip White, by into a successful play, and then Hammer snapped up the rights and invited American producer Robert Lippert to join them as production partner. Lippert, an old hand at this sort of thing, provided the money to hire Hollywood tough guy Richard Conte for the role of an aging race car driver, determined against all the advice to enjoy one last season at the top. Conte, clearly more comfortable playing gangsters than heroes, made an aggressive but ineffectual leading man. Lippert also provided a love interest in the shape of Mari Aldon who was used to better effect by Raoul Walsh in *Distant Drums* and here makes a curiously pasty-faced and unappealing leading lady, who even in a state of décolletage can't distract Conte from his piano playing!

Coulouris was cast against type as a lively and good-natured Italian driver, happily singing opera in the bathroom and flirting with chambermaids. Of course the moment Coulouris announces he is to marry his childhood sweetheart and that the next race will be his last, you know it isn't going to end well. True to form, an off-screen crash sends Coulouris to the local hospital where, swathed in bandages, he duly expires. Barely a third of the way into the narrative, and not a dry eye in the house, the film has Conte, grim faced and granite jawed, trying to win the championship for his dead friend. The irrepressible Renee Glynne was the continuity girl, a role she had on many of the early Hammer movies. She remembered working with Coulouris very well:

> He was a big name actor for Hammer and of course we all knew he had worked on some big, big films in America but you would never know it from the way he behaved, and he was treated just the same as everyone else. I suppose he may have needed the money to come to work on such a low budget

film but he treated it very professionally. He was very proper in a way that reminded me of Christopher Lee, not pompous but a little standoffish until you got to know him, then he would tell such wonderful stories about Hollywood and the people he worked with.

By anyone's standard *Mask of Dust* is a routine programmer staged without much feeling by Terence Fisher, a director whose best work would lie in Hammer's atmospheric horror movies. It was shot on location at Goodwood racetrack and featured some of the more familiar names of contemporary British motor racing including Alan Brown, John Cooper, Reg Parnell and Sterling Moss, the only one of the professional drivers to get a speaking role. To open the radio play and ensure a suitably Transatlantic feel, Lippert had his regular scripter Richard Landon flown to London but the film never really develops an international feel and looks and feels very British and low budget. The stock footage is well integrated but unless you have a particular passion for racing cars of the period the race sequences overstay their welcome. Even the device borrowed from the radio of using BBC commentator Raymond Baxter to narrate much of the action fails to enliven proceedings. Still with such unsympathetic leads it would be a surprise if Coulouris didn't steal the show and in *Mask of Dust* he is exceptionally good, clearly enjoying the opportunity to play such a gregarious character.

Coulouris took on another comic role, a befuddled vicar at a loss to understand Dennis Price's machinations, in one of the best comedies of the time, the Boulting Brothers' *Privates Progress*. Coulouris doesn't actually appear until near the end of the film but it's nice to see him keeping company

Privates Progress

65

with such reliable performers as Richard Attenborough, Terry-Thomas and Ian Carmichael. The film was well-made and -received which is more than can be said for *Tarzan and the Lost Safari* (1957). Hailed as the first of the "modern Tarzans," *Lost Safari* blazed onto the screen with the far from inspiring tagline "Adventure takes to the Air in a Safari in a Luxury Plane." Sadly the film reflected the same lack of imagination. The somewhat lame storyline has Tarzan swinging to the rescue of the five members of the titular safari, a party of socialites stranded in the jungle when their plane crashes. The villain of the piece is a white hunter, a leering Robert Beatty, who intends to sell the interlopers to the Oparian tribe as human sacrifices. *Tarzan and the Lost Safari* was "modern" in the sense that it was the first movie featuring Edgar Rice Burroughs' creation to be shot in full Cinemascope, making use of location work in Congo and Uganda—a relative novelty for a series that rarely left the comfort of California. In all other respects this outing added little to the oeuvre, with a wooden Gordon Scott, a former army trainer and Las Vegas lifeguard, taking up the loin cloth discarded by his far better known predecessors Johnny Weissmuller, Buster Crabbe and Lex Barker. In fact this was Scott's second bash at the part having previously starred in *Tarzan's Hidden Jungle* and he would go on to four further sequels before ending his career in Italian "sword and sandal" movies. H. Bruce Humberstone, best known for the Charlie Chan movies of the 1930, flatly directed the film. The acting is without distinction by normally reliable performers such as Wilfred Hyde-White, Peter Arne and Yolande Dolan. Coulouris, marking an inauspicious return to MGM (they distributed the film), is simply along for the ride and apart from looking hot and bothered is given very little to do; his name doesn't even feature in the movie's publicity, an indication of how transient Hollywood fame can be.

Staying with a jungle theme, Coulouris was promoted to top billing for his next role, which after a lifetime of playing villains, marked his first proper brush with horror movies. The producer-director team of Cuido Coen and Charles Saunders was responsible for a series of low budget thrillers throughout the 1950s with titles such as *Kill Her Gently* and *Murder Reported*. Saunders wasn't noted for his sense of style but his work was consistent and reliable and he was a classic example of a "journeyman director" coming up through the ranks to direct programmers for companies such as Eros and Hammer, before moving on to Fortress Film Productions in 1954 for a series of potboilers starting with *A Time to Kill*. (Fortress Films is a nearly forgotten name in the annals of British film history but deserves a footnote for its choice of leading ladies. Between 1954 and 1957 Fortress managed to find employment for Hazel Court, Yvonne Romain, Vera Day, Melissa Stribling and Shirley Eaton.) By 1957 Fortress had graduated from thrillers to horror movies and commissioned Coen and Saunders to bring *The Woman Eater* to the screen, based on a script by Brandon Fleming and inspired largely by Roger Corman's exploitation movies for AIP.

Fleming's script is pure drive-in fodder: An overzealous scientist, Dr. Moran, on an expedition to the Amazon witnesses the ritual sacrifice of a scantily clad native girl to what appears to be a large and rather agitated tree. Some years later Moran has relocated to the south of England, bringing with him a native witchdoctor, Tanga, as well as the actual tree itself! From here the story deviates little from the accepted formula with Moran, clearly deranged, sacrificing Home Counties lovelies—allegedly to benefit mankind though it is never explained how. Prior to each sacrifice, Tanga drums out a catchy beat to get the girls into the mood. Thereafter duly enthralled, with their dresses ripped rather fetchingly, they are "absorbed" by the tree. Throughout the process, the good doctor looks on with an expression that suggests his motives are less than noble. The heroine, played by pneumatic starlet Vera Day, becomes embroiled in his experiments while the local police scratch their heads and mutter about how terrible the whole thing is.

The link between sexuality and science (and madness for that matter) has always been explicit in the fantasy genre. From *The Cabinet of Dr. Caligari* to Bela Lugosi's Dr. Mirakle in *Murders in the Rue Morgue* and beyond, mad doctors have drooled over pallid heroines, usually bound on some sort of operating table. In *The Woman Eater* Dr. Moran follows down this well-worn path. Apart from the overtly sexual sacrifices, exploitation rears its head in Moran's midnight walk through London's seedier neighborhoods with Coulouris ignoring the more conventional temptations in favor of stalking potential victims;

Coulouris and Joyce Gregg in *The Womeneater*

and where else would one find compliant females but in the fleshpots of the red light district in Soho? To his considerable credit Coulouris gives a thoroughly watch-able performance, managing to convey not only Moran's lunacy but also his sadness; indeed one feels that Vera Day has been rather beastly in judging him so harshly. Despite outward appearances Moran patently thinks of himself as a "lady killer"—in both the allegorical and literal sense! Moran is clearly a passionate man, as demonstrated by his relationship with Margaret, the doting housekeeper and former paramour who obviously still holds a candle for her employer. Despite her lingering attraction to him, Moran treats his ex-lover with something approaching contempt: "There was a time when you trusted me," she whimpers, only to be dismissed with a curt, "My dear Margaret, I have never trusted you or another woman with anything I didn't want anyone else to know."

Actress Joyce Gregg, who shows the unrequited love simmering beneath the surface with just the hint that it may one day explode, ably demonstrates Margaret's tight-lipped frustration. Things are clearly going to get a bit sticky when Margaret is introduced to her successor, an airhead blonde whose sole qualification for the job is a slightly used hula skirt and a winsome smile. Interestingly, this on-screen triangle was also mirrored to some extent off-screen with Coulouris taking a fatherly interest in the young actress. Vera Day remembers:

> George was lovely and we got on very well but I remember Joyce Gregg wasn't very friendly and I tried not to have too much to do with her. I really don't think she liked me very much and I remember one day she said to me: "You need to lose that cockney accent if you want to get on in this business." Just like that, I was very upset. George would have none of it. "Don't you dare," he said, "that's what makes you unique!"

Day, just starting her career, recalls sharing her anxieties about the quality of the film with Coulouris and being offered some reassurance: "He told me not to worry too much about it and no one is going to remember this in a year's time!"

With the most hackneyed of scripts, Coulouris had to make the most of the limited opportunities it offered. Like his illustrious predecessors in similar work, Karloff, Lugosi and Atwill, he chose to play the role absolutely straight, avoiding the self-mocking camp that was to become a feature of latter day mad scientist movies. In a carefully mannered performance we see Moran's sanity stretched as tight as a drum, threatening at any moment to erupt into full-blown madness. Coulouris is excellent, with his staring eyes and seedy appearance, he captures Moran's fall from grace with iron resolution.

There is a fine score from Edwin Astley who later did the music for Hammer's *The Phantom of the Opera* and some good photography from veteran Ernest Palmer whose cinematography for *Blood and Sand* won him an Oscar in 1941. Of course the stock footage, seemingly obligatory in all 1950s films, is poorly integrated but in a low budget horror film it doesn't really mar the enjoyment. Sadly "woman eating" remains something of a disappointment for even the most undemanding of viewers and the amateurish quality wasn't lost on the cast as Vera Day admitted:

> It was very hard to take it seriously. It didn't look real when we did it and looking at it on the screen it is really obvious there is a hard working technician in there pushing the arms backwards and forwards. Like all these things you hope they will sort it out in the editing but I don't know how we managed to keep a straight face.

The fact that the victims are required to more or less walk into its tentacles could be said to be part of the charm but the mechanics of how the creature actually digests the sacrifices are kept mercifully vague. Saunders had his own way of compensating for the poor effects, as Day suggested, "He put in so many boob jokes to distract people from the awful monster!" The inconsistencies of the plot are left unresolved; why Tanga would agree to move to Hampshire is never touched on or indeed how an eight-foot killer tree have got through customs in the first place. *The Woman Eater* benefits from a healthy dose of bad taste, has the same kitsch entertainment value as *Attack of the Crab Monsters* or *The Beast with a Million Eyes*, and certainly deserves to be watched.

The film opened in the U.S. in July 1959 with a campaign that promised, "See the nerve-shattering Dance of Death! See *The Woman Eater* ensnare the beauties of two continents! See the hideous arms devour them in a death-embrace!" By then Hammer's Technicolor horrors had erupted and Saunders' film looked quaintly old fashioned. If it had enjoyed greater success in the U.S., Fortress may well have emerged as Britain's answer to AIP but the film failed to gain the exposure it needed, though it enjoyed a brief run as a supporting feature for Richard Gordon's *The Electronic Monster*.

The Man without a Body seems to carry on where *The Woman Eater* leaves off. "A diabolical dream comes true! Who is his Next Victim?" screamed the trailers but sadly it is less fun and represents a step down in almost every respect. Although it was released later, Coen shot *The Man without a Body* at Twickenham prior to *The Woman Eater* and he was clearly aiming at the same market. Coulouris again enjoyed top billing as Karl Brussard, a powerful and ruthless millionaire inflicted by the one thing it seems his money can't prevent, an incurable brain tumor. In seeking an alternative to the Grim Reaper, Brussard isn't too concerned with either the cost or the ethics. The principal idea, with modest refinements, had been seen before in *Donovan's Brain* where an honest scientist keeps the brain of a dead millionaire alive long after the body has passed its "sell by" date. *The Man without a Body* reworks the premise with a rather more fundamental approach; why bother with the complexities of brain transplants when you can take the whole head? Enter Dr. Merritt, an earnest but under-funded scientist who has managed the rather grotesque feat of transplanting heads between monkeys. But even with token efforts to present Merritt as a misguided but honest scientist, sympathy is in short supply and the camera skirts the thin line between exploitation and bad taste, dwelling too long on the living head of a disemboweled monkey. It is not just the animal experimentation that leaves a bad taste; too much screen time is given to the sexual shenanigans between Brussard and his mistress, the mistress and the chauffeur, Brussard and his wife, the wife and Merritt's assistant, and so on.

The film really takes off into ghoulish fantasy when Brussard enlists the help of broken-down scientist Dr. Brandon for the role of body stealer, or more correctly "head stealer," to procure an appropriate donor. Given a choice of great men in history he opts for Nostradamus, whose head (and body) are conveniently located in an under-guarded crypt. Amongst the more bizarre moments is Brussard going through customs with the aforementioned head in his hand luggage. The scientists succeed in reviving the long dead philosopher who naturally enough is less than thrilled by the prospect of a transplant. For a film

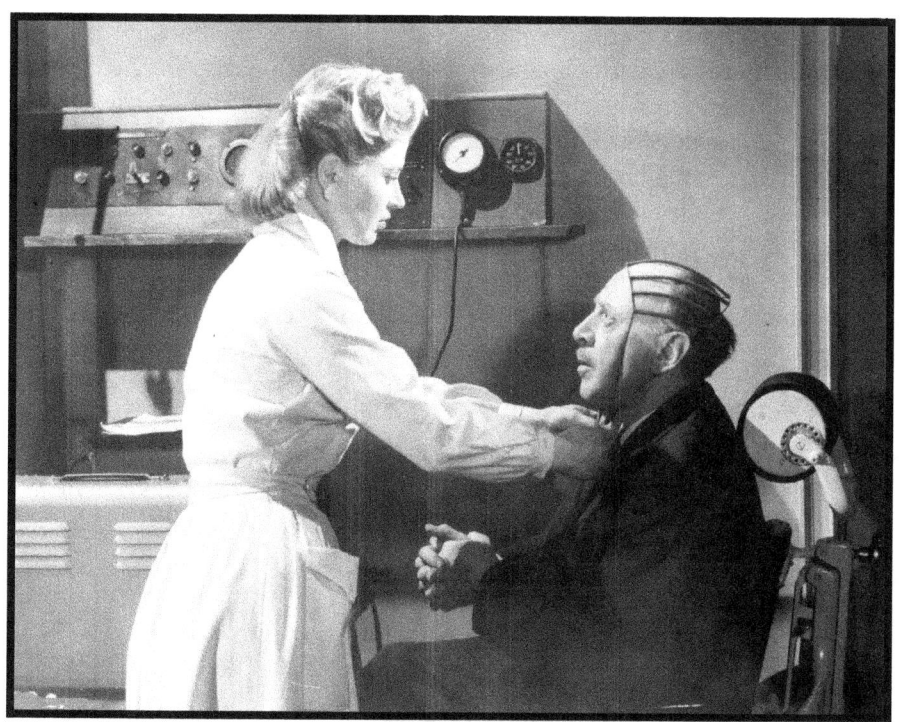

Coulouris as Brussard in *The Man Without a Body*.

which at its best can be described as far fetched, the last third becomes positively weird, a bizarre hybrid of every bad Frankenstein/monster-on-the-loose movie you are ever likely to see. Despite the ludicrous plot it is nearly possible to see why Coulouris would have been attracted to Broussard, a braggart, a bully and a real throwback to Pharaoh Coffin without the grandeur but with all the flaws of arrogance and egotism, plus an unhealthy dose of sexual immorality added. Murder, blackmail and sexual abuse all fall within his job description.

Squared-jawed Robert Hutton brings an amiable charm to Merritt, little more than a routine hero/doctor role. Despite the ludicrous plotting he manages to keep a straight face. Coulouris had in fact met Hutton briefly when they were both at Warner Bros., where the latter was a contract player. (Hutton would later find his stamina tested to the limit in *The Vulture* and *Trog*.) The film also features Nadja Regin, who decorated British films like *Don't Panic Chaps* and *Goldfinger* before finding more gainful employment as a script reader for Hammer.

The straight-faced dramatics of the cast are undermined by the unintentionally hilarious script and Poverty Row budget. The lack of money shines through in every scene, most notably in the laboratory sequences where the sight of Nostradamus' head suspended in a tank isn't enough to distract from the lack of scientific equipment.

The credit or blame for this preposterous film is shared for tax reasons between nominal Brit Charles Saunders and the actual director, American-based W. Lee Wilder, the younger and less talented brother of Billy, who was making the first of three films featuring Coulouris. A more inspired director might just have pulled off something entertaining but Wilder either wasn't up to it or sufficiently interested. With its lifeless soundtrack and dull photography the film struggles to hold the attention for its modest 80-minute running time.

The reviews were surprisingly positive. Kine Weekly summed up, "Hocus pocus which has an element of sex, becomes a bit heady towards the end but the few laughs in the wrong place should not prevent it from throwing a scare into the industrial nine-pennies." *The Man without a Body* represents the nadir of Coulouris' film career, a Z-grade movie that everyone involved would disown and the public avoided.

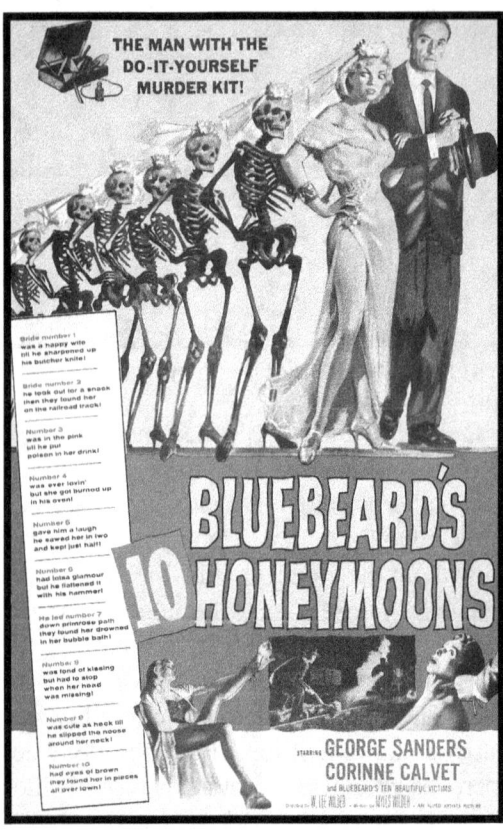

Unfortunately Coulouris' later collaborations with Wilder—both filmed in England—show the same lazy plotting and inconsistent direction. In 1958 Wilder had the actor assume a convincing American accent to play a U.S. Colonel in his espionage thriller *Spy in the Sky* set in Vienna, about which the less said the better. Marginally more interesting is *Bluebeard's Ten Honeymoons*, the story of the notorious serial killer reduced to another of Wilder's low budget comic thrillers. Although it is an improvement on their previous collaborations, Coulouris is reduced to a brief cameo while George Sanders plays the titular murderer with his trademark indifference. Wilder, once again milking the tax incentives, has England standing in for Paris but struggles to find humor or suspense in the workmanlike script by son Myles. The film has nothing to commend it apart from the gimmicky casting of Corinne Calvet, Jean Kent and Patricia Roc, Gainsborough's three leading ladies reunited after over a decade apart, sadly in a vehicle that had nothing of the panache of their earlier work.

Robert Hutton interviewed by Tom Weaver, was asked if Coulouris seemed pleased to work in these sorts of movies. He replied:

> Over there in England it is completely different from Hollywood. Over here if you made a movie like that, they'd say, "The guy is washed up, he's finished." But over there the main thing is to work. They couldn't care less if the movie has a 50-cent budget or a 50-million dollar budget, as long as you worked.

Coulouris' son George remembers his father was ambivalent towards not only B movies but films in general:

> Dad saw these films as potboilers; he made them because he had to but he didn't really like them very much. He seldom went to see any kind of films but he understood the difference between film acting and stage acting. He certainly took all of them very seriously though and always tried very had to do good work even if he didn't think the script merited it.

Coulouris' next role was as a minor crime boss in the routine thriller *Kill Me Tomorrow* shot again at Southall Studios. Hollywood actor Pat O'Brien stars as a washed up reporter whose son needs a life saving operation. O'Brien's desperation to get the money leads him into the murky quarters inhabited by Webber (Coulouris). With such an underwritten script, the actor had little opportunity to do anything more than add another thoroughly unpleasant hood to his rogue's gallery. Webber, who uses a seedy nightclub as a front for his nefarious activities, committed perhaps his worst crime when he introduces the ever-smiling crooner Tommy Steele to English audiences! This was another inferior effort which despite a spirited performance from Coulouris would have slipped into deserved obscurity if not for two minor points of interest. Firstly, *Kill Me Tomorrow* was (along with the cult favorite *The Trollenberg Terror*) the last film shot at Southall. The old studio, reeling from the decline in cinema audiences, was closed permanently soon afterward and demolished the following year. Secondly, the film marked the collaboration in the director's chair by those two great journeymen of British Bs, Francis Searle and Terence Fisher. Both spent most of their careers fashioning supporting features and low budget programmers; the latter of course would go on to become the father figure of Hammer horror. Indeed *Kill Me Tomorrow* would be Fisher's last movie before he reported for work on *The Curse of Frankenstein*.

In terms of quantity Coulouris could have no complaint about his films, as he was in near constant employment. In terms of quality, he was a long way

Coulouris and Herbert Lom in *I Accuse*

from *Citizen Kane*. English audiences were still keen on war films and Coulouris had a short run under fire starting with *Seven Thunders* (U.S. title *Beast of Marseilles*), a better than average prisoner of war drama with some nice twists. Sadly Coulouris, playing a Frenchman, had little to do, but the locations at Bouches-du-Rhône in France probably compensated to some extent. Coulouris retained the accent and added a military uniform to play a French officer in *I Accuse*, a worthy but uninspiring retelling of the infamous Dreyfus affair, the trial of a Jewish officer in the French army wrongly accused of treason. Then there was *No Time to Die* with such British stiff upper lips as Leo Genn and Anthony Newly, aided and abetted by Victor Mature, re-fighting the North Africa campaign with Coulouris as an Italian POW commandant.

None of these films were of much value and film producers in Britain seemed blissfully unaware of the untapped potential they had at their fingertips. Their counterparts in Hollywood adopted an out of sight, out of mind attitude and the screen career of one of cinema's great heavies was slowly allowed to wither away in efforts like *The Big Money* which sounds like a *film noir* but is actually another one of those dimwitted Rank comedies that appeal to no one but the British. This one was a routine vehicle for comic actor Ian Carmichael, normally cast as an upper class twit who this time slips across the class divide and plays a working class twit who steals a suitcase from a sinister looking clergyman, played by a sinister looking Robert Helpmann, only to find it stuffed with counterfeit banknotes. The bumbling Carmichael is soon mooning over barmaid Belinda Lee while finding new and increasingly "comical" ways of laundering the cash. The villains of course want their loot back and are soon on his trail, as are likeable rogues Coulouris and Michael Brennan who try to con him out of his ill-gotten gains. Directed by John Paddy Carstairs, the film is well acted by the leads, particularly Coulouris whose turn as the dodgy Colonel is easily one of the highlights, but the script is weak and the story predictable.

Coulouris continued the run of uninspiring film work playing Alan a'Dale, one of the middle-aged merry men in *The Son of Robin Hood*. England is once again under the thumb of a cruel tyrant and looking to the offspring of the late outlaw for salvation; the twist is that the "son" of the title is actually a daughter, with all the allegedly "comic" misunderstanding that this entails. Hollywood star June Laverick plays Ms. Hood but it is all fairly routine with Coulouris asked to do little more than look perplexed. Then Ralph Thomas, on a rare departure from comedy, recalled the actor for the straight-faced drama *Conspiracy of Hearts* starring Lilli Palmer and Sylvia Sims as unlikely nuns defying the Nazis' firing squad. Ronald Lewis plays an anxious Italian officer torn between duty and compassion, with Coulouris, as a sympathetic Italian, relying once again on his fretful expression to cover for a lack of characterization.

Sharply contrasting with this film work, Coulouris had a burgeoning reputation on the stage. In the decade or so since relocating to England, the actor enjoyed the most consistent and successful period of his stage career; working with directors of the caliber of Sam Wannamaker and Peter Ustinov in works by Clifford Odets and Ibsen. It was Ibsen's *Enemy of the People* that provided the actor with one of his most memorable stage roles. Opening at the Theatre Royal in Lincoln on March 2, 1958, the play attracted the attention of the influential critic Kenneth Tynan who identified Coulouris as a "visiting star" but noted, "not since *Citizen Kane* has this burly actor hit so full a stride." Amongst the other highlights from the period was *The Ghost Writers* by Ted Allan, with Coulouris avenging himself on Hollywood by playing a loud mouthed Californian film producer. The play also featured a young Andree Melly.

Despite the success, Coulouris was reluctant to commit to a company or theatre for a long period of time and there would be no more Mercury or RSC seasons on his résumé. More significantly, he remained stubbornly on the outside of London's theatre elite and as a consequence was seldom called on to play in the West End and never worked with any of the major recognized stalwarts of the English stage. Coulouris enjoyed leading roles but the plays were more often than not imported rather than by his beloved Bard. Coulouris was too intelligent not to realize this would affect his standing and his legacy as an actor, and he raged against the injustice of it throughout his life. The paradox is that he did nothing to remedy the situation, arguing that this sort of politicking and back-slapping had nothing to do with acting. Later in his life he would have long conversations with his close friend at the BBC Brian Deane who remembered:

> George was friendly with Ralph Richardson but not the others, the whole Binkie Beaumont crowd. Beaumont was the most important theatre impresario in London and he was at the centre of a clique; if you weren't part of that scene you

simply didn't get asked. George had no time at all for that, or Olivier or Gielgud. This attitude put George on the outside. He never played at the National Theatre, although Ken Tynan was a great friend, because Olivier was in charge. I think he resented that.

Coulouris on family holiday in 1953

The family was now well established in the Vale of Health and Coulouris continued happily with his never-ending home improvements while Sunday afternoons became open house for family and friends. Amongst the guests were politician Michael Foot, later the leader of the Labour Party, author John Steinbeck and film director Sidney Lumet. George relished these occasions and he loved playing host. Daughter Mary Louise characterizes her father as "a family man, he loved having friends and his children around him—a very Greek characteristic." Coulouris continued to play tennis and cricket, he was extremely fit and as Mary Louise recalled he would find ways of channeling his tremendous enthusiasm:

> Dad never seemed to get tired no matter what he was doing; he had enormous energy. He would get very excited when things were going well and he was busy and he would rave about how wonderful it was to be an actor and what a noble profession he was in. When things weren't going so well he would be more moody and pace up and down trying to make things happen. Even when he wasn't acting he would embark on massive building projects at home just to keep busy. He would be there banging in nails, bursting open his finger and carrying on regardless. He was so focused on getting things done.

The early 1960s on the whole were not a good period for Coulouris as a film actor though two movies stand out, not because of any inherent quality but because they echo back to previous days. 1960 featured Coulouris in *Surprise Package* with his old mentor Noel Coward in a comic caper which has something to do with an American gangster, Yul Brynner, stealing the crown jewels of the exiled King of Anatolia and hiding out in an exotic Greek island. Coulouris is the heavy who had engineered the King's earlier overthrow. Even a good Hollywood director like Stanley Donen couldn't make much of the material. Then a year later Coulouris played a small role in Nicholas Ray's sprawling epic *King of Kings* which marked his last professional association with Orson Welles who, bloated and practically unemployable, was reduced to providing the voice over. Coulouris himself could only salvage a little dignity from his fleeting role as an Arab camel driver.

The only really memorable film of the period was *Fury at Smuggler's Bay*, the rollicking tale of 17th Century ship wreckers on the desolate Cornwall coast. Directed by the flamboyant John Gilling, whose best work would come for Hammer in 1966 with *Plague of the Zombies* but who also fashioned their early action movie *The Pirates of Blood River*. The film was intended as a ripping adventure yarn combining the best elements of Gainsborough and Hammer's swashbucklers—indeed the film is so successful at the latter that it is often mistakenly identified as a Hammer film. Peter Cushing stars as the terse Squire Trevelyn in a cast that includes Bernard Lee as the cutthroat "Black John" and William Franklin as the roguish highwayman, "the Captain," clearly modeled on James Mason's role in *The Wicked Lady*. Lee is the villain of the piece, leading his gang of thugs onto the beaches, plundering the stricken ships and murdering the survivors. Billed sixth, Coulouris is Lejeune, a sympathetic scallywag played with a twinkle in his eye and although technically on the wrong side of the law quickly elicits audience empathy. Compared with Black John, Lejeune is a model citizen. Romance is provided by the Squire's son, John Fraser, and Lejeune's daughter, the stunning Michele Mercier. Comic relief comes from Miles Malleson, and Liz Frazer, better known for comic roles, is also featured. The rugged coastline and history of Cornwall had already provided a backdrop for many a Hollywood epic—including Hitchcock's classic *Jamaica Inn*—but the film fails to take advantage of the natural drama of the location and background. Gilling, who also co-produced and wrote the film, has to take much of the blame for the limp direction and talky script.

Coulouris as Shylock in *The Merchant of Venice*

Coulouris' first love, the stage, continued to offer the artistic challenges denied to him on film and television. At the Tower Theatre in North London he made a return to directing with a version of *The Male Animal* by James Thurber and Elliott Nugent, then followed it with a successful adaptation of Strinberg's *The Father* in which he also played the Captain. Then in 1962 he enjoyed a short season consisting of the Restoration farce *Lock Up Your Daughters* and *The Plough and the Stars* at the Mermaid Theatre in South London, not quite the West End but the quality was good. Coulouris supplemented his regular appearances with an engagement for Mary, Her Royal Highness the Princess Royal, at the Georgian Theatre in Richmond, playing scenes from William Congrieve's *The Way of the World* and *Tartuffe*. The following year he celebrated a return to the Bard, creating a memorable Shylock at the Flora Robson Playhouse in Newcastle-on-Tyne. Shakespeare was obviously very important to the actor and it was during this run that Kate O'Mara, who played his daughter, saw just how seriously Coulouris took his stage work. He may have been relaxed around the set of *The Woman Eater* but his approach to stage drama was very different, as O'Mara recalled:

> I found George very remote and unapproachable. He was absolutely no help to me and went out of his way, literally, to

be obtuse. I would run on stage to do a father and daughter scene with him and he was nowhere to be found, he made a point of being in a different place every night. I daresay it was all very good experience for me but I doubt if we exchanged more than two words to each other either during rehearsals or off stage.

In 1964 Coulouris returned to Broadway for *Beekman Place*, his first appearance on an American stage since 1948, and followed it the following year with *The Condemned of Altona* at the Vivian Beaumont Theatre in New York. In 1967 he accepted an offer to return to Los Angeles and play Voltaire in *The Sorrows of Frederick* at the Mark Taper Forum. He spent the rest of the decade in London in plays such as *The Outcry*, *The Last Analysis* and most memorably as Big Daddy in Tennessee Williams' *Cat on a Hot Tin Roof*. This decision to use London as a base meant that Coulouris was available for more film roles, and between 1965 and 1970 he made no fewer than eight movies including his long overdue return to the horror genre. The first of these movies was an action film for veteran director Don Chaffney, *The Crooked Road*, starring Robert Ryan and Stewart Grainger, two Hollywood leading men who had both known better days. Set in the small Balkan state of Orgagna, the loose plot has Ryan's hard nosed reporter planning an elopement with the local dictator's wife. Shot on a shoestring budget in Yugoslavia it was a pointless waste of time.

Far more interesting was England's Amicus Productions *The Skull*. Amicus was just beginning to emerge as a serious rival to Hammer. Directed by future Oscar-winning cameraman Freddie Francis, *The Skull* was an adaptation of Robert "*Psycho*" Bloch's short story *The Skull of the Marquis De Sade* and stars Peter Cushing as an antique

Arlene Has Poor Play In 'Beekman'

By Jack Gaver

NEW YORK (UPI)—Samuel Taylor has made a couple of pleasant contributions in the area of drawing room comedy in the past, but "Beekman Place", which opened at the Morosco theater Wednesday night, is not destined to join that company.

The play, presented by Stevens Productions, Inc., Samuel Taylor and Bonfils-Seawell Enterprises, is a tired, almost trite and ever-predictable work that has only a fraction of the wit and airiness that such an offering needs to make it succeed.

There are skilled players of the proper type at hand, notably France's Fernand Gravet and our own Arlene Francis, but the author has let them down most of the time.

Such good actors as Leora Dana and George Coulouris have thankless roles. Now I know why Madeleine Carroll, replaced by Miss Dana, left the production during its try-out tour.

The Skull

collector called Maitland whose acquisition of the aforementioned skull unwittingly releases the evil essence it contains. Coulouris appears only in the film's prologue, a rare period outing for Amicus, which features "resurrectionists" digging up the Marquis' body and inadvertently triggering a bloodbath. Cast as Dr. Lunde, Coulouris finds himself possessed with the Marquis' spirit and unable to control his homicidal inclinations brutally murders his friend and his mistress. The action then moves to contemporary London and continues more or less where it left off, with the skull unleashing considerable mayhem, possessing the hapless Maitland and becoming curiously animated during the cycle of the full moon.

Francis was a director who like Coulouris had no particular affection for the horror genre and he kept his tongue very much in his cheek when filming *The Skull*. "I have a rather unique sense of humor and I think it comes out on the screen," he admitted. "I couldn't take these films too seriously, to be honest." The director certainly needed a sense of humor; the skull bobbles along clearly on wires and later the camera is actually placed inside creating a unique point of view. That effect, far from undermining the tension, acts as a comic release and works extremely well. Francis later showed his ability to build genuine frisson in the dream sequences where Maitland is forced to put a gun to his temple. If the film has a flaw it is in the flimsy script—the penalty for adapting a short story—and it seems to run out of ideas after 60 minutes; the whole piece in fact would be more suited to one of Amicus' multi-episode films of later years. Producer Milton Subotsky did manage to assemble a starry cast to support Cushing including Christopher Lee, Jill Bennett, Patrick Wymark, Michael Gough and Patrick Magee, all lending considerably more than the feather-light premise deserved. Coulouris, who could easily have played any of the more central roles, makes the most of his limited screen time as yet another unhinged medical man. It was a minor contribution but a memorable one—at least from Francis' perspective:

> George couldn't have been with us for more than a few days but I remember he was a complete lunatic, but lovely. He just talked incessantly, very distracting I suppose but I enjoyed it.

The Skull is an effective thriller and enjoyed some reasonable notices. The *ABC Film Review* commented, "Evokes a brooding atmosphere filled with a sense of evil," while *Time Out* added, "The whole film is directed by Freddie Francis with much technical panache."

Coulouris next film, *Too Many Thieves*, isn't as remarkable. Peter Falk in a dry run for his *Columbo* character is an eccentric, raincoat wearing insurance agent on the trail of some Macedonian art treasures. The film was cobbled together from two episodes of a forgotten television series and dumped into theatrical release by an unenthusiastic distributor. An interesting cast including Britt Ekland, David Carradine and Coulouris fails to make the final result the least bit interesting.

Coulouris moved quickly on to *Arabesque*, a wannabe Hitchcock comic thriller directed by Stanley Donen and starring Hollywood heavyweights Gregory Peck and Sophia Loren. It was interesting to see Coulouris back in an A movie even if he was forced to resurrect his dodgy foreigner act, this time bedecked in Arab robes as "Ragheeb." The film was praised at the time; certainly the photography by Christopher Challis is stunning and merited his British Academy award, but the whole production is a little dated now. Peck in a role that demands Cary Grant is wooden and charmless, while Loren is—Loren.

Coulouris stayed with comedy for a cameo as a peasant in Basil Dearden's enjoyable romp *The Assassination Bureau* before reporting to Spain to appear as a Mexican in his first Western since *California*, *The Land Raiders* but the actor's accent is the only convincing thing about the effort.

The pattern of Coulouris' film career seems to have been set by these movies. Always a character actor, as he aged he had moved from the powerful and threatening bully into a frailer more fussy character, usually with an impenetrable accent. With only one or two exceptions his screen parts would be less important, essentially cameo roles providing a familiar but not wholly

Nigel Davenport threatens Mr. Sturdevant (Coulouris) in *No Blade of Grass*.

identifiable face. One is reminded of the old adage "there are no such things as small parts, only small actors," and Coulouris proved again and again that whatever the size of the role he could not be written off as a "bit part" player.

In 1969 Coulouris signed on with director and former matinee idol Cornel Wilde; the two had last worked together 25 years earlier in *A Song to Remember*. The film *No Blade of Grass*, based on John Christopher's highly regarded novel, begins with the premise that a virus has destroyed all the cereal crops in the world. Endless shots of pollution and death follow, accompanied by news footage of starving millions in the Third World and the general breakdown of civilization. Nigel Davenport plays an architect fleeing to Scotland with his family to avoid the ensuing anarchy. Along the way they encounter a number of self-serving and murderous characters—which presumably was Wilde's way of saying something meaningful about the state of society. Coulouris surfaced briefly as Mr. Sturdevant, a humble shopkeeper who resorts to extreme measures to protect the contents of his gun shop. Sadly the film wasn't a success: Christopher's ponderous tome makes for a cynical and depressing film, erratically directed by Wilde who seems uncertain if he is pushing a message or making an action picture.

Given the reputation Coulouris had in Hollywood, it's odd that Hammer hadn't taken advantage of his availability since the release of *Mask of Dust* over 15 years earlier. *Blood from the Mummy's Tomb* didn't really make up for the lost opportunity but it was a start. Coulouris was cast as a tomb raider called Berigan, part of an expedition to find the lost tomb of Tera in a story loosely adapted from Bram Stoker's *Jewel of the Seven Stars*. The film opens with a particularly nasty flashback involving the mutilation and entombment of Queen Tera, aka "Queen of Darkness" or "she who has no name."

Tera's hand is cut from her arm and thrown to a pack of ravenous dogs; moments later the dogs are slain, their throats cut. The same fate befalls the priests while the hand, somewhat the worse for wear, scuttles away. These killings are inter-cut with a sleeping woman, Margaret (Valerie Leon), whose wrist scar implies that these events are more than just a dream. It seems that Margaret was born at the very moment her father, Professor Fuchs, entered the tomb and pronounced Tera's name. Is it coincidental that she is the spitting image of the dead Queen? Of course not— this is a Hammer film.

Tera's spirit is intent on using Margaret's body as a vehicle for her reincarnation but first she needs to assemble five relics looted by each of the original explorers. A series of set-piece murders follow with the Egyptologists getting their comeuppance in graphic fashion. Of the five, Coulouris has by far the most interesting part. Berigan, unhinged by his experiences in the desert, is confined in a lunatic asylum, where, rather bizarrely, he is permitted to keep his ceremonial snake in the cupboard! His warders, played with insidious nastiness by James Cossins and David Jackson, take great delight in tormenting "Old Snakey." The late David Jackson, who spends most of his screen time with Coulouris, remembered the actor with affection:

> He was a very nice man, perhaps a little quiet at first, but then it's always difficult coming into a film where you don't know anyone. We were a little in awe of a man who had been in *Citizen Kane* but he had no airs and graces at all. As soon as he found out I was from Manchester he chatted away about all the places we had in common. In fact it was impossible to shut him up! It was a confusing sort of film for a number of reasons and our scenes were shot near the end of the process when everybody was a little bit tired and maybe a little shell-shocked. George was full of life and full of stories about the theatre and Hollywood, particularly Hollywood; I think we needed that energy to get us through.

Jackson also remembered Coulouris' undying love of cricket, specifically the fortunes of the England team;

> He absolutely loved it, more I think than acting or so it seemed. I don't know if this is true or not but someone said that he had

it written into his contracts that he didn't have to work during England's test matches!

Blood from the Mummy's Tomb was a troubled production and actually came close to being abandoned completely. First the intended star Peter Cushing dropped out after only one day shooting when his wife's health seriously declined, and he was replaced on short notice by Andrew Keir. Then with only one week of filming left the director Seth Holt died of a heart attack. Holt who was overweight and a heavy drinker had not been in the best of health for some time; in fact producer Michael Carreras had not been able to obtain insurance before starting the picture. His untimely death left Carreras with the dilemma of closing down the film or finding a new director to finish the remaining scenes; in the end Carreras took over the last five days of filming. The remaining scenes principally involve Berigan and his murder in the asylum, and Carreras did a passable job of mimicking Holt's style; of all the deaths, Berigan's certainly stands out. Left alone and bound by his guards, Berigan is defenseless as the spirit of Kera closes in; he thrashes and twists desperately to free himself as his chilling screams ring out. Then there is an ominous silence. Berigan ends up a crumpled heap, his throat ripped out, the horror effectively underscored by the drips from a bottle of water.

By all accounts Holt left his producer something of a jigsaw puzzle in the cutting room and Carreras had to use a lot of guesswork to assemble the final cut. Despite the misfortunes the film turned out to be a better than average entry into the generally dire Hammer mummy series, thanks largely to an intelligent script by Christopher Wicking and the atmospheric cinematography of Arthur Grant. *Blood from the Mummy's Tomb* offers audiences a more complex scenario than the more familiar Hammer world where good and evil are clearly defined and the triumph of the former over the latter is preordained. By eschewing the trappings (and wrappings) of mummy pictures Wicking's script scores by presenting his vengeful corpse not as a shuffling bandaged creature but as the beautiful Valerie Leon, all eye lashes and heaving bosom. He also wrings considerable value out of the self-serving Corbeck, a team member keen to keep the relics for himself; this neatly dispenses with the other great mummy film stalwart, the embittered Egyptian. It also means that Tera can be largely self motivated and not at the beck and call of anyone. This independence of action is diluted somewhat by having the usual stalk and scare body counting of the expedition but at least the director shows some creativity in the staging of the deaths, even if a staggering amount of throat ripping goes on.

Unfortunately the stunning but bland Valerie Leon doesn't really make the most of her role; cast for decorative reasons she doesn't invest the role(s) with the appropriate depth and sensuality. The rather gimmicky last scene closes the film on an air of ambiguity that runs the length of the whole movie. The film was premiered at the National Film Theatre in London, as part of a belated tribute to the studio, and critics were split over the film's qualities. *The Times* was less than generous: "It shows no sign of any directional distinction at all, and the script makes a fearful hash of Bram Stoker's excellent novel." *Variety* on the other hand found the film "Polished and well acted," while *The New York Times* thought it "Tremendous fun, skilful and wonderfully energetic." Unfortunately Hammer was finding it increasingly difficult to get its horror films onto the major circuits either in Britain or America. The traditional Hammer formula looked quaintly old fashioned in a world dominated by the likes of *Clockwork Orange* and *The Devils* and for all its promise *Blood from the Mummy's Tomb* was unleashed as the supporting feature for *Doctor Jekyll and Sister Hyde*, neither film achieving the attention it deserved.

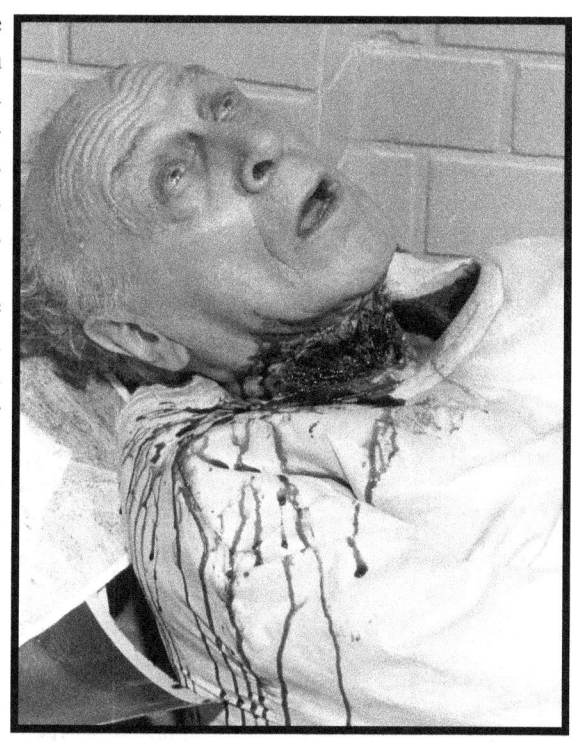

Coulouris' gruesome death from *Blood from the Mummy's Tomb*.

Coulouris probably couldn't have cared less, as he had no time for this type of movie. "Dad really didn't like the Hammer films at all," George, Jr. remembered. "He couldn't see the value in them. He never let this affect his performance though." The early 1970s saw the withdrawal of the Hollywood majors from the UK following a series of big-budget failures including *Ryan's Daughter* and *The Charge of the Light Brigade*. The larger American companies, concentrating on home grown subjects, started the wave that would lead to *The Godfather*, *The French Connection* and *The Exorcist*. British film companies, with a confidence born out of ignorance and/or desperation, rushed headlong to fill the gap, and horror films enjoyed an unprecedented boom.

Coulouris hopped from Hammer straight into another horror movie, *The Horror of Snape Island* (sometimes called *Tower of Evil*), a gruesome stalk and slash movie from producer Richard Gordon, best known for his low budget horror and science fiction films of the late 1950s and 1960s, including the late-night favorite *Fiend without a Face*. Gordon's best work includes the Boris Karloff thrillers *The Haunted Strangler* and *Corridors of Blood* (both 1958) and extended into the 1970s with the cult movies *Horror Hospital* and *Inseminoid*.

The one consistent factor throughout his career was his use of faded names, either character actors or stars from the golden years who had fallen out of fashion with modern filmmakers. Respected actors of the stature of Dennis Price, Derrick de Marnay and Derek Farr, now available at a reasonable price, gave Gordon's movies a gloss that belied their budgets. By the early 1970s Coulouris now fell into this category and his film pedigree meant more to producers like Gordon than it did to filmgoers.

The Horror of Snape Island opens with its most famous sequence, a flashback showing how a gaggle of Americans students, including the darkly exotic Candice Glendinning, were slaughtered in a remote lighthouse—after the obligatory reefers and coupling. One student (Robin Askwith, using an excruciatingly bad accent) gets skewered by a Phoenician ceremonial spear. Coulouris also appears in the prologue, cast against type as John Gurney, a craggy, weather-beaten fisherman rather than an authority figure or scientist. Arriving at the fog-shrouded island with his son Hap, Gurney sets up the scene nicely by muttering ominously, "There are things to do, Hap. It's been left long enough." The fact that they are armed with clubs and ropes suggests this is not a reference to some DIY repairs! No sooner have Gurney and Hap (granite-faced Jack Watson) started prowling around the island than they encounter severed hands, naked corpses and decapitated heads. Gurney Sr. then stumbles across the aforementioned Glendinning, bloody and psychotic, and promptly gets hacked to death for his trouble.

The film then cuts to the present where a stately Dennis Price of the British Museum is excited by the unexpected appearance of that spear in the midst of all the carnage. A team of special investigators is rustled up and dispatched to Snape Island to check out what appears to be a simple case of Baal worship. The whole archeological thing is something of a red herring as another boatload of potential victims is dropped into the lap of a vengeful "beast" skulking in the caverns below the island. By now the British censor was relaxing his paternal grip on filmmakers, and producers were quite freely pushing the boundaries of acceptable taste. *The Horror of Snape Island,* unusually for a British film even in those enlightened times, happily juxtaposes sex and slicing, with one teenager (Glendinning) breaking the previous taboo of blood on naked breasts—at least in some markets (a suitably clothed version was provided where appropriate).

Coulouris as John Gurney in the prologue of *The Horror of Snape Island.*

Having set the tone in the opening reel, director Jim O'Connelly more or less follows the same pattern for the rest of the running time, with Hap's assertion that "the island has a bad name, always had," hiding the fact that a hirsute and lunatic offshoot of the Gurney clan is lurking in the shadows. The dialogue becomes annoying at times—far too self-consciously hip, as are the fashions with archeologists prowling around crypts in knee boots and hot pants! Sadly the island itself is all too obviously recreated in the studio, though O'Connolly works hard to create the appropriate tension, helped considerably by the lurid cinematography of Desmond Dickinson and some seasoned performers (including Bryant Haliday and Jill Haworth, as well as Mark Edwards who had played the lead in *Blood from the Mummy's Tomb*). Once again Coulouris wasn't given a great deal to do but Richard Gordon had no doubts about his contribution:

> I had first met him on the set of *Kill Me Tomorrow* but it was only an informal introduction, as I did not participate in the making of that picture. I was always aware of him because of his Hollywood credits so when our casting director suggested him, I jumped at the opportunity. I always had a fondness for character actors, especially those from an earlier era. If there was someone available who also had a Hollywood background or some recognition value for the States like George Courlouris—so much the better! Actually with

hindsight we should have considered him for the role that Jack Watson played but Watson had already been signed.

Whatever his reservations about this type of film or doubts about the role, Coulouris never let it show on set or on the screen, as Gordon recalled:

> We signed George for six days over six weeks and he was a complete professional; having agreed to play in *The Horror of Snape Island* he treated it with respect. He was a genuine eccentric but you couldn't help liking him, but he never stopped talking! He wanted to speak mainly about Welles, the Mercury Theatre and *Citizen Kane* and he was very proud also of his stage work but less enthusiastic about his Hollywood roles.

Coulouris' next film, also in the fantasy genre, is even more offbeat than *The Horror of Snape Island.* Michael Moorcock's surreal novel *The Final Programme* introduced the bizarre character of Jerry Cornelius, a futuristic secret agent-cum-adventurer of ambiguous gender and dubious fashion sense. Robert Fuest, who had directed the equally surreal *Dr. Phibes* movies for AIP, seemed the ideal choice to create a psychedelic world where Amsterdam has been accidentally turned into "28 miles of white ash" by the USAAF, Trafalgar Square has become a gigantic rubbish dump and all hope rests with an artificially created hermaphrodite ape man! *The Last Days of Man on Earth,* as it was retitled for the U.S., is every bit as weird as it sounds. Jon Finch dons a ruffled opera shirt and velvet jacket to play Cornelius, with Jenny Runacre playing the formidable Ms. Brunner who has the disturbing habit of absorbing her partners after lovemaking. Coulouris plays Dr. Powys, one of three identically outfitted scientists trying to acquire the computer programme that will, we are told, create "a new messiah, born of the age of science." Graham Crowden and Basil Henson are the fellow mad doctors who all get their comeuppance, after an orgy of soft lens and color filters herald the morphing of Brunner and Cornelius into the new superman. There are some eye-catching cameos from Sterling Hayden, Patrick Magee and a totally out of control Hugh Griffiths. The film was a step up for Coulouris in terms of screen time and, as the voice of doubt amongst the scientific zealots, he offers a conviction to his pseudoscientific mumbo-jumbo lacking throughout most of the film.

Fuest's visual style and offbeat sense of humor was first demonstrated in *The Avengers* television series and then carried to its logical conclusion in *The Abominable Dr. Phibes* but by the time the sequel was made the novelty had worn off. Some of Fuest's designs were certainly strikingly realized: a wall that is a vertical chessboard and, depending upon the move, becomes either a

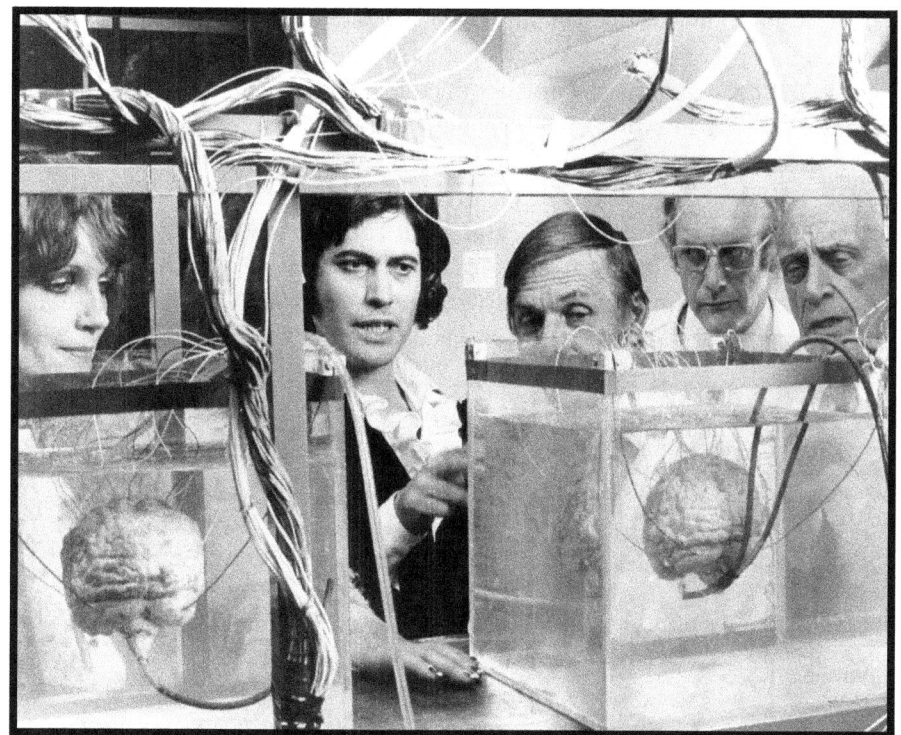

Jerry Cornelius (Jon Finch) is searching for the *Final Programme* with the help of Jenny Runacre, Basil Henson, Graham Crowden and George Coulouris.

door or a death trap; coloured silk tunnels; a pinball arcade of inflatable plastic decor and girls running inside giant plastic balloons. But in trying to look too clever, Fuest overloaded his film with in-jokes, lame humor and ponderous silences; the result is visually striking but largely incomprehensible. Even when re-cut by the normally astute Roger Corman for American audiences, watching the film was an exhausting and disheartening experience. Disowned by Moorcock and hated by critics, *The Last Days of Man on Earth* was then ignored by filmgoers.

Proving he could still attract Hollywood, Coulouris offered a reliable supporting presence for Franklin J. Shaffner, best known for *Planet of the Apes* and *Patton*, who cast the actor in a small role in his overwrought prison drama *Papillon*. Set in a French penal colony the film stars Steve McQueen and Dustin Hoffman and feels more like an endurance race than "the greatest adventure of escape ever filmed!" Thirty years earlier Coulouris would undoubtedly have played a sadistic prison governor or brutal guard, but in his declining years was given the small role of Dr. Chata, described as a "sort of Hindu" and who, despite an affable nature, has been incarcerated for slaughtering his wife and children. Coulouris at least had the honour of stealing a scene from the charismatic Mc-

Queen while simultaneously hinting at Chata's sadness and regret. It is a moving cameo of a broken man in a film, which proved enormously popular.

Coulouris sought out by another notable director, Britain's *enfant terrible* Ken Russell, was hired or a small part as yet another doctor in the closing scenes of his biopic *Mahler*. Russell's reputation for the bizarre and visionary rested largely on his interpretations of the life stories of famous composers: Mahler followed on the heels of Elgar, Debussy and Tchaikovsky. Along the way Russell managed to make deeply personal statements out of *Women in Love*, *The Devils* and *The Boyfriend*. Conceived as a big budget extravaganza, *Mahler* was originally partly financed by German backers but when the deal fell through at the last minute a considerably scaled down—but no less eccentric—movie was made.

Of course the film features the trademark Russell imagery and disturbing visuals, and the director took full advantage of Mahler's conversion from Judaism to Catholicism to introduce an anachronistic Nazi element. In one scene, a jackbooted Cosima Wagner confronts the composer, and in another sequence Mahler, imprisoned in his coffin, is forced to witness his widow's flamboyant sexual encounters with her Nazi lovers. As with all Russell movies *Mahler* is littered with in-jokes, pastiche and self-indulgent humor but the stunning cinematography of Dick Bush, the emotive score and occasionally shocking visuals more than make up for the lapses. The casting of Coulouris was a deliberate move by Russell, who selected the actor specifically because of his Hollywood past, though he resisted the temptation to have the screens best-known Nazi playing one of Mahler's tormentors. Instead he appears in a tiny role as the doctor hurrying to tell Mahler that he has only months to live. Russell spends much of the movie parodying Hollywood, referencing his own films, silent movies, Groucho Marx films and so on; his stated intention with this last sequence was to pull out all the stops and "out Hollywood Hollywood." Russell's solution was to stage a climatic reconciliation between the mismatched lovers and have his hero dismiss the news of his impending death with a cheery "You can go home, Doctor. We're going to live forever" before walking into the sunset. Quite simply he wanted to deliver as much bittersweet schmaltz as he could get away with and the casting of Coulouris was a deliberate part of the over-the-top exercise.

Despite two decades of B movies Coulouris was still readily identifiable in the public mind with his classic roles in *Citizen Kane* and *Watch on the Rhine*— indeed more than one reviewer referred to him as a "Hollywood veteran." Russell himself always thought of *Mahler* as one of his best films; predictably perhaps given the director's handling of the subject matter, it was never given a full release in the States and was rather indifferently handled elsewhere.

In 1974 Coulouris became caught up in the slew of *Exorcist* rip-offs that flooded out of Europe following the phenomenal success of the William Friedkin movie. It is tempting to suggest that Coulouris' primary motivation in appearing in *L'Antichristo* (aka *The Tempter* or *Deliver Her from Evil*) was a chance to revisit some of the art galleries and museums of Italy. Certainly the version of the film, which crept into American cinemas offered the actor little else in the way of compensation for his time and trouble. The director, Alberto de Martino, who would later make the *Omen* rip-off *Holocaust 2000*, is probably best known for his *Gladiator* movies. Italian actress Carla Gravina plays Carla who, confined to a wheelchair at the age of 12, allows a brooding resentment and jealousy of her father (Mel Ferrer) to fester into all-consuming hatred. Clearly the girl has issues and the baffled Ferrer sends her for a number of crackpot cures until she is introduced to a smooth psychoanalyst who glibly announces that, since she has no physical injury, he can cure her completely with some hypnotherapy. Before you can say "Beelzebub," Carla is alternating between her suppressed past as a witch burned at the stake by the Inquisition and her current life, wandering the countryside in a dreamlike trance, seducing and murdering boyish German tourists.

An outbreak of the demonic clichés follows: verbal abuse, green bile, heads rotating 360 degrees and assorted poltergeist activities are enough to convince a dubious Bishop Oderisi (a tired-looking Arthur Kennedy) that he has a genuine case of possession on his hands. An urgent appeal is issued to the Vatican's top exorcist, a mysterious Austrian priest called Father Mittner (Coulouris). Its obvious parallels with the Friedkin film aside, *L'Antichristo* offers little that is new and, despite its unpleasant reputation for extremes in both language and imagery, is probably more restrained than *The Exorcist*. Certainly the decision to cast an actress in her 20s as opposed to a 12-year-old is a concession to good taste. Anyone approaching the film now because of this reputation will be disappointed; talky and slow for most of its running time, *L'Antichristo* owes much of its infamy to the "goat orgy sequence" depicting Carla's initiation into Hell—a sequence actually cut or reduced in most versions. Those deprived of the complete version don't miss much; the refusal of Ms. Gravina to appear nude forced restraint on an unimaginative director who resorted to the comical use of an over-elaborate wig and gaffer's tape. In truth the whole sequence consists of a prop frog getting its head ripped off, a goat receiving the pleasure of Carla's tongue (mercifully off screen) and much writhing and naked bottoms. All told, the "infamous orgy" is something of a let down.

Coulouris was spared this indignity and does lend the film considerable gravitas in what is essentially the Max Von Sydow-Father Merrin role, following this well-worn path as Mittner takes over the exorcism for the last third of the film. Mittner's presence is actually introduced long before he makes this formal entrance, looming out of the shadows in a particularly comic entrance. The character, still unnamed at this point, is then glimpsed several times from moving cars or in the corner of the scene, collection box in hand as he canvasses alms for the poor. Confusingly he is seen in the hypnosis-induced flashback sequence, creating a flashforward within the flashback! As the movie continues, Mittner has to endure trials of fire, rain and serpents, all of which Coulouris takes in his stride. While it was nice to see him back in a role that demands a strong physical presence as well as a commanding intelligence, the decision to overdub his voice with that a gravelly German actor detracts from his performance.

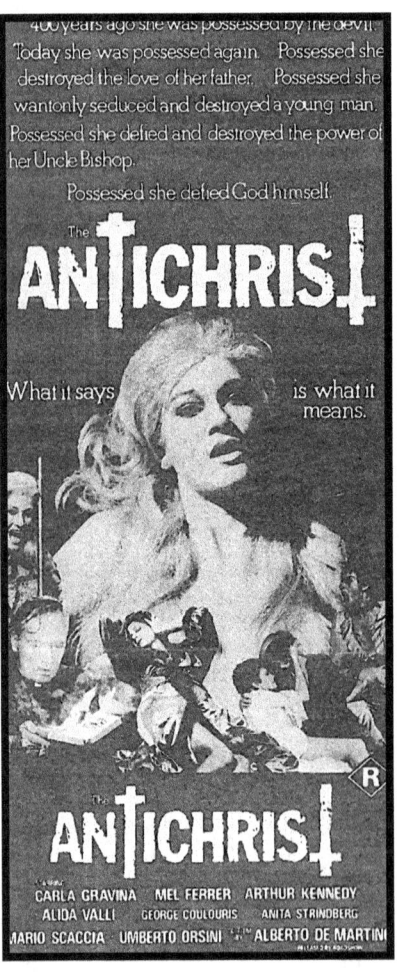

L'Antichristo isn't without its strengths; the cinematography is excellent, as are the lavish sets and a musical score one would expect from Ennio Morricone. The less said about the special effects, the better. Veterans Arthur Kennedy and Alida Valli give solid performances as does Coulouris, which is more than can be said for the younger members of the cast, all of whom struggle to make any sort of impression. But by far the worst offender is Mel Ferrer who spends half the film looking like he wants to be somewhere else and the other half looking like he is! Cut by 16 minutes for its English language release and shabbily dubbed to often-comical effect, even the limited ambitions of the director wither away. Amongst the general outpouring of scorn for the film, the critic for London's *The Observer* made an astute observation: "Decades of strong, undervalued acting have left Mr. Coulouris with a face of monstrous tribal wisdom, an agreeable focus of interest, for once, amid reeking plagiaristic trash."

Coulouris returned to the relative sanity of Pinewood studios just outside London, a move that wasn't exactly from the ridiculous to the sublime but close. Coulouris had first met Sidney Lumet when he was an actor on Broadway in the 1930s and although they had not worked together they had stayed in touch. Lumet's acting career never took off but he proved himself a capable director on television and later in films such as *12 Angry Men*. In 1974 he was in England to direct a lavish version of Agatha Christie's *Murder on the Orient Express*. Backed by EMI, the film was an unfashionable attempt to revitalize a subgenre that had lain moribund for almost a decade, and lift the stately whodunits of Christie into the realms of lavish budget mainstream movies. Albert Finney took the lead as Hercule Poirot, torturing the vowels as he attempts to get his tongue around a cod Belgian accent and simultaneously unravel a seemingly unsolvable stabbing on the isolated Orient Express. Lumet's impressive cast includes Sean Connery, Anthony Perkins, Ingrid Bergman, John Gielgud and Martin Balsam—all stars of Hitchcock thrillers—supplemented by Michael York, Vanessa Redgrave and Jacqueline Bisset. Filling out the supporting roles are English stage actors Colin Blakely, Denis Quilley and Wendy Hiller who had appeared in *Outcast of the Islands*.

In such company Coulouris was inevitably well down the cast list, playing a tousle-haired doctor scampering about in the wake of Finney and fellow investigator Martin Balsam as they gently interrogate the suspects and slowly deconstruct Christie's overelaborate puzzle. At least Coulouris was rewarded with plenty of screen time,

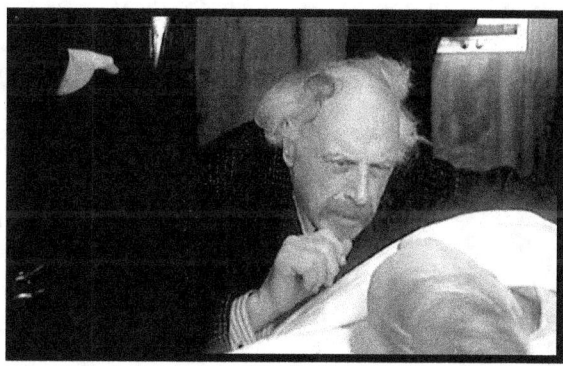

Dr. Constantine in *Murder on the Orient Express*

pondering and postulating excitedly only to end up baffled and exasperated by Finney's thought processes. It is a good part and the elegance of the sets, Lumet's unhurried direction and the rich acting make it a diverting two hours of unchallenging entertainment. Despite being quaintly old fashioned, *Murder on the Orient Express* proved a surprise hit at the box office and spawned a number of inferior look-alike movies over the next few years. The film also represented Coulouris' last sizable role in a significant movie.

By now George Coulouris was in a financial position where he could comfortably retire, but the thought never occurred to him. For Coulouris, work was his life, a view reinforced by Elizabeth Coulouris, the actor's second wife, who said:

> It wasn't about money; if something came up that he didn't want to do, he would tell his agent to ask for more money than the producers would be willing to pay. When he came back to Britain and things weren't going so well he saw films as a way to earn a living; as long as the script wasn't too awful he would just do it. Later on he did films because he needed to keep working.

Coulouris continued with cameo appearances; he was amongst the guests in the sex comedy *Percy's Progress*, sedately directed by Ralph Thomas. The

film, a sequel to the popular *Percy,* followed the general trend in British comedy films to become broader and bluer, and detailed the misadventures of the world's first penis transplant patient, energetically played by Leigh Lawson, supported by Judy Geeson and Julie Ege. Sadly it was all a lot less entertaining than it could have been, though there were a number of entertaining cameos from such reliable performers as Vincent Price and Bernard Lee. Far less interesting than the title suggests, *Shout at the Devil* was a strictly by the numbers wartime yarn loosely modeled on *The African Queen* but with none of the latter's charm or quality. Roger Moore and Lee Marvin play the sort of characters they could have handled in their sleep. Then there is Richard Lester's dire comedy about the mob, *The Ritz*, which turned out to be depressing unfunny and a massive box-office dud. As a mafia Don, Coulouris was at least afforded the dignity of dying in the opening reel.

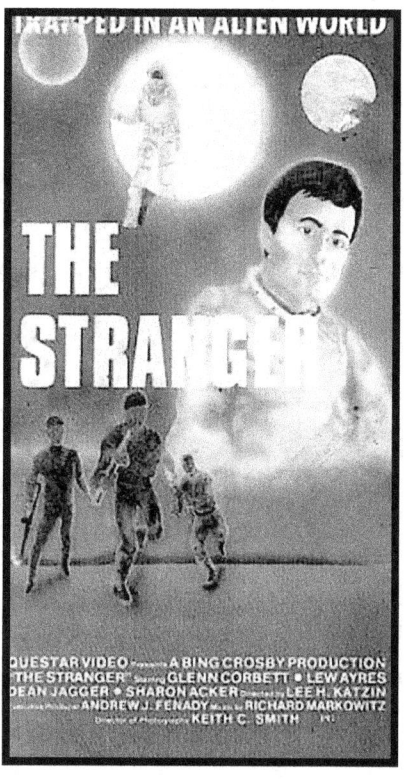

By the mid-1970s Coulouris had to endure an enforced slowing down of his stage commitments as his age caught up with him. Increasingly and much to his disgust he had to resort to television to keep working, a medium he still reviled: "television has wrecked acting because it's impossible to make a stirring success." One can understand his point but in fairness he was never well served by his choices. *The Stranger* is a good example, a 1973 TV movie starring B-movie veterans Dean Jagger, Lew Ayres and Cameron Mitchell. It was more or less a straightforward remake of the 1969 film *Journey to the Far Side of the Sun* about an astronaut who finds himself on a parallel version of Earth. Despite the intellectual pretensions the end result was pretty poor and mercifully the proposed series never materialized. His advancing years had done nothing to mellow Coulouris, who continued to rage against an establishment that he thought still pigeonholed him as an outsider:

> I'm never in line for an ordinary part; an English barrister, say, with some sensible line to deliver. Some silly bastard always says, "Coulouris? He's a foreigner isn't he?"

Coulouris had played guest roles in the popular shows *Dr. Who*, *Haunted* and *The Prisoner*, as well as a series called *Search* for NBC, but they did little to dispel the actor's deeply held belief that television was in every way inferior. In 1984 he did have one television credit remarkable mainly for what it represented. *Hart to Hart* was ABC's lightweight detective series featuring an amateur husband and wife team who each week find themselves embroiled in all sorts of mayhem. Robert Wagner and Stephanie Powers played the leads as only middle-aged, bronzed Californian movie stars can, and the show remained a ratings winner for a number of years. Coulouris' guest role came towards the

Coulouris and Patrick McGoohan in *The Prisoner*, 1967

end of the run when the producers were trying to revamp the formula and were sending their leads to exotic locations. Coulouris, who by then was very much aware of his own mortality, took advantage of the opportunity to return to the Greek village where his father had been born, his first visit since the 1920s, a sign that he was at last reconciled to his heritage. Surprisingly and much to his delight the actor met people who remembered his father, as well as long lost family members who had been following his career with interest since the 1940s.

In 1976 Louise, Coulouris' wife of 46 years, died. It must have been a tremendous blow for the actor but he was determined that he would not allow it to be the closing statement on his life. At the time Coulouris was in good shape, mentally and physically, and although he was working less, he had no intention of slipping gracefully into retirement. He continued to discuss new projects both on the stage and in film, undertook his DIY repairs and decoration around his cottage and always created the impression that he was busy doing something. Coulouris also read vociferously: European history was a favorite but the family remembered that a trip to the local library would result in a sack load of books on all subjects from biographies, to travel and even keeping pets! With his determination to keep going it probably surprised few people when the actor announced his intention at the age of 74 to marry Elizabeth Donaldson, a close neighbor in Hampstead. Elizabeth told a touching story of how they first met:

> I had recently moved into the Vale of Health and wanted to borrow some tools for a bit of gardening work but we didn't really get to know each other until a few years later after Louise had died and some of the people in the Vale organized an "open gardens" day. We got to chatting and he asked me if I wanted to come round for a drink sometime. I remember I did and George was there looking after his grandchildren, the little boy needed a diaper changing and George was a bit lost about how to do it. I was just as confused and I think in the end we wrapped a towel around him and sat him up.

This image of Count Teck de Brancovis defeated by a baby's diaper is an endearing one and, as Elizabeth remembered, it was a softer side to the actor she would see many times:

> George loved his family very much. He said that he hadn't really thought about children; he had been an only child so families didn't really matter to him but Louise wanted children and George went along with it. He said it was the best decision he never made. He loved his grandchildren.

Coulouris was some 28 years older than his new wife, a situation that neither of them really noticed. "It didn't seem to matter at all," Elizabeth says, "George was so energetic and vivacious that I was barely conscious there was an age difference." The relationship brought new vigor to the actor and in 1977 he made a triumphant return to Hollywood to play *King Lear* at the Globe Theatre, his first appearance on stage in three years. Audiences who traveled to the Hollywood Hills to see the performance in the open air theatre had to endure extreme howling winds and driving rain which didn't seem to have affected the performances but must have given a resonance to the storm scenes. In 1978 Coulouris appeared fit and strong, so much so that Elizabeth struggled to keep up, but she remembered the warning signs had started to appear:

> George was a great letter writer; he would write pages and pages and he started to find it not difficult exactly, but he said his hand writing was getting funny. At the same time he found he couldn't get out of his chair as he used to; he would get

breathless going up the hill. He hated drugs and medicines; he wouldn't even take an aspirin if he didn't have to. He went to see a specialist and he said it was his heart so George was fitted with a pacemaker. Actually he had to undergo three operations; the first two they fitted didn't work properly for some reason, and three operations in quick succession were physically arduous, even for George. After a little while it was obvious there was still something wrong; he finally saw a geriatric specialist who knew just by looking at him that he had the earlier signs of Parkinson's disease.

When the extent of Coulouris' illness became all too clear the actor sat down to recall his memoirs:

I want to talk about acting and its possibilities. This is my last chance to do so. I have found out the truth about the nature of acting and now it's too late to put to practical use as I lie here half paralyzed by Parkinson's.

Understandably perhaps, given his personal circumstances Coulouris was in no mood to be generous, and his writings reveal a characteristic frankness:

Another great cause of mediocre acting becoming ridiculously over-praised is that the critics no longer perform the function. In the olden days a critic had seen every performance of a Shakespeare play several times, so that when one reads *The Guardian* notice of Sir Frank Benson's *Richard III* and *Richard II*, one gets an essay showing the play was psychologically hundreds of years ahead of its time and the performances assessed in these terms. Nowadays the critics yap ecstatically about Olivier or Gielgud.

When he wasn't writing Coulouris was still looking for work; his body may have been weakening but his voice was as strong and versatile as ever. In 1981 when Brian Dean, now working as a radio producer for the BBC, was preparing a series of readings of the ghost stories of Algernon Blackwood, he sought out previous versions of the ghoulish tales:

Algernon Blackwood had recorded his own version of the stories some years earlier and I listened to these and thought about that distinctive voice and who would be the best actor to do the new versions; the voice I heard in my head was George Coulouris, he was so perfect. I phoned him up and asked if he was familiar with the stories; he listed them all off the top of his head!

Dean found Coulouris the complete professional who refused to let his illness get in the way of his work:

> I booked two days in the studio, which is more than I would normally allow for this simply because of George's age but he didn't need it; he was perfect and needed very little direction from me. Parkinson's was in the very early stages I think but he was very relaxed; he liked to wear carpet slippers in the studio, but he was very cheerful, never stopped talking and telling stories about his career and so on. He was a real joy to work with.

Broadcast as part of the BBC's *A Book at Bedtime* series, Coulouris' renditions of Blackwood proved to be something of a revelation and the network reported much better than anticipated listening figures. Coulouris entered into the spirit of things promoting the show with a suitably macabre interview with the *Radio Times*:

> When I was a boy it was the habit of the lower middle-class families to take their children to see dead bodies. I remember gazing at one yellowed old lady while the adults recited the details of the dropsy she suffered. And when I saw my grandfather's body I cried out, "He's not dead, his eyes are open," which they were.

Coulouris was aware that his condition would continue to deteriorate; his regular diet of tomes from the library now included medical books as the actor sought to educate himself on his condition. In the meantime he intended to work as long as possible. In 1984 he made his last stage appearance, appropriately as Lear in a short run close to his home at St. George's Theatre in North London. But he was determined it wouldn't be his swansong; even when he no longer had the stamina for a long play he was still thinking of new projects. Dean recalled:

> George called me and asked if I would be interested in staging a one man show with him at the New End in Hampstead, a sort of question and answer thing. He said he would set the whole thing up if I came in and asked the questions. It never came off for one reason or another. We also talked about him playing Hobson in *Hobson's Choice* again for radio which he

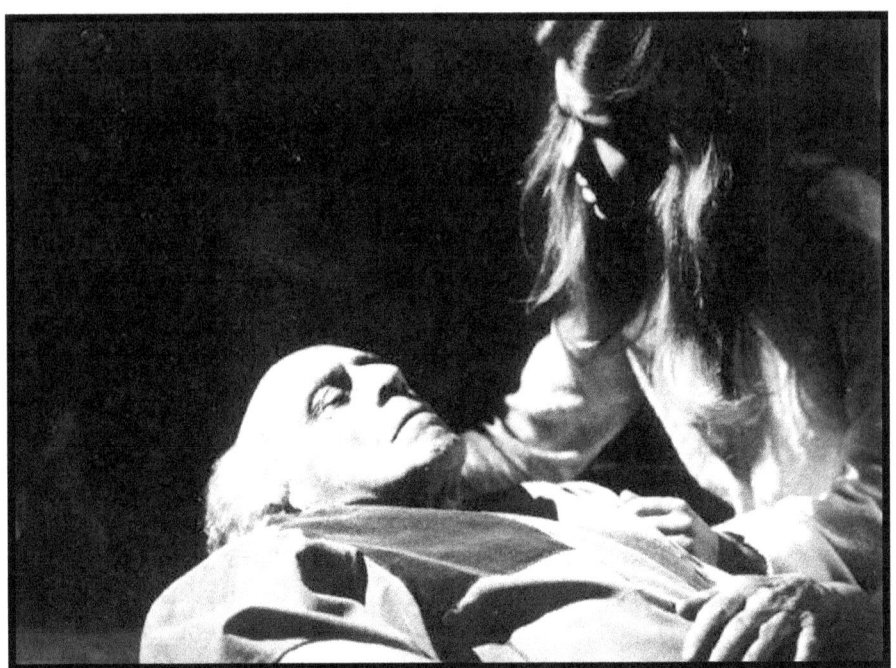
Coulouris as King Lear

was very keen on but again it didn't come off. George never stopped. He refused to give up.

The family of course had to witness Coulouris' decline first hand; George recalls his father feeling "very angry about his illness," adding that, "Parkinson's robbed him of his ability to express himself which he found unbearably frustrating." It is a view reinforced by Elizabeth:

> He didn't shout or throw things around but he was irritated and frustrated by the disease. He resented I think contracting Parkinson's after the normal age span for these things but I wouldn't say he got angry. He didn't tremble or anything like that but it affected the muscles in his neck, so speaking was difficult; his hearing was also going which caused him a lot of irritation. He felt trapped in a body that was letting him down; he couldn't get it to do what he wanted to do.

Deprived now of his most potent tool, his voice, Coulouris poured out his rage in his own writing, recording a vitriolic attack on his whole profession:

> I now realize what a miserable business I have been in for over 60 years. A business where I can't remember telling the truth

> about a job, a part in a film or a play when I was interviewed for the prospect of the job, too frightened of not getting it, and later on to protect my growing bank balance by not getting it. I listened to variegated morons give me their opinions of plays etc. which I knew to be asininely stupid and pretentious.

Despite the frustrations Coulouris never gave up hope of a cure. In 1987 he and Elizabeth traveled to Bucharest after seeing a television documentary on the remarkable work being done with children suffering from brain defects. George researched their work and convinced by the results spent six weeks undergoing tests and then treatment but without any noticeable improvement. Elizabeth sadly noted, "he was probably too old, the advances were all made with children whose brains are perhaps more pliable." By then he had played his last screen role in *Mussolini: The Untold Story*, a rather grand docudrama for American television. Coulouris played the small part of DeBono and was largely lost amongst the star names, George C. Scott, Robert Downey and Raul Julia amongst them. Looking frail and tired it wasn't the exit he deserved but it was an earnest enough effort and the production values were remarkably good for television.

Coulouris knew the end was coming; in 1984 he started to write the notes for what he hoped would be his autobiography. Because of his illness, progress was extremely slow; he spent hours tapping away at the keyboard when it was increasingly difficult to focus and formulate his thoughts. With Elizabeth at his side, he managed to produce a number of essays on his early life, one of which was used as part of an exhibition called "Images of Salford," which recalled his childhood. It was later published in *The Guardian* in England and revealed that after all this time he had softened his view of his father:

> For most people Hollywood is a realm of fantasy; I landed up there, but found its brand of fantasy pale by comparison with my junk-filled memories of Salford; and even the fabulous Orson Welles could never displace my father as the most colourful character in my life.

A brief chapter outline is all that exists now to suggest how Coulouris would have structured his memoirs. If his essays had followed this closely, they would have been passionate and uncompromising. As it is, Coulouris left only teasing insights into his thinking:

> Only by working on a part to create this electric atmosphere is acting worth doing instead of spending one's lifetime listening a la Gielgud to the sound of your own voice. Some wiseacre said, "More good actors have been ruined by having beautiful

voices than by any amount of whisky." I only have to think of Orson Welles and Gielgud to see how true this is.

George Coulouris died of a heart attack on April 25, 1989, after battling Parkinson's disease for over a decade. In England the broadsheets all covered his death: *The Guardian* lamented the loss of his "elegant villainy" while *The Independent* informed readers he was "best known for his sly or scary rascals in American films." The same paper asserted that he was never as good in films as he was on the stage and that he never created a film character to compare with his great theatrical roles, concluding, "Shylock, Big Daddy etc; Coulouris had the flourish to fill them, sometimes to overflowing but always compelling." The *Daily Telegraph* described him as an "ubiquitous, if underrated character actor of considerable presence whose somewhat sinister features tend to be more familiar than his frequently misspelled name."

In an era when fame is so transient, Coulouris' reputation continues to grow. To mark the centenary of his birth in 2003, the Salford Museum and Art Gallery held an exhibition on his life and work accompanied by two lectures by Brian Dean. It was followed by a special screening of *Appointment with Venus* for many of his family and friends. Ian McKellen, who was brought up in the north of England, has talked about his admiration for the actor, and as recently as January 2005 the *Toronto Star*, in an article on Johnny Depp, made the observation:

> As a character actor, he plays with extraordinary vocal talent, postural, gestural and choreographic—in the same league as John Lithgow, Denholm Elliott, and George Coulouris.

George Coulouris was cremated at Golders Green Crematorium in London in a non-religious service. According to his wishes it was followed by a small gathering at the Bird House in Hampstead. His friend, American actor Ted Reed, said a few words but otherwise there was a notable lack of showbiz at the event. That is how Coulouris would have wanted it. He was an actor who hated the pomp and posing so often associated with that side of the business. He never wanted to be part of a movement or a new wave, and he never stayed long enough anywhere to let his work get boring or routine. Elizabeth Coulouris summed up the man perfectly:

> George never compromised, you know, he was always honest with himself and others. He loved his work and he enjoyed his life; he lived it to the full and always tried to get as much out of every situation as he possibly could. Life came naturally to him; he didn't have to work at it.

Coulouris never received the professional acceptance he thought he deserved. He certainly had earned admission to that rare group of theatrical greats but perhaps in the end he was afraid of being unworthy; or maybe he was more comfortable as an outsider. His great stage roles may not have survived but his remaining radio work reveals a sensitive and thoughtful side to this most physical of actors. His contribution to cinema hasn't been marginalized; at his peak he was amongst the best screen heavies in Hollywood and he could have gone on to enjoy a long and distinguished career. Hollywood viewed him as a villain, usually playing one-dimensional characters, but Coulouris did so with such intelligence and depth as to make them the most real and threatening characters in the movies. Over scores of British films he demonstrated his range, turning easily from broad comedy to melodrama with equal aplomb. The fact that he never finished his autobiography is tragic but his method and approach are already there for all to see; acting for Coulouris had to be fresh and dangerous, and he brought this vitality and individualism to everything he did.

André Morell: Flesh and Blood

Although he made many films that have stood the test of time, André Morell is best remembered for a handful of movies he made for England's Hammer Films in the 1950s and '60s, providing a depth and humor rarely glimpsed in B movies. Indeed so memorable was Morell's contribution to that oeuvre that his work with such prominent directors as Alfred Hitchcock, David Lean and Stanley Kubrick is frequently overlooked in favor of *The Plague of the Zombies* or *The Mummy's Shroud*. Morell is actually much more than a Hammer horror star; in fact of all the actors who appeared in the company's extended repertory troupe—including George Coulouris—Morell had the best theatrical pedigree and his name appeared prominently on playbills that included Laurence Olivier, Michael Redgrave and John Gielgud. More than that, he was also a major television star; his work for the BBC in the formative years of live dramas made him one of the most popular and versatile actors on the small screen, and he turned his hand easily from the doomed lover in *Othello* to the ice-cold torturer in *1984*. It was on television that André Morell scored arguably his biggest personal success, playing the lead in *Quatermass and the Pit*, which launched the unassuming actor into what today would be considered the "superstar" category.

In the cinema, Morell never regarded himself as anything more than a jobbing actor; he took the roles that either interested him or paid the taxman. He is quoted as saying he enjoyed his film work—or most of it—but cinema in general and Hammer in particular did not appreciate what a considerable talent it had. While Peter Cushing, another of the BBC's alumni, was penciled in for practically all of Hammer's leading roles, Morell was left to slog it out in the second features and, with the possible exception of *The Hound of the Baskervilles*, he never appeared in a recognized Hammer classic.

This image of Morell as a utility performer in movies shouldn't be taken as a measure of his values; he took his work very seriously and set high standards, which extended to those around him, and he could be intolerant of anyone whose efforts fell short. In his personal life he also could be demanding and sometimes difficult but his friends remember him as wonderfully urbane and witty. It is these qualities that shine through in every film he made; from the sprawling epic *Ben Hur* or the taut thriller *Seven Days Till Noon,* Morell made the film more memorable simply by being in it.

Cecil Mesritz was born in London on August 20, 1909, and by no stretch of the imagination could his childhood be described as conventional. Certainly he was never encouraged to pursue theatrical ambitions; if his parents André and Rosa had their way their son, who later took the name André Morell, would never have set foot on the stage. Rosa Mesritz (nee Lamb) was a direct descendant of Lady Caroline Lamb, the notorious socialite whose very public obsession with Lord Byron scandalized London in the 19th Century. André Mesritz was more of a mystery; the family oral history portrays him as a musician, or possibly a composer, and of Dutch origin but he had no stronger connection with the theatre. Mesritz certainly wasn't rich and while there was money on Rosa's side it didn't extend as far as this branch of the family tree. The Mesritz's were not wealthy but they were respectable, and acting at the time was still not considered an appropriate career. Young Cecil, who always was bright and intelligent, would be instructed to find a trade, engineering or perhaps law.

In 1914, with the outbreak of WWI, the boy was sent to his grandparents in the relative comfort and seclusion of Bath, the affluent town some 100 miles west of London best known for its hot springs and impressive Georgian architecture. It was here that the boy was first exposed to the lifestyle that only extreme wealth could provide—even in the midst of war—from servants and nannies to lavish meals, the very best in clothes, furnishings and toys.

His parents' personal relationship was already on the rocks and one suspects that the decision to evacuate young Cecil had as much to do with shielding the boy from the emotional breakup as any danger posed by the Kaiser. Even when he had a family of his own many years later, he was seldom disposed to talk about his childhood, and whenever the subject was raised it was swiftly brushed aside. The only happy memories he cared to share were of a precocious five-year-old enchanting his grandparents with a rendition of *The Boy Stood on the Burning Deck*. At some point while Cecil was staying in Bath, his parents separated and later divorced, and the upheaval at home meant that the boy would be 11 before he was allowed to return to London—long after the end of the war. Even then, far from being welcomed into the bosom of a family, he was immediately dispatched to that uniquely British middle class institution, the boarding school, in this case Belmont College.

Rosa seems to have disappeared from the family scene soon afterward and the suggestion is that she died soon after the boy returned to his father. The records show that Morell left formal schooling at age 15, which may have coincided with the death of his mother but certainly marked a significant turning point for the youngster. He had never shaken off the feeling of delight he experienced with his early "performances" in Bath, but Mesritz made it perfectly clear that his son would have to pay his way in the world. At a time when most thespians of his generation were studying technique at the Royal Academy of Dramatic Arts or one of London's many private acting schools, Cecil was spending his days learning the fine points of engineering. During the evenings and weekends he perfected his craft as a spear-carrier and scenery changer with the amateur dramatic society at the St. Pancras People's Theatre.

After fours years of this double life and still acting under the name of Cecil Mesritz, he joined an amateur group in Bermondsey, South London, a repertory company in the days when everyone had to learn and perform a variety of roles in a new play every week. Despite the lack of formal training and the obvious stresses and strains involved with this type of rapid turnaround, he still attracted attention. When the drama critic of the *South London News* saw the production of Pirandello's *Perhaps You're Right* in April 1934 he wrote:

> Cecil Mesritz, who is proving himself one of the finest amateur actors in London, was brilliant as Lamberto Laudisi. In this performance he excelled, so much so that I was sorry when he left the stage for the others of the cast seemed at once to feel as a child does without its mother.

Over the next two and one-half years, André Morell honed his art in places like Brighton, Margate and Liverpool, appearing in literary dozens of plays ranging from the light comedy of P.G. Wodehouse's *Good Morning Bill* to murder mysteries like *Death at Court Lady*. The actor's scrapbooks reveal an almost unbroken list of plaudits from the provincial press: "finest performance of the season," "a brilliant performance," "perfect timing" and so on. For anyone who is only familiar with the actor's film work, the range Morell displayed on the stage will come as a revelation. He successfully tackled everything from the classics to modern farce, even succeeding in pantomime, playing a memorable Tweedledee in Lewis Carroll's *The Charm of Alice*. The *East Kent Times* was particularly impressed with this performance: "He certainly lifts it to an even higher plane. His performance is as near flawless as one could desire."

Making steady progress through Britain's provincial theaters, Morell inevitably attracted the attention of casting directors in his native London. In September 1936 he was contracted as Cecil Mesritz to understudy the popular leading man Owen Nares in *Call It a Day* at the Globe Theatre. By the time the play opened in October, he was listed in the credits as the much more familiar André Morell. On December 30, 1936, he made his West End debut when Nares fell ill, having to cover at both the matinee and evening performances. It was not exactly the fairytale of overnight stardom but Morell proved himself a capable stage performer and he soon enjoyed top billing in small London productions of *Burnt Pig* at the Portfolio and *Sweet Aloes* at the "Q" Theatre. Stardom beckoned when he was engaged for the title role in *Matador*, which had its world premiere in Edinburgh in March 1937 before embarking on a British tour.

In September 1937 Morell consolidated his position as a West End star by appearing in a huge hit, *The Last Straw*, a grim murder mystery in which he played a character described as "a cad guaranteed to let any and every side down with the maximum bump." He was now in constant demand, invariably in London, and his impressive credits included *They Came by Night,* again with Owen Nares, *Believe It or Not* at Richmond, *Quiet Wedding* with Glynis Johns, and the leading role as a gentleman sleuth in *Open Verdict*. By then, having adopted the professional name of André Morell, he decided to change it legally by deed poll. Morell was a great admirer of the Irish writer George Bernard Shaw and it seems likely that the name was taken from the character in Shaw's *Candida*.

In August 1938 Morell accepted an invitation from the legendary impresario Tyrone Guthrie to join the Royal Shakespeare Company at the Old Vic, one of the most prestigious theatres in London. Guthrie had been appointed director at the RSC in 1936, a position he would hold for nearly a decade, and he is widely credited with attracting the cream of English acting talent. At the Old Vic that season Morell shared the stage with John Gielgud, Alec Guinness, Anthony Quayle and a young Richard Wordsworth. Opening with Horatio to Gielgud's Hamlet, Morell moved on to the larger role of Faulkland in Sheridan's 18th-century comedy *The Rivals*; but it was in the next play that he really proved his worth, playing the upstart playwright Tom Wrench in *Trelawney of the Wells*—a role he would always consider a favorite.

The season was a popular success and helped cement Morell as one of the leading lights of the London stage. Guthrie took to the younger man immediately and signed him to appear in the RSC's forthcoming tour of Europe playing in *Hamlet* and *Henry V* to audiences in Lisbon, Milan, Florence and Rome.

Despite the demands of the stage Morell found time to take part in *Sun Up*, an experimental television production for the BBC, which also starred Dame Sybil Thorndyke. Working almost exclusively on adaptations of existing plays or classic novels, the BBC's limited resources were then turned to *Pride and Prejudice* (1938), with Morell playing Wickham, the romantic lead, and *Lady Precious Steam* (1938), featuring a walk-on by a young Dennis Price. As part of a series called *Theatre Parade*, Morell also recreated his roles in *Trelawny of the Wells*, costarring Freda Jackson, and *The Rivals* with Eric Portman, as well as a more ambitious staging of *Cyrano de Bergerac* starring Constance Cummings and James Mason. These early television movies were shot quickly and looked cheap and stagy; they were broadcast live in black and white with a running time of 60 to 70 minutes. At the time, broadcasts were restricted to the London area with an estimated audience of some 30,000-40,000 television sets. It was the

Curigwen Lewis was Elizabeth Bennett to Morell's Wickham in the BBC's 1938 *Pride and Prejudice*

inauspicious beginning of a relationship with the small screen that would serve the actor well for the next three decades.

In July 1939 Morell was back with the RSC at the Old Vic as part of Robert Donat's company (including Stewart Grainger, Constance Cummings and Andrew Cruickshank) to stage *Romeo and Juliet, Devil's Disciple* and *St Joan*. Morell's burgeoning career as a juvenile lead seemed secure until fate intervened.

On September 3, 1939, Britain declared war on Nazi Germany. At first life seemed to continue largely unchanged; the weather was excep-

tionally hot and in London the crowds were flocking to the parks and open air markets. The RSC was enjoying yet another successful season, although bookings were down due more to the temperatures than the shadow cast by Adolf Hitler. This was the period known as the "phony war" which consisted largely of rhetoric and posturing by the respective governments.

It wasn't to last and, by the start of the following year, air raids were a nightly occurrence and the threat of German invasion was all too real. Morell was still at the RSC, playing Olonzo for Marius Goring in *The Tempest* in a fine cast including John Gielgud (as Prospero), Jack Hawkins, James Donald and Jessica Tandy. But the war was taking its toll and *The Tempest* has the dubious distinction of being the last play staged at the Old Vic prior to its closure for the duration. In June 1940 Morell, along with close friends Jack Hawkins and Andrew Cruickshank, took his leave of the RSC and volunteered for the Royal Welsh Fusiliers, receiving his commission in March 1941. Tyrone Guthrie took a reduced company into exile in Lancashire, in the North of England, well away from the Blitz but shorn of most of its young men.

Initially Morell was stationed at the regiment's base at Worthing, a seaside resort on the English Channel, which had celebrated its best days—possibly its only good times—during the 1800s, and had been in a long, slow decline. Despite the ever-present threat of a German landing, Morell spent the best part of a year "communing with nature and guarding the Cissbury Ring" (an Iron Age fortress of no strategic importance whatsoever). By early 1942 Morell had enough of cooling his heels and volunteered for active service overseas, which at that stage of the war meant North Africa or the Far East. The actor was transferred to the First Battalion Rajput Regiment of the Indian Army and took part in operations on the North West Frontier and later in the infamous Burma Campaign against the Japanese, with all the rigors and hardships that accompanied life in what became known as the "Forgotten Army." Morell finished the war on a small island, some 800 miles east of Sir Lanka in the Nicobar Group, commanding a company of infantry with "three thousand Japanese soldiers and precious little else."

As the tide turned in the Allies' favor, Tyrone Guthrie organized a new company that would take the RSC into the postwar era. He eventually recruited actors of the caliber of Laurence Olivier, Sybil Thorndyke and Ralph Richardson. As early as July 1944 he wrote to Morell, suggesting, "There is a reasonable chance that there would be something interesting to offer." Unfortunately, with the war against Japan still raging, Morell wasn't released from the army until the following year, by which time the Guthrie-Olivier company had written itself into history by appearing in Hamburg's Schauspielhaus a mere two weeks after the German surrender. The actor's formal discharge, dated January 21, 1947, granted him the honorary rank of major; by which time he already had returned to England and the London stage.

In the summer of 1946 Morell produced a short run of *The Dragon and the Dove* and followed it with an appearance in *Three Silent Men* opposite Patricia Roc, but it wasn't until October 1946 that he reestablished some of the lost momentum. *Happy as Kings* opened at the Arts Theatre in Cambridge and was successful enough to merit a transfer to the West End. Barely pausing for breath he then starred in a massive hit, *Boys in Brown*, at the Duchess in London, playing a benevolent prison governor trying to implement progressive reforms at an institute for young offenders. In 1949, Gainsborough made the hard-hitting drama into a disappointing film with Jack Warner playing the lead. Morell enjoyed another London stage hit with the Battle of Britain drama *English Summer*. The *New Statesman* was moved to describe him as "a highly accomplished actor with a much wider range than this sort of realism allows…just the right note of responsible maturity with just the right touch of boyishness."

Staying in London, Morell replaced Clive Brook as Henry Hutton in Aldous Huxley's *The Giaconda Smile*, a bitter morality tale adapted from his own short story. Morell's character, described as "a sensual, cultured hedonist," set tongues wagging when he married a much younger woman soon after the death of his invalid wife. He is then was tossed into a cell after the police discovered that the unfortunate woman was poisoned, and is saved only after his new wife confesses to the crime. For a play that relied heavily on melodrama rather than tension for its impact, *The Giaconda Smile* was a surprise hit in London and enjoyed a long run in the West End. (It moved to Broadway in 1951 with Basil Rathbone in the lead.)

A London run, no matter how successful, didn't offer the sort of financial remuneration available from films and almost as soon as he returned from the army Morell's agent was urging him to explore cinematic opportunities. He had made his film debut in the all male cast of *13 Men and a Gun*, a quota quickie shot in 1938 by Italian-born producer-director Mario Zampi, who would helm a series of well-received comedies, including *The Naked Truth* and *Too Many Crooks* starring Terry-Thomas. *13 Men and a Gun* is a talky war movie starring Arthur Wintner, a popular star following his success as Sherlock Holmes in *Murder at the Baskervilles* (1937). Wintner played Holmes five times, in a characterization many consider definitive, but he is wasted here in a routine drama, which, at a mere 65 minutes, barely qualifies as a B feature. For Morell, whose love of travel would be an important influence in his choice of film work, the opportunity to spend four weeks in the Italian locations with Clifford Evans and Howard Marion-Crawford was worth more than the limited challenges offered by the trite script.

Morell then slummed through a handful of minor roles in forgettable movies while concentrating on establishing his theatrical career. It wasn't until after the outbreak of the WWII that he made arguably the highlight of his brief film career to date. The irrepressible Mario Zampi had been interned as a potential enemy alien but his company, Two Cities Films, threw itself happily into the patriotic effort. *Unpublished Story* starring Richard Greene and Valerie Hobson was a contemporary thriller about investigative journalists hot on the trial of Nazi Fifth columnists in Blitz-stricken London. Set soon after the disastrous evacuation of British soldiers at Dunkirk when invasion paranoia was at its height, *Unpublished Story* progresses at a stately pace trying to balance the action with the need to highlight the danger posed by Nazis in the backstreets of London. It doesn't quite succeed either as entertainment or propaganda despite the worthy performances. Morell and Greene were already on active duty, but the director, Anthony Havelock-Allan (Hobson's husband), took advantage of a government directive allowing key personnel to be released from the service if the film was deemed to be in the national interest. Despite six weeks leave of absence from his regiment, Morell didn't have much more than a featured role adding some flourish to the otherwise stoic acting. A U.S. release by Columbia

kept the British flag flying on the other side of the Atlantic and gave Morell some American exposure, but soon afterwards Morell was posted overseas and his film career seemed to have stalled almost as soon as it started.

In a press interview during the 1950s Morell said, "After the war I thought I would never get another film part, I am not a smooth faced juvenile," and his priority in civilian life was rebuilding his career on the stage. By the time he was ready to resume screen acting there was actually very little work to be had. By 1950 the British film industry, crippled by unnecessary expansion and damaging protectionism, had stuttered almost to a complete halt. Many leading lights, both in front and behind the cameras, beat a path to Hollywood rather than feed on the scraps available in their native country, while British studios released actors and technicians from their contracts. By the time production started to pick up again the projects were far less ambitious and the scale more modest. Cinema may have missed out on Morell as a juvenile lead but by the time he returned to films, the 41-year-old had developed a maturity and air of authority combined with distinguished looks that made him a natural for professional men, doctors, lawyers and senior army officers.

In *No Place for Jennifer*, he played a sympathetic lawyer in a "tug of love" melodrama about divorcing parents (Leo Genn and Beatrice Campbell) and their disbelieving daughter (12-year-old Janette Scott yanking the heart strings in the title role). The film was released a year later in the U.S. by the tiny Stratford Pictures Corporation but the tepid and overly sentimental drama found few fans. Morell switched to the medical profession and was rewarded with more screen time in British Lion's soap opera *Flesh and Blood*. Set in Scotland and starring Richard Todd and Glynis Johns, the story follows three generations of a family as they struggle with poverty, death and scandal. Amongst those wrestling with a Scottish accent are Freda Jackson, George Cole and Ursula Howells but Morell had the additional burden of some rudimentary makeup, supposedly aging his character from a strapping youth to a pasty-faced senior citizen. The film is notable now for the first professional association between Morell and his future wife Joan Greenwood but in all other respects it is best forgotten.

Morell was better served by his next movie, which marked his first collaboration with David Lean, then one of the most promising talents still working in British films. Morell first met Lean soon after coming out of the army, at a party hosted by Constance Cummings. Having just seen *Brief Encounter,* Morell was waxing enthusiastically about its virtues, unaware that the director was in the room, and what could have provided an embarrassing moment actually was the basis for a long friendship. Lean cast Morell as a lawyer in *Madeline,*

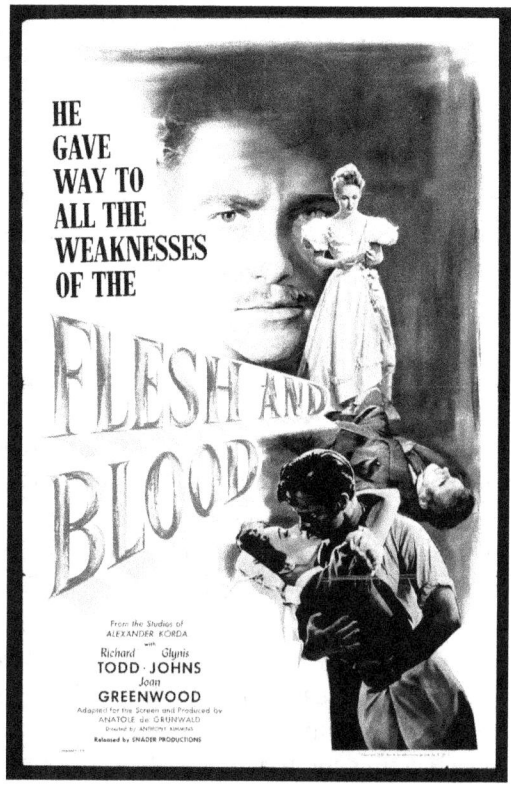

the true story of the 21-year-old Glaswegian Madeline Smith who was accused but never convicted of murdering her penniless French lover Emile L'Angelier. Smith, born into comfort and wealth, scandalized Victorian society not so much by her pursuit of physical gratification but by her readiness to betray her own class to get it. The fact that she callously disposed of this inconvenient lover when a much more appropriate partner appeared added spice to the whole mix. While frowning on Smith's behavior, the newspapers of the day turned on L'Angelier and characterized the unfortunate victim as an inscrutable foreigner who got what he deserved, largely ignoring his agonizing death from rat poison. The *crime passional* was made all the more gripping by the somewhat foolhardy decision of the couple to document their passion in a series of explicit love letters, and much of the carefully edited highlights found their way into the public domain. The verdict seemed a forgone conclusion with Smith facing the death penalty, until the jury returned that uniquely Scottish verdict of "not proven"—meaning that innocence had not been established but there was insufficient evidence to convict. Smith left Britain for America in the face of undiminished interest in her case in the form of endless magazine articles, books and fictionalized adaptations. She lived long enough into the 20th Century to see Hollywood producers vie for the screen rights but died in 1928.

The story seemed to have all the elements for great cinema—illicit passion, class conflict, courtroom drama and murder. David Lean had no difficulty persuading the Rank Organization, the only major studio still operating in England, that it would make a splendid vehicle for his then-wife Ann Todd. Having previously starred in a well-received theatrical version written by Harold Purcell, Todd—despite her age, 41—was accepted by Rank in the leading role. Yves Montand had been an early choice for the role of her lover and fellow countryman Gérard Philipe had been auditioned but the part eventually went to the largely unknown Ivan Desny. Lean began shooting exteriors in Glasgow's Blythswood Square—outside of Smith's actual home—in April 1949 before retiring to Pinewood for interiors. Morell joined the production there, playing Smith's defense counsel with what seemed an impossible task, while Barry Jones was cast as the prosecutor. Lean and his wife had a volatile relationship, on and off the set, and seemed locked in a destructive battle of wills over their respective visions of the story. The disharmony affected the cast and crew, and the tension on the set was not improved by an electrician's strike that prolonged the already exhausting schedule to 21 weeks. Lean, bored or perhaps just annoyed by the emotional aspects of the case, immersed himself in detail; the Victorian background is beautifully recreated and shot—at the expense of the drama. The actual trial, which should have been the climactic set piece, turns out to be something of a damp squib with Lean's fussy direction and Todd's glacial acting combining to diffuse all the dramatic tension. On the plus side, these scenes do include Morell delivering a powerhouse performance as the battling lawyer, using all his credibility and guile to save his client. Morell's closing summation is an impressive three and one-half minute *tour de force*. The *Evening News* sent a reporter to the set for that scene, noting that the actor achieved the rare accolade of spontaneous applause from the veteran—and by then exhausted—crew. Morell's efforts garnered some of his best film notices to date; the *Sunday Pictorial* hated the film but conceded, "There is a long court room scene which gives Andre Morell brilliant opportunities as Ann's defending counsel." The decision by Lean not to commit one way or the other on Smith's guilt seems to have annoyed cinemagoers as much as the critics and *Madeline* died at the box-office, with Lean branding it "the worst film I ever made."

It would be quite a challenge for any actor to move upward from David Lean but that is exactly what Morell did when he reported to perhaps British cinema's most celebrated filmmaker, Alfred Hitchcock. The Californian-based Hitchcock had devised a plan to alternate his work in Hollywood with films shot in his native country and began the experiment with the unsatisfactory *Under Capricorn*, starring imported leading players Joseph Cotten and Ingrid Bergman. The director seemed on much safer ground the following year when he returned to England to make what seemed a textbook Hitchcock thriller, *Stage Fright*. Adapted from Selwyn Jepson's novel *Man Running*, the film is essentially an old fashioned English whodunit with all the standard elements: a man accused of murder on the run from the police while an amateur detective tries to clear his name. The fact that the sleuth is in love with the suspect adds to the drama but the tired old standard of "innocent man in the wrong place at the wrong time" is turned on its head by having the seemingly blameless hero revealed at the climax to be the actual killer. To trick audience expectations, Hitchcock playfully rewrote the conventions of the genre with a falsified flashback that outraged cinema purists but did little to improve one of his lesser efforts.

With the money coming from Warner Bros., the leading players were selected more for their international appeal than their suitability. Jane Wyman, erstwhile wife of Ronald Reagan, was flown from Hollywood to play the would-be actress on the trail of the real killer—against the advice of all her friends and family. Marlene Dietrich was cast as the scheming cabaret diva whose plot to dispose of an inconvenient husband triggers the series of events. Richard Todd, an Oscar nominee for *The Hasty Heart*, plays the dimwitted lover seemingly manipulated into the role of fall guy. Comic relief is provided by Alastair Sim as Wyman's eccentric father, while Michael Wilding, best known as husband number five of Elizabeth Taylor, plays the likeable detective more interested in landing Wyman than catching criminals. Wilding, who also appears in *Under Capricorn,* plays a character called Wilfred Smith whose nickname "Ordinary" sums up everything you need to know about the actor. Morell was cast as Inspector Byard, the first of what would prove a profitable sideline as dogged policemen but, despite being in nominal command of the investigation, he was given very little to do. That didn't stop his becoming the target of Hitchcock's mischievous nature. Suffering from a wound received during the war, Morell found standing for long periods of time uncomfortable and asked the director if he might be seated during his key scene, the interrogation of Dietrich. Hitch was happy to oblige but made sure he played the entire scene seated with his back to the camera! At least there was the consolation of working with Marlene Dietrich who plays the role to the hilt and shimmers across the stage in a series of increasingly glamorous costumes. Morell and Dietrich hit it off famously and caused a minor stir on set when word got out that the actress had been visiting his apartment after shooting. The actor was single and had something of a reputation as a ladies' man, so the inevitable conclusions were drawn. Morell was too much of a gentleman to ever comment publicly but his standing amongst the crew was considerably enhanced!

Appropriately for a film set in the theatre, Richard Todd gets his comeuppance in the final act as the curtain falls, literally. Filmed during the summer of 1949, *Stage Fright* didn't prove the return to form that Hitchcock had hoped for; the plot is paper thin, the need to stop the action to accommodate yet another tune from Dietrich undermines the action, and Jane Wyman makes a distinctly unappealing heroine. The diminutive Richard Todd plays a largely colorless hero, a long way from Cary Grant and James Stewart, but things pick up when he is unmasked as a twitching psychopath—suggesting cinema gained a lackluster leading man at the expense of an entertaining villain. Morell's contribution went largely unnoticed, as did the enjoyable cameos from Joyce Grenfell, Miles Malleson and Kay Walsh. The critical and financial failure of *Stage Fright* left Hitchcock so dissatisfied with filming in England that he wouldn't shoot there again for 22 years (except for *The Man who Knew Too Much*, which had some location work in London).

Hitchcock bounced back from the disappointment of *Under Capricorn* and *Stage Fright* with *Strangers on a Train*; Morell on the other hand went to work with a director whose reputation, at least in his chosen field, was almost as great as Hitchcock's. Terence Fisher had begun working at Gainsborough Studios in 1936 when it was still independent from the Rank Organization, and he continued to learn his trade there after the studio came under the control of Rank and his head of production, Sidney Box. Amongst the better-known efforts that benefited from Fisher's expertise as an editor were *The Wicked Lady* and *Master of Bankdam*. He made his directorial debut away from the studio and relatively late in life at the age of 44 with *Colonel Bogie*, a light comic ghost story, before returning to Gainsborough for meatier stuff like *The Girl in the Painting*. Two years later Fisher, like many at Gainsborough in particular and Rank in general, had a reputation for being a technically proficient, dependable but uninspiring filmmaker. When Fisher was selected for *So Long at the Fair*, it was considered just another assignment but the film came along when Gainsborough was on the decline and Sidney Box was fighting to save the studio and his reputation. The failure of his prestige productions *Christopher Columbus* and *The Bad Lord Byron* had undermined Box's position and Rank's poor investment decisions had effectively ended the company's policy of allowing artists and producers a free rein. The relationship between the Gainsborough boss and his corporate masters was difficult, and the pressure on Box was enormous; to say that a lot was riding on the success of *So Long at the Fair* is an understatement.

The film was conceived as the directorial debut of Sidney's wife Muriel Box, Gainsborough's most reliable writer. Rank then insisted that it be shaped into a vehicle for Jean Simmons, one of the few recognized box-office stars still contracted to the company. Simmons, who would soon decamp to Hollywood, enjoyed an enormous success in *The Blue Lagoon*, which made her indispensable to the project—and she knew it. Deciding that she didn't want her star status entrusted to a debutante, Simmons had Muriel Box ousted from the director's chair and replaced by the more reliable Terence Fisher. The latter had by coincidence also replaced Box on an earlier attempt to direct, *The Astonished Heart*, which was shot on sets adjacent to *Madeline* while Lean was at Pinewood. Anthony Darnborough, a highly experienced producer and long term associate of Box, would share Fisher's director credit on the film—as he had on *The Astonished Heart*—and help him navigate the increasingly choppy waters surrounding the movie.

The script for *So Long at the Fair* centers on Simmons' character, Vicky Barton, who is on holiday in Paris with her brother Johnny. The background is the Great Exhibition and Paris is awash with tourists but, despite the crowds, Simmons is left alone and isolated when Johnny disappears without a trace. Playing on the twin English obsessions of crime and xenophobia, Barton faces not only the possibility of foul play but also the disbelieving and suspicious behavior of every foreigner she meets. The only crumb of comfort comes from fellow Rank contract artist Dirk Bogarde, then just a promising young lead, playing a struggling English artist who naturally believes her tale of woe. Augmenting leads are a pre-Disney David Tomlinson, a coquettish Honor Blackman and Morell in another character study as the skeptical Dr. Hart, who seems to know more than he admits. For anyone interested in spoilers, the hotel owner (Catherine Nesbitt) is lying!

The film is a bit of a mixed bag; there is no chemistry at all between the leading couple but Simmons makes a suitably vulnerable heroine and the supporting cast is uniformly good. Fisher, either by inclination or design, seems more interested in the romantic tryst so there is little effort to build any sustained tension other than the natural discomfort of the situation. The second unit did a creditable job of filming the obligatory tourist shots of the *Folies Bergere* and the Eiffel Tower but there was insufficient money to send any of the leading players to Paris and the crude rear screen projection undermines the best efforts of the cast.

Despite the best efforts of the publicity department to suggest the film was based on real events, it is nothing more than a loose reworking of *The Lady Vanishes* and the conceit later cropped up as the basic plot for Hammer's *Kiss of the Vampire*. Curiously Les Bowie who picks up a credit for special effects on *So Long at the Fair* would later fulfill the same function on *Kiss of the Vampire*. (Trivia buffs might like to know that the star of that Hammer film, Edward De Souza, played the Bogarde role in a BBC version of *So Long at the Fair*.) Given that Morell has practically nothing to do, the film is an important one only in terms of his future career; not only as a precursor to his later work with Fisher but also for his introduction to Darnborough who, as a producer, would employ Morell in two subsequent movies—the first of which, *Trio*, went into production almost immediately.

Darnborough had a particular fondness for English author Somerset Maugham whose short stories were ideally suited for the compendium style movies so favored by horror filmmakers in the 1960s and 1970s. Darnborough successfully initiated the formula with *Quartet* directed by Ken Anakin in 1948; and *Trio* would be followed by his third and final adaptation, *Encore*, in 1952. In *Trio*, Morell is featured in the last and longest of the three stories, "Sanatorium," set in an austere tuberculosis clinic in Scotland, where many colorful characters are confined. Essentially it is a slight story about a relationship between a retired army officer (Michael Rennie) and an impressionable young girl (Jean Simmons). Flatly directed by Harold French (Ken Annakin helmed the first two segments), *Sanatorium* may have worked as a 15-minute story but the at-

tempt to spin it to almost a full hour and introduce a raft of peripheral characters simply defuses any emotional engagement. Morell's appearance, predictably as a doctor, comes long after the audience has lost all interest and the actor is given little to do beyond looking vaguely concerned.

Trio turned out to be the last film to carry the famous Gainsborough Lady marquee; Sidney Box, worn down by years of in fighting over projects and squabbling with accountants, requested an extended leave of absence. The new head of production at Rank, John Davis, generally described as J. Arthur Rank's hatchet man, took the opportunity to close the company down and terminate all the contract artists and staff. Overnight the famous old studio ceased to exist and amongst those left looking for work in the austere environment of post-war Britain was Terence Fisher; two years later he would find something like a permanent home at Hammer.

Morell was making slow progress in his film career, however, the BBC was offering much more interesting prospects. Cashing in on his stage success, Morell was cast as Bassanio in a broadcast of *The Merchant of Venice*, followed by the title role of *Othello* with Stephen Murray as Iago and Laurence Harvey as Cassio. Proving his range, Morell enjoyed significant success with the television adaptation of *An English Summer* and *Crime Passional* directed by George More O'Ferrall and costarring Morell's close friend Michael Gough. Morell would go on to play such diverse parts as Stockman in Ibsen's *Enemy of the People* and Boss Mangan in *Heartbreak House;* by the early 1950s he was being hailed as one of the best and most versatile actors on British television. It was the success of these television performances rather than the work for Lean and Hitchcock that brought Morell to the attention of the Boulting brothers, then in the process of casting a new thriller called *Seven Days to Noon*.

Although Roy and John Boulting are probably best known for their satirical comedies such as *Privates' Progress* and *I'm Alright Jack*, they had proved, with their adaptation of Graham Green's *Brighton Rock* (U.S. title *Young Scarface*), that they could make gripping contemporary dramas. *Seven Days to Noon* came from an original story by James Bernard and Paul Dehn and draws on the growing public unease about atomic weapons and in particular the distinctly real threat of nuclear war. Barry Jones, Morell's courtroom sparring partner in *Madeline,* took top billing in the role of Professor Willingdon, a scientist who absconds from Britain's atomic research program with a bomb big enough to destroy the centre of London. Willingdon appeals as more a friendly grandfather figure than a zealot but he writes a carefully worded letter to the Prime Minister threatening to detonate his bombs unless there is a public commitment to destroy all atomic weapons. Scotland Yard, in the shape of Morell's Superintendent Folland, initially dismisses the letter as a hoax only later realizing that Willingdon is as dangerous as he is desperate. The film then evolves into a manhunt with Folland's taskforce playing cat and mouse with the scientist

while the clock ticks down to the deadline. Willingdon at first does very little to avoid capture; later after the police publish his picture the pace picks up and the build-up to the climax is as tense as any Hollywood thriller. John Boulting milks this time pressure for all he is worth, while his understated direction and black and white cinematography create a disturbing pseudo-documentary style, underpinned by the stark shots of desolate London streets.

Second-billed Morell is in good form as Folland, creating a determined but human character out of the blandly written policemen and presenting a fine foil for Barry Jones' twitchy scientist. During the early stages of the film Boulting uses the development of these two heavyweight characters to engage and hold the audience attention and relies almost totally on his cast for impact. As a finely drawn study of a man losing his grip on sanity, predictably it was Jones who captured all the best notices but Morell, with less to work with, offered a performance of no less depth. His anxious expression in some of the scenes achieved a hint of realism when he developed appendicitis during the last week of filming and relied on painkillers to get him through the last days. Made and released by Alexander Korda's London Films, *Seven Days to Noon* treated its subject with seriousness and maturity, a long way from the monster on the loose movies that so typified cinema's response to the nuclear threat in the 1950s. The basic premise, a nuclear device detonated in a city centre, was as relevant then as it is today and it struck a cord with contemporary audiences and critics alike. Reviewers on both sides of the Atlantic praised not only the entertainment value, but also the decision of the filmmakers to opt for character actors rather than stars. (James Bernard on the writing credit is better known as Hammer's composer in residence; his work here earned him a share of the film's "Best Motion Picture Story" Oscar.)

Morell took time off from film and television work to direct his own production of *The Mayor* at Wyndhams Theatre in the West End but it struggled to find an audience and the actor was only too happy to renew his acquaintance with the Boultings when they offered a reprise of Superintendent Folland in a sequel called *High Treason*. Having tackled the menace from within the Establishment, Folland and his team were now called on to battle an external threat in the shape of ruthless communists determined to bring down the British Government. The precarious state of finances at London Films drove the Boultings to the Rank Organization, which was keen to cash in on a proven hit and guaranteed the producers a major circuit release—as well as a modest increase in the budget. The script, written by Roy Boulting and Frank Harvey, opens with a spectacular explosion on an arms ship, the work of undercover saboteurs working on the London docks. Although they are never identified as such, Boulting leaves his audience in no doubt that the villains of the piece are communists—a topical concession to the anti-Soviet feeling sweeping England. When the police and security services start to show too much interest around the docks, the conspirators launch plan B, attacking power stations at strategic targets and effectively paralyzing Britain's national grid. With a trail of death and destruction to follow, Folland is soon on their tracks and the conspiracy widens to include a Member of Parliament. Finally the gang is confronted in a bloody shootout at London's Battersea Power Station. Morell was as watch-able as ever, this time playing second fiddle to Commander Brennan of the Secret Service (Irish actor Liam Redmond). Boulting once again allows the interaction between the characters to add depth and texture to a well-paced thriller. The documentary feel is also retained and the director doesn't shy away from showing the grim side of 1950s Britain; London's bombed-out docks and slum areas lend the film an unsettling air of realism. Amongst the cast of *High Treason* is Anthony Bushell, a close friend and associate of Laurence Olivier, who would carve a career playing officious army officers; here he is true to

High Treason

type as Major Elliot. Joan Hickson and Geoffrey Keen also join Bushell. With the lack of recognized star names and a presentation that is arguably too British, *High Treason* could conceivably have been consigned to the un-releasable file of U.S. distributors if not for the executives at Arthur Mayer-Edward Kingsley Inc. Having previously released *Seven Days to Noon*, the company was shrewd enough to realize that, pitched correctly; they could ride the same anti-communist wave identified by their English counterparts. Opening in the States in May 1952, *High Treason* garnered favorable reviews; amongst the more prominent was *The New York Times*, which found it a "first rate chase film…goes careering through tight places with the velocity of a train."

Morell finished 1951 at Rank working for Betty Box, sister of Sidney, in the spy thriller *The Clouded Yellow*. Cast as the urbane Chubb, an "M"-type head of the British Secret Service, Morell is called into action when a former agent "appears" to have committed a murder. The film is every bit as "Hitchcockian" as it sounds right down to the innocent man accused, lovers on the run and a climatic chase across the wilds of northern England. Trevor Howard plays the disillusioned special agent and Jean Simmons, in her third film with Morell, is the girlfriend who makes his life on the run significantly more tolerable. In a nice touch, Barry Jones, also in his third film with Morell, plays a seemingly harmless butterfly collector. Director Ralph Thomas was no Hitchcock but the chase (beautifully photographed by Geoffrey Unsworth) rattles at a good pace through rural England.

Morell's next film, directed by Terence Fisher, was also a thriller and, while the actor is restricted to a peripheral role, it has the distinction of marking his first association with Hammer, a production company that would play a major part in his film career.

The company had been around since the Thirties mainly as a film distributor under the banner Exclusive Films; the more familiar Hammer Film Productions was incorporated as a wholly owned subsidiary in 1948—just at the time the rest of the industry in England was giving up the ghost. Hammer's secret weapon was its charismatic head, James Carreras, who never seemed short of a moneymaking idea and was one of the few producers in Britain to recognize that brand familiarity could entice the public into cinemas. At a time when television was still regarded as the natural enemy of cinema, Hammer executives would regularly trawl the archives of the BBC looking for suitable subjects to turn into undemanding entertainment. These movies would be distributed in England through Exclusive and in the U.S. under a series of ad hoc arrangements. The focus was very much on safe options—thrillers or comedies—and this solid if unexciting operating model meant that, by the early 1950s, Hammer could boast some eight productions a year of their own, with many more being released through Exclusive.

Fisher's first film for Hammer had been *The Last Page*, a murder melodrama featuring former Rank starlet Diana Dors and released by Robert Lippert in the U.S. as *Man Bait*. Lippert had agreed to finance a package, which gave him North American, rights in exchange for a substantial contribution to the budget and an "above the title" star familiar to American audiences, in this case George Brent who had been so memorable in *The Spiral Staircase*. Lippert was a quickie king in the days before American International Pictures made it fashionable and specialized in churning out formula movies for the lower end of the market. He recognized the quota legislation in England, which guaranteed a market for a minimum number of British films, gave nimble-toed producers the opportunity to partner British companies with scripts but no capital to get their films made. Lippert found in James Carreras a man after his own heart and their second movie, also directed by Fisher, was a mystery thriller with an aeronautical backdrop, *Wings of Danger* aka *Dead on Course*, written by John Gilling and starring Zachary Scott.

By the time Fisher sat down to plan the third in the series, he was pretty much considered as the in-house director at Hammer—more a reflection of his economical use of the camera and reliability than any inherent talent. The next collaboration between Lippert and Hammer was *Stolen Face*, a more ambitious effort, not in terms of budget but certainly in its themes. *Stolen Face* was also the first time the names Fisher and Hammer were linked on a fantasy project, and one that traded on unashamedly sensational and horrific images.

The script, a bizarre love triangle, was based on a story by émigré Hungarians Alexander Paal and Steven Vas. The former had produced *Cloudburst* for

Hammer and would go on to made *Man Trap*, *Four Sided Triangle* and *Countess Dracula*. *Stolen Face* is the story of renowned plastic surgeon Phillip Ritter who, as a result of a weekend in the company of a beautiful but troubled concert pianist, Alice, develops a deep rooted obsession. The film's early sequences establish Ritter as a decent sort, happier with *pro bono* work with the needy than pandering to the desiccated but wealthy harridans who patronize his private practice. He does diagnose that something is missing in his life, at least until he meets and falls for Alice. Fisher's montages of schmaltzy images are so sickly that it is something of a relief when things go awry and Alice absconds; later she admits she is inconveniently engaged to her manager David. As the country's leading light on facelifts Ritter doesn't waste too much time pining over his unrequited love; instead he decides to create his own version and the opportunity appears when he is called in to operate on a horribly scarred lowlife, Lilly. With admirable economy we learn everything we need to know about Lilly's character and background by the news that she is an inmate of one of Her Majesty's prisons for women and she was "banged up in the Blitz." Unfortunately this isn't just puppy love, Ritter's infatuation borders on psychotic; first he alters Lilly's appearance, then her clothes and musical tastes until she has effectively become Alice, at least superficially. Sadly Lilly has retained her unfortunate taste for the sleazy side of life and soon resorts to type—rather letting the side down, you might say. Ritter offers Lilly everything that money can buy but she can't shake off her gutter-level predilections for both drink and men and rebels against her kindly but misguided benefactor.

The theme was a genre standard; everything from *The Bride of Frankenstein* through *Horror Circus* to *Corruption* used or re-used the same elements. One of Ritter's trite homilies, "A physical deformity might cause someone to become unbalanced and commit a crime," could have been lifted from Boris Karloff in *The Raven* (1935). Had Fisher concentrated more on Ritter's obsession and less on the class divide, *Stolen Face* could have been a classic of the genre. Instead Ritter comes unstuck not because he meddles in things "best left alone" but because he picks a working class tart rather than a nice girl. In fact all the lower classes are portrayed as self-serving louts while the worst thing you can say about the polite middle classes is they are "misguided." Even Ritter, who is clearly deranged, receives forgiveness at the end and gets the girl—the right girl. Lilly, on the other hand, who is the victim after all, ends up under a train! *Stolen Face* is every bit as interesting as it sounds; the entertaining confusion of identity scenes and the climatic catfight between the two "Alices" is almost worth the price of the ticket. Of course the U.S. Production Code frowned on adultery, so the leading players had to be—technically—single during their liaison, and of course crime could not be seen to pay; so when the lovers walk off into the sunset at the end of the film, they had to do so out of step rather than arm in arm.

Stolen Face is graced with the presence of two fading Hollywood names, Lizabeth Scott playing Alice(s) and Paul Henried as Ritter. The latter had of starred in the classic *Casablanca* but his career faltered with his outspoken criticism of Senator McCarthy's House of Un-American Activities committee. Lizabeth Scott was contracted to producer Hal Wallis and had been built up in the Forties as a femme fatale in a series of film noir movies where she was dubbed "the threat"—a effort to create the sort of on-screen mystique attached to Veronica Lake and Lauren Bacall. Scott's career lost momentum when the infamous *Confidential* magazine cast doubts on her sexuality and, despite winning a lawsuit against the rag, her career never recovered.

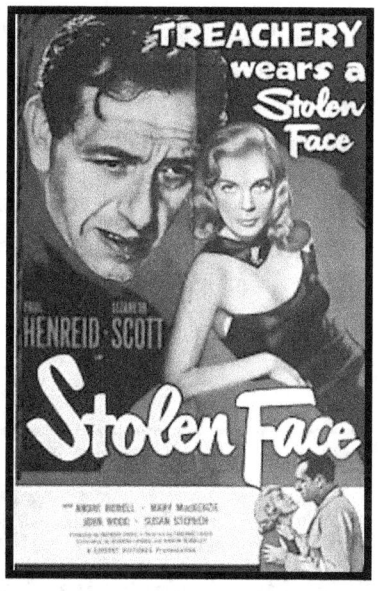

The film is fascinating but runs nearly a third of its time before Morell's character, David, Alice's fiancé, is even mentioned; thereafter he is kept literally on the sidelines. David is one of those "decent sorts" that exist purely as a plot device and his contribution can be measured by the fact he doesn't even merit a surname on the credits. True to form—this was the 1950s—when he realizes that his true love has fallen for another, he gives her up with barely a murmur. All very poignant but not too challenging for an actor of Morell's caliber, and he spends most of his screen time watching Alice from the wings, looking vaguely concerned. With only a superficial characterization Morell had to use all his subtlety and skill to make anything out of his role, but he managed to create a great deal with the smallest gestures. This is particularly true in the scene where he begins to suspect Alice's affections lie elsewhere. When Ritter phones her house and David answers, Alice instructs him to say she is too busy to speak to him; David's obvious confusion is met with a curt dismissal of Ritter "as just someone I met." With the briefest of looks, Morell conveys everything his character is feeling, not only his understanding of the situation but his deep sadness. It has already been made abundantly obvious that Alice does not love David and Morell's gentle underplaying makes it equally obvious that David is aware of the fact. When asked about the film only a few years later Morell summed up his contribution to the film with "I do very little in it indeed" before remarking that he could remember nothing else about it.

Running only 72 minutes, *Stolen Face* was shot for a pittance at the tiny Riverside Studios; Hammer had vacated their rural base at Down Place and taken temporary residence in central London next to the Thames. The company made three films there before returning the following year to Down Place now rechristened Bray Studios, which would remain their production home for over a decade. Interestingly *Stolen Face* was the first Hammer film to win a major West End premiere, opening at the Plaza in May 1952 where it was greeted with the type of derision mainstream critics tend to reserve for low budget or exploitation subjects.

Far from being frustrated by the limited screen time in his films, Morell regarded any film as a bonus, provided he was free to concentrate on his first love, the stage. The hard work paid off when Tyrone Guthrie handed him the opportunity of a lifetime. Guthrie had returned to the RSC to direct the temperamental Donald Wolfit's 1951-52 season productions of *Tamburlaine the Great*, *The Clandestine Marriage* and *Timon of Athens*, with a company that included Richard Pasco, Robert Shaw and John Neville. One of the great eccentrics of the British stage, Wolfit was the archetypal barnstorming actor-manager whose declining years were captured in the film *The Dresser*. The 50-year-old actor clashed constantly with his director and the management of the Old Vic until he finally—and theatrically—walked out half way through the season. Morell answered the call from Guthrie and agreed to take the title role in *Timon of Athens*, generally regarded as one of the most obscure and difficult works in the Bard's canon. Wolfit's loss was certainly Morell's gain and, despite insufficient time to prepare for the role or to work with the other actors, the play was the hit of the season with both the public and critics. At the age of 43 Morell was hailed as a major star on the West End stage.

Role to 'Trio' Star

BURBANK, Calif. Andre Morell, noted British actor known to American audiences for his outstanding performances in "High Treason," "Seven Days to Noon" and "Trio," has been set for a major role in "His Majesty O'Keefe," starring Burt Lancaster. He will play a trader who runs the affairs of a small Pacific island.

As well as plaudits, the success brought Morell to the attention of Hollywood. After completing the run at the Old Vic, he accompanied the RSC on their national tour including *King Lear*. During this run an executive representing the independent production company Hecht-Lancaster stopped by to discuss a role in the film *His Majesty O'Keefe*. Company founder Burt Lancaster had title role, but Morell was offered an interesting supporting part and a lengthy sojourn in the film's South Pacific location. It was an offer too good to miss and Morell committed to the film—as soon as he had discharged his obligation to the RSC.

In the meantime the actor supplemented his income with low-budget British movies including *The Tall Headlines* aka *The Frightened Bride* for Raymond Stross Productions, adapted from his own story by Audrey Erskine-Lindop and directed by Terence Young. A torrid melodrama masquerading as a social statement, it concerns the fate of the Rackham family forced to abandon their home after the eldest son is executed for murder. The family members hope that moving to a new area, avoiding social contact and becoming distinctly tight-lipped whenever the subject is raised, will help them to forget their shame and shake off the stigma. History appears to be repeating itself when the other son's wife disappears in mysterious circumstances and all the old tensions and fears erupt. Morell plays the father George, an ordinary and rather dull man suddenly thrown into a situation that he can't understand or control. Judged purely on the acting the film is a tremendous success with Morell in a splendid performance as the gentle man railing against the injustice of his plight but unable to do anything about it. Distinguished actress Flora Robson lends commendable support as his tormented wife, with Michael Denison in a dual role as the murderer and then the brother whose anti-social behaviors triggers the crisis. The cast however is undone by some shamelessly exploitative direction from Young and an unnecessarily complex script by Erskine-Lindop. Former Rank leading players Dennis Price and Mai Zetterling pop up in supporting roles, the latter playing Denison's victim, the one truly sympathetic role in the film. *The Tall Headlines* was picked up for release in the U.S. by Beverly Pictures and released on a double bill with Francis Searle's lamentable comedy *The Caretaker's Daughter*.

The New York Times was unimpressed: "Audiences who relish the steady infiltration of quality British imports will do well to avoid this pair of fly-by-nights…at least (*The Frightened Bride*) can claim some sterling, muted emoting by those infallible veterans Flora Robson and André Morell."

Another B picture from the period was *The Secret*, a tale of diamond smuggling in the seaside resort of Brighton on England's South Coast. A very minor thriller, the principal selling point—at least in the British market—was popular child star Mandy Miller, though the film is notable for the involvement of two American refugees from the McCarthy witch hunts, Sam Wanamaker and director Cy Enfield. Shot on the tiny soundstages at the Brighton Film Studios, *The Secret* does benefit from some nice color photography by Jack Asher which makes the most of the seaside resort's tawdry glamour and a committed performance by Morell as Inspector Lake, a thinly veiled version of Folland. The typecasting continued in *The Golden Link* with Morell as Inspector Blake of Scotland Yard in a dreary thriller directed with workmanlike competence by quickie specialist Charles Saunders whose most memorable work would be *Woman Eater*.

Andre Morell and Greta Gynt star in the BBC production *It Is Midnight, Dr. Schweitzer*.

Television continued to offer Morell respite from low budget thrillers. Shortly before he took up duties for Burt Lancaster, he donned a bushy wig and bushier mustache for the title role in the BBC's production of *It Is Midnight, Dr. Schweitzer*, featuring 24 hours in the life of the renowned humanitarian whose work in Africa has become the stuff of legend. Costarring Douglas Wilmer, Reginald Tate and Greta Gynt, the play was broadcast live on February 21, 1953. Unfortunately no copy was ever made so it is impossible to assess Morell's performance but the play did have a more lasting significance on Morell's career; it was his first contact with producer-director Rudolph Cartier who would be responsible for two of his most memorable appearances. The theatre too continued to offer challenges; in 1954 he directed his own version of *The Sultan's Turret* at Wyndhams Theatre in the West End, with no more success than his previous venture. In May 1954 he did enjoy another critical and popular triumph with Ibsen's *The Master Builder* at the Nottingham Playhouse even though it was to be overshadowed in the summer by the release of *His Majesty O'Keefe*

The film had been shot in 1953 and actually opened in the U.S. in early 1954, offering Morell rare exposure to audiences who would not normally be caught dead watching imported, low budget B movies. It wasn't until August that British cinemagoers got their chance to see one of their favorite television actors propping up a major Hollywood movie for the first time. Morell played Alfred Tetens, employed as an agent for a German trading company and by all accounts the first white man on the remote Pacific island of Yap. That situation doesn't last long and Tetens is soon joined by American adventurer David O'Keefe, a fortune hunter cast adrift by his mutinous crew and washed up on the tropical paradise. O'Keefe realizes that there is money to be made from the island's natural resources but first he must overcome the hostility of the natives, slave traders and German expansionists. Tetens first befriends O'Keefe and then guides him through the delicate Fijian politics; the two men become business partners and together stand up to the villains. After seemingly endless fight scenes, O'Keefe triumphs, but realizes when Tetens is slain by the Germans that there is more to life than commerce. The story is based on fact (both the O'Keefe and Tetens characters did exist) but the filmmakers turned the story into a simple-minded action movie where their wit stretches no further than playing "Deutschland Über Alles" whenever the Germans come on screen.

Director Byron Haskin, who sandwiched the film between much more interesting assignments on *War of the Worlds* and *The Naked Jungle*, seemed happy enough to rely on Lancaster's grinning exuberance and the admittedly stunning scenery, gloriously captured in Technicolor. However good the film looked on the screen the actors had to work hard. Lancaster later recalled:

> It was so tough working in that humidity that one day I actually watched fungus grow on my clothes. Every day blazing sun or tropical rain beat down upon us and at night the only entertainment was movies flown in from the Warner exchange in Auckland.

Financed by Warner Bros. at $1.5 million and shot exclusively on location, this was by far the biggest movie Morell had been involved in and he took third billing, behind Lancaster and British starlet Joan Rice as O'Keefe's Fijian bride. Rice is a winsome heroine and Morell offers sterling support in a role that could easily have been a cipher but instead comes across with genuine warmth and affection. Tetens' death is a thoroughly moving moment in a film where emotional engagement is rather limited.

The critics had little appreciation for their efforts; the magazine *America* noted, "the finished product is definitely spotty, as though it had bitten off more than it could chew, and is more notable for bloodshed than it is for social significance." The *New Statesman* at least recognized that "the film has some superb photography and a number of good performances—particularly from André Morell...and from Joan Rice." Morrell met up again with Rice soon afterwards when they appeared in a charity gala at the Theatre Royal in Drury Lane, rubbing shoulders with fellow thespians Sybil Thorndike, John Gielgud, Hazel Court, Peter Ustinov, Margaret Lockwood and John Neville.

Association with big budget movies can only be good for the profile and Morell found himself elevated to that rare group of British character actors regularly supporting Hollywood epics. His next film was made by what was nominally a British company but one with its eyes very much on the U.S. market. Warwick Films had been founded in London in 1952 by two ex-patriot Americans both of whom would come to greater prominence in later years: Cubby Broccoli of James Bond fame and Irwin Allen who would go on to practically invent the disaster movie with *The Poseidon Adventure* and *The Towering Inferno*. Broccoli and

Morell visits Camelot in *The Black Knight*.

Allen came to England initially to take advantage of the lower production costs and tax subsidies but their stated intention was always to make international films with the scale and scope of their Hollywood counterparts. *The Red Beret* starring Alan Ladd was their first effort and established the formula for the next decade: all-male heroes, decorative heroines, action-adventure plots and exotic locations. *Hell Below Zero* also starring Ladd followed, then in 1954 the company announced their first foray into the world of costume adventure, *The Black Knight*. Despite a script by Bryan Forbes, *The Black Knight* illustrates lame-brained filmmaking at its worst with a hodgepodge of historical ideas loosely tied around the myth of Arthur and Camelot—without the benefit of a logical narrative or character development. Ladd plays a lowly blacksmith called John who, complete with Arkansas accent, sets out to avenge himself on some renegade Saracens, win the hand of his lady love and prove himself as a knight—all in the space of 85 minutes! Forbes managed to telescope together several centuries of history and includes such anachronisms as Vikings, Druids and Saracens battling the Knights of the Round Table for control of England. Allen and Broccoli regarded Alan Ladd's diminutive presence an essential part of the funding package but with an Oscar for *Shane* decorating his mantelpiece, the actor was reluctant to make yet another action movie. Euan Lloyd, later to become a distinguished producer in his own right, was then a young assistant to Cubby Broccoli, and he remembered:

> Alan had already made two films with us and he really didn't want to do another one, he just wanted to go home to his ranch, I think. It took all of Cubby's powers of persuasion to get him to stay but I really don't think he enjoyed the experience but he was a professional and got on with it. We had such a marvelous cast and the locations in Spain were gorgeous, certainly the rest of the cast and crew all had a lovely time.

Tay Garnett, who directed *The Postman Always Rings Twice* (1946), had the cream of British acting talent to choose from and made some interesting choices. Peter Cushing who, like Morell, was an established star on television, played Sir Palamides, a black-hearted villain who, together with his surly cohort King Mark of Cornwall (Patrick Troughton), corner the market in gnashing of teeth and scenery chewing. Lending support is theatre actor Harry Andrews as the Earl of Yenil and Anthony Bushell, for once out of army uniform, playing a curiously wooden King Arthur. Darkly exotic Patricia Medina who, despite making a career out of playing exotic slave girls, was actually born in far from glamorous Liverpool, provides the obligatory love interest as Yenil's daughter Linet. With so much colorful villainy on hand it is a little disappointing that Morell was brought into play the one dimensional Sir Ontzlake, a loyal subject of the King and something of a mentor figure to the blacksmith. Sir Ontzlake appears soon after John has been labeled a traitor and a coward—a simple misunderstanding naturally— and realizes that the best hope to save the kingdom is to help the younger man achieve his knightly ambitions. In the blinking of an eye John has mastered the art of hand-to-hand combat and the rules of chivalry, and emerges as the avenging Black Knight. From then on it is a straight head-to-head between John and Sir Palamides, whose plans also include the modest aim of the destruction of Christianity. Morell was allowed to wear armor, ride horses and sword fight—real boys adventure stuff but hardly professionally challenging. As Euan Lloyd remembered, Morell certainly didn't think he was there just to make up the numbers:

> Andre Morell was a wonderful actor, he brought depth and richness to everything he did, and he was also an extremely nice man. We were lucky to get him because he brought great presence and sincerity and he also had a tremendous voice, which is a marvelous asset for any actor. Everyone these days talks about Richard Burton's voice but you know Morell was just as good, it gave him tremendous dignity and gravitas.

Morell later gently mocked the fact that he had to stand in a trench to shoot his scenes with Ladd to compensate for the action hero's lack of stature, but if he was in any way concerned about the quality of the film he certainly didn't let it show. Lloyd spent a lot of time with Morell as the actor waited to be called to the set:

> André seemed to be really enjoying the location and the atmosphere; he was such a nice man and great company. He took everything very professionally and was very committed to his craft. I don't think he ever gave less than 100 percent.

Shot on location at the castilles at Manzanares el Real, Castilla la Nueva and the Palace of El Escorial as well as South Glamorgan in Wales, the film is great fun in a lively comic book sort of way, with Garnett keeping his sights aimed well and truly at pantomime level. The critics of course hated it but the public seemed to catch on to the tongue in cheek humor and the film returned good box office. The story was remade in 1963 as *Siege of the Saxons* starring Janette Scott and Ronald Lewis and featuring footage from the original.

The critics posting dismissive reviews of *The Black Knight* passed over Morell's contribution he was soon to appear in a production which would not only prove his versatility but achieve a level of notoriety that exists to this day. By 1954 Rudolph Cartier had established himself as one of the most daring and inventive producers at the BBC and, while his productions had enjoyed critical and popular success, the Austrian born producer-director didn't really capture the public's imagination until he mounted his ambitious production *The Quatermass Experiment*.

Until then drama on British television showed the same lack of imagination and innovation that had existed before the war; entertainment was considered secondary to making worthy productions. Technically the productions had achieved some success, but artistically they still consisted of studio bound, talky adaptations under the supervision of a producer who would present the action rather than direct the actors. Cartier's stated intention was to shake the complacency out of the BBC drama department and spice up the staid formulas with new elements — innovation and excitement. Cartier struck the first blow with the *Quatermass* series, written by Nigel Kneale and starring Reginald Tate in the title role. The terrifying account of Britain's first space mission and a disastrous encounter with an alien organism electrified audiences as never before; this was the defining moment in the development of television in Britain. Not only were cinemas and pubs running near empty during the broadcasts, the police reported a massive decline in crime statistics! The small screen was seen for the first time as the preeminent force in popular entertainment. The Kneale-Cartier team returned to the classics for its next production, a conventional adaptation of *Wuthering Heights* with an unlikely Richard Todd as Heathcliffe and Yvonne Mitchell as Cathy. Cartier was then handed a project

Morell in the BBC's version of *1984*

that the BBC had been considering for sometime without ever getting close to production, George Orwell's *1984*.

Orwell's book had sat on the bookshelves for six years without causing much of a stir; his nightmarish version of a totalitarian Britain under the heel of the omnipresent "Big Brother" triggered intellectual debate without attracting anything remotely resembling controversy. Whilst recognizing the value, no one at the BBC could see how the book could be successfully translated into entertaining television until the project fell into Cartier's lap. The producer immediately saw the potential in Orwell's world where freedom to think—let alone act—was punishable by torture or death. An early draft by Hugh Falkus was rejected and Cartier floated the idea to Nigel Kneale, offering the writer a free hand to push the boundaries of acceptable taste as far as he was prepared to go. With Kneale working on the script the BBC executives demonstrated their faith in Cartier by handing him their biggest budget to date for a single play—some $11,000—and a contract to bring the book to life for two live transmissions. The hero in Orwell's story is Winston Smith, a low level clerk in the Ministry of Truth who commits the ultimate crime in the Britain of the future, falling in love. Branded a traitor to the ideals of Big Brother, Smith is taken into Room 101, deep in the heart of the Ministry of Love where he is tortured into signing a confession by Inner Party Official O'Brien before being released a broken man. *The Black Knight*'s leading heavy, Peter Cushing, took the role of Smith, with Yvonne Mitchell playing his lover Julia. The cast also included Donald Pleasance as Smith's obsequious neighbor Syme, as well as nearly 60 other actors spread across 22 sets and supported by a small orchestra. André Morell was cast against type as the play's main villain, O'Brien, the Inner Party's chief interrogator and of course custodian of the terrors in Room 101. Although the part offered Morell less screen time than Cushing, the actor's presence dominates the last third of the play—a white-haired and refined torturer with that marvelously cultivated voice urging, teasing and ultimately threatening an increasingly desperate Winston to betray the woman he loves. Morell's rich and soothing tones are an effective counterpoint to the tortures to come. "By itself pain is not always enough," he purrs. "What happens in Room 101 is the worst thing in the world."

The tension reached breaking point when O'Brien unleashed Smith's particular nightmare, rats, onto his captive's face. Producing an ominous looking mask O'Brien went on to explain the mechanics of Winston's fate:

> The mask...fits over the head, leaving no exit. When the plastic door is raised up, the rats will shoot out like bullets. It was a common punishment in Imperial China...

Peter Cushing's autobiography records that the animals were originally plucked from the London sewers specifically for the play but released when Cartier found them more inclined to semi-slumber under the hot studio lights. An unnamed BBC technician had the bright idea of getting some tame white rats from the pet shop, dying them a dirty brown and then, in the era of political incorrectness, depriving them of food until after the broadcast. The effect was truly startling, with the starved rats shrieking wildly at the morsels dangled in their cage off screen; it was one of the most horrific images seen on British television. Cushing's sensitive and credible playing of Smith and Morell's truly chilling turn as O'Brien made compulsive viewing, never more so when Morell in his best paternal pose told Smith:

> My poor friend, you are almost well. Look at my eyes. It is not enough to obey Big Brother. You now know what is needed. Who it is you must love?

The literate script and the taut direction from Rudolph Cartier transformed Orwell's heavy-handed satire into a powerful and chilling vision and the program was unleashed on an unsuspecting public on December 12. Broadcast live with some filmed inserts, *1984* produced such extreme reactions that the scheduled repeat performance the following Thursday was under threat of cancellation. The headlines were staggering: "TORTURES ON TV HORRIFY WHOLE NATION" ran one paper, with another claiming, "TORTURES ON TV START

BIGGEST PROTEST STORM" before going on to add that "it brought the biggest flood of protests the BBC has ever known." Another journalist found that "the play reeks of decadence and corruption." A spokesman for the BBC confirmed that they had received "hundreds" of calls from angry viewers and the archives reveal that one viewer alleged, "the persons responsible for putting on the play are Sadists and readers of Horror Comics." The country's rulers jumped on the bandwagon and five Conservative Members of Parliament tabled a motion in the House of Commons, accusing the BBC of "pandering to sexual and sadistic tastes." Amidst all the uproar *The Times* television critic was one of the few who noticed the performances and was unconditionally impressed, particularly with Morell who he thought "had just the right tone of controlled fanaticism." The actor himself was nonplussed by all the attention; a decade later on the BBC chat show *Late Night Line Up* he said:

> I was completely astounded at the violence of the outcry against it...in spite of all this outcry they (the BBC) believed in what they had done and had the guts to repeat it.

Executives at the BBC had to think long and hard about the second broadcast but the fuss ensured that the audience was even bigger than before. Cartier, in a shrewd publicity stunt, revealed to the press than he had taken the precaution of laying on extra security after threats were made to disrupt the performance. By all accounts the second broadcast was inferior to this predecessor and several members of the cast claim that it lacked the spontaneity. There may be some truth to this but it is this version that the BBC recorded for posterity and when it was aired again in 1994 to mark Rudolph Cartier's passing it revealed an undiminished power to shock.

By the middle of the 1950s film production was still coming in fits and starts but the industry was recovering, though it would never again scale the heights of the immediate postwar years in either quality or quantity. In the meantime actors and technicians could always find work on television; indeed many of the major studios now turned their soundstages over to the growing demand from the small screen. Morell never signed a long-term contract with any of the British studios nor the London based subsidiaries of American majors, and he never regarded himself as anything more than a jobbing film actor with assignments to be fitted in between theatre arrangements. With television now expanding into regular series and one-off plays, Morell adopted pretty much the same approach to the small screen. Over the next few years he happily accepted guest roles in some of the more popular shows, including *The Buccaneers*, a swashbuckling adventure show starring Robert Shaw.

Like their film counterparts, American television companies were taking advantage of the low production costs and ready access to talent in Britain.

Morell picked up higher profile work on *The Rheingold Theatre,* also known as *Douglas Fairbanks, Jr. Presents,* which was shot at Bray with Terence Fisher directing many of the episodes. The show also utilized the talents of former Gainsborough man Bernard Knowles as well as John Gilling, Arthur Grabtree and Francis Searle. Morell was featured in the episode *The Assassin*, which also starred Brian Wilde and was directed by Don Chaffey. NBC's contribution was the *Lilli Palmer Theatre,* or as it was more properly known *Lilli Palmer presents The Quality Theatre*, with the Swedish star acting as hostess for some 33 half hour episodes all shot in the UK. A mere footnote in television history, this particular show has considerable curiosity value for aficionados of the horror genre as a proving ground for many now familiar names: Melissa Stribling, Christopher Lee, Clifford Evans, Michael Gough, Michael Ripper, William Franklinand and Andree Melly amongst them, as well as established talents like Flora Robson, Ernest Thesiger and Ursula Howells. More recognized theatre names also appeared, including the blacklisted exile Sam Wanamaker and George Coulouris who starred in an episode called "Flight One-Zero One." The production company behind the series was Towers of London, aka the infamous Harry Allan Towers who also line produced many of the episodes. Towers would become better known over the next two decades for his association with Jess Franco and a slew of quickie horror movies. Morell appeared in two episodes for Towers: "Atlantic Night," a recreation of the Titanic saga where he manned the ship's bridge as Captain Arthur Welch, and in the spy story "The Immigrant" with Laurence Payne and Christopher Lee.

This increased exposure on the small screen kept Morell's name in front of casting directors and his ability to play cultured villainy led directly to his first job for Val Guest, a B movie called *They Can't Hang Me*. Written by noted journalist Leonard Mosley, *They Can't Hang Me* tried to mine a similar vein as the earlier *Seven Days to Noon* and purported to be "a thrill-a-minute story behind today's atomic headlines!" Despite all the hype it was far less interesting than it might sound.

Morell played a top civil servant called Pitt who, convicted of murdering a prostitute and sentenced to hang, pronounces the film's title from the dock. It would be more grammatically correct if Pitt had declared, "They won't hang me," as it seems he has access to information concerning the security of the country—in particular a spy in the nation's top nuclear research station. The film's ace detective (Anthony Culver) is very much in the Folland mold, this time trying to unravel the mystery before Pitt's appointment with the gallows; Terence Morgan represents the security services and lends more physical support. Amongst those watching anxiously are Yolande Dollan (Mrs. Guest in real life) and Ursula Howells as Pitt's wife. Guest, one of the most interesting and prolific of Britain's journeyman directors, crafts a minor film that lacks its predecessor's gritty tension; the promise of the opening scenes is never fulfilled

Inspector Brown (Terence Morgna) visits Pitt (Morell) one final time in *They Can't Hang Me*.

and it quickly settles into the B movie bracket. Morell conveys the arrogance of a man who thinks he is too important to hang and delivers a suitably unsympathetic performance, but he is given too little to work with and fails to turn Pitt into a really interesting character. Culver and Morgan are both capable actors but neither have the screen presence to carry the film.

Morell closed 1954 by making his first brush with the horror genre in *Three Cases of Murder*, again for Alexander Paal. This was yet another compendium film, this time linked by a vaguely supernatural theme. Morell appears in the best segment, "Lord Mountdrago," written by Ian Dalrymple and based on a short story by W. Somerset Maugham. Orson Welles, wallowing in his self-imposed exile from Hollywood and desperate for cash, took the title role in a play which also features Alan Badel and Elizabeth Sellars. Badel is the one consistent factor throughout the film, appearing as different characters in all three segments. The story is simple enough: The arrogant and overblown politician Mountdrago (Welles of course) uses all his bluster to demolish the arguments of a younger rival, Owen, during a parliamentary debate. Owen (Badel) is no mere political animal and after confronting his tormentor vows revenge by "crushing your proud spirit." From then Mountdrago starts to suffer a series of dreams where he is subjected to ridicule by his peers: in one he is at a din-

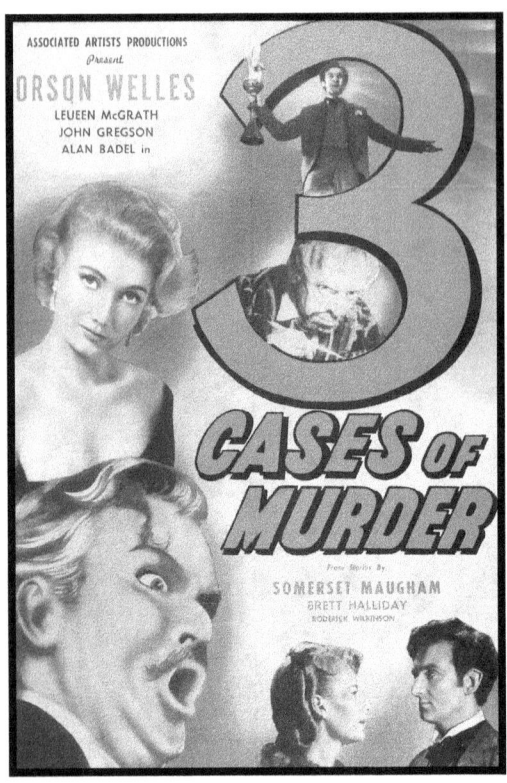

ner party without his trousers; in another he bursts into song in the middle of a parliamentary debate. During the day Owen adds to his discomfort with his knowing smirks and veiled remarks until, in a fit of desperation, Mountdrago decides the solution to his problem lies in direct action and he resolves to kill Owen. Morell's role benefits from his natural gravitas to add the voice of reason as the psychiatrist who suggests the whole thing is a figment of the beleaguered Mountdrago's imagination. "We are all not just one self but many," he tells his patient, "and one of your selves in you has taken on Owen's form in your mind to punish you."

Despite top billing, Welles isn't the star—the Hollywood legend was clearly inserted for his marquee value; nevertheless he gives a commanding performance in a role he could probably have played in his sleep. Morell in an even smaller role looks relaxed and comfortable playing opposite another iconic figure but again doesn't have too much to tax his abilities. Although they don't share a scene, the film also features the venerable Arthur Wontner who had starred in Morell's very first film *13 Men and a Gun* in 1938. The 80-year-old Wontner appeared briefly as the Leader of the House of Commons in what would prove his last film appearance. Overshadowed by Ealing's *Dead of Night,* Paal's suspenseful little film deserves more attention than it gets but, as with most of compendium movies, *Three Cases of Murder* is a mixed bag: two interesting stories and one extremely labored comic relief. Predictably rumors abound that Welles himself directed his last sequence but in fact the reins were tightly held by George More O'Ferrall, the distinguished English director who already had a long and successful career in television. Beautifully photographed on Shepperton sets by distinguished cinematographer Georges Périnal, the film attracted some complimentary reviews when it opened in New York in March 1955 but it was considered a little too sedate to attract a wide release.

Despite his theatre commitments, Morell remained in demand in films and, unlike many of his contemporaries, continued working in A movies. Anthony

Darnborough offered Morell the chance of a comedy in 1956 with *The Baby and the Battleship*, one of a slew of British movies that sprang up in the 1950s gently mocking the armed forces. In this case the title probably tells you everything you need to know about the plot: Able Seaman "Knocker" White finds himself holding the baby after a shore visit in an Italian port and he and his  best friend "Puncher" Roberts conspire to keep the infant hidden away below decks on HMS *Gillingham*. Before long the entire crew has adopted the baby and conspires through a series of comic episodes to keep the infant hidden from the officers. Richard Attenborough and John Mills, obligatory for this type of film, play Knocker and Puncher respectively with all the unbridled enthusiasm British casting schools insist is appropriate for broad farce. Rather more serious work awaited Morell in *The Man Who Never Was,* directed with some distinction by Ronald Neame and starring Clifton Webb. In this true story of a plot by British Intelligence to dupe their German counterparts into believing the invasion of Europe is eminent, Morell passes through as a government official who adds suitably solemn words of caution.

Morell was back in boys' adventure country with another war movie, *The Black Tent*, turned out by Rank to their tired old formula. The producers suggested they were making a frothy mix of passion and adventure set against the shearing desert heat but delivered instead yet another cliché-ridden action story, this time featuring a wounded British soldier stranded behind enemy lines when his unit retreats without him. The love interest appears soon after he receives succor from some sympathetic Bedouins and, in particular, the beautiful daughter of a local sheikh. Earning the respect of his hosts, he persuades the sheikh they can best help their own cause by waging war on the Germans. Second-string matinee idol Anthony Steele heads a cast that includes Donald Sinden and Donald Pleasence, while Morell plays the desert warrior Salem ben Yussef convincingly enough to be singled out for positive notices by critics who struggled to find anything worthwhile to say about the film. The Libyan deserts look absolutely stunning but the movie is indistinguishable from a host of similar films churned out by Rank.

Morell stayed with the North African theme when he was engaged by Warwick Films for the latest installment of their campaign to create a new

Morell in *The Black Tent*

Hollywood in England or (more accurately in this case, Morocco). Terence Young's *Zarak* is another one of those closing days of Empire movies so beloved by British filmmakers in the 1950s when the Empire itself was actually dwindling away. Stomping around like the proverbial fish out of water in the title role is Hollywood beefcake actor Victor Mature, whose acting consists of barking orders and scowling out from under his turban. Zarak Khan's blood feud with his despot father Haji Khan is threatening to explode across the North West Frontier while the British, playing both ends against the middle, attempt to engineer a peace in their own interests. When Zarak falls for one of his father's favorite wives, the beauteous Salma, it looks pretty much like the whole frontier might get sucked into their domestic dispute. Mature was never an actor who took himself or his image too seriously and, while his smirking self-depreciation hardly lends credibility, he is considerably more entertaining that the wooden turns from Patrick McGoohan and Michael Wilding as they scour the hills without much enthusiasm for the elusive Zarak. The pneumatic Anita Ekberg plays Salma, who's wildly erotic dancing provides one third of the promised "Pillage, Plunder, Passion." Morell, on the other hand, missed out on all three and contributes only in a minor supporting role amongst the stiff upper lip Brits.

The film achieved something of a cult following as the only movie where the title character is flogged to death but apart from camp value it is worth a mention for two reasons. Firstly, some of the action sequences were cannibalized by distributor Columbia to spice up Hammer's *The Brigand of Kandahar* directed by John Gilling. Secondly, *Zarak* served as something of a proving ground for many of the personnel whom Broccoli would use in his James Bond series, including director Young, who would helm *Dr. No*, a film which also features the skills of *Zarak's* director of photography, Ted Moore, writer Richard Maibaum and actress Eunice Gayson. Audiences who like a bit of gratuitous violence, larger than life entertainment and scant intellectual challenges will find much to enjoy in the film.

Mature was slightly less out of place but probably no more credible in his next outing for Warwick, *Pickup Alley* aka *Interpol*, directed with gusto by John Gilling. The rugged star plays drug enforcer Charles Sturgis on the trail of an international smuggler (Trevor Howard) and his reluctant accomplice Gina (Anita Ekberg in far less exotic but more contemporary costumes). Shot on location throughout Europe as well as New York, Howard just needs a pet cat to be right at home as a Bond-style villain but Mature lacks the charisma to make his secret agent rise above the

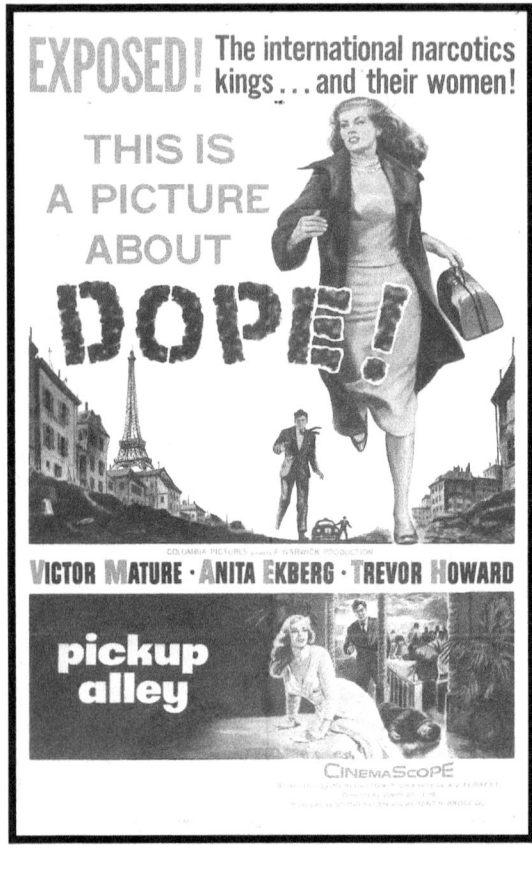

routine. Morell was reduced to yet another cameo appearance and, while the whole thing is a more down to earth story than the Warwick costume epics, it's also a lot less fun.

In the years following *Madeline,* Morell maintained a close friendship with David Lean. After the director's marriage to Ann Todd fell apart, Morell extended the freedom of his spare bedroom to Lean and later acted as best man for his fourth marriage, to Leila Matkar in Paris. In between, Morell and Lean, together with close friends Michael Gough and Peter Bull, made an unlikely quartet of men about town, enjoying their freedom in a society that was finally shaking off the constraints of a wartime economy. The two men would remain great friends and, except for a few years at the end of the 1960s, maintain a lengthy correspondence wherever they were in the world.

Morell popped up in an unbilled cameo in Lean's *Summertime* (1955) and then signed on for a brief but significant role in what would prove to be one of cinema's more enduring classics, *The Bridge on the River Kwai* (1957). The inspiration came from Pierre Boulle's book of the same title, with its fictionalized clash of personalities and cultures against the backdrop of the Pacific war. The setting is a prisoner-of-war camp in Burma where the British, under the command of Colonel Nicholson, are put to work by their captors building a bridge for the Imperial Japanese Army's trains. Boulle's focus is on the clash between the British and Japanese and his story never leaves the confines of their jungle prison. To persuade Columbia to invest nearly $3 million in the production, Lean and producer Sam Spiegel had to expand the story. A number of crucial changes were made, the most significant of which was the introduction of Commander Shears, a U.S. Naval officer. Shears begins as an inmate in the camp but after a successful escape is persuaded by British Special Forces to return as a guide for a small team of saboteurs.

The new subplot allowed Lean to hang a whole series of enhancements on his narrative, including a love interest for Shears, which provides the film's only significant female character as well as lightening the overall tone for a least a few scenes. The new subplot allows for the creation of the film's most spectacular scene, the climatic destruction of the bridge, an incident absent from the book. This commando mission also allowed the introduction of Colonel Green, played by Morell, the affable commander of "Force 316," specialists in "sabotage, demolition, that line of country". The team is led in the field by Morell's former real-life comrade-in-arms, Jack Hawkins, while the Colonel himself adopts a benign but fatherly supervision from the team's exotic training camp. Morell's scenes, which come in the middle of the movie, were actually shot towards the end of filming and by staying well away from the prison camp location, the actor was spared the hardships that had dogged most of the production. Indeed by the time Lean came to shoot the last of the prison camp scenes his relationship with his English actors, including star Alec Guinness and James Donald, had deteriorated to such an extent that the director was barely on speaking terms with his cast. After nearly seven months in the jungle, the director's outburst after calling "cut" on the last of the prison camp scenes indicated his frustration:

> Now you can all fuck off and go home, you English actors. Thank God that I'm starting work tomorrow with an American actor. It'll be a pleasure to say goodbye to you guys.

The American in question, and the actor with whom Morell would share his scenes, was William Holden, one of the biggest stars in the world who was paid a staggering $300,000 up front plus 10 percent of the profits to lend his name to the film. Holden's stake in *Kwai* would set him up for life. Morell certainly seems to be enjoying his on-screen banter with Holden and Jack Hawkins, helped no doubt by the beauty of the location, a coastal idyll far removed from the rigors of the jungle. This was the setting for Force 316's headquarters, the sort of commando operation where tea is sipped on the veranda while men are trained to kill in the gardens. Over the space of a few minutes Morell does enough to bring Green to life. Having coerced Shears into joining the mission, described as a "little hike in the jungle," Green warmly shakes him by the hand, saying, "Good show. Jolly good show." After establishing that there is a relaxation on the military protocol of saluting etc., Green criticizes Shears for being precisely four minutes late and then indicates the discussion is moving on by hitting a little bell on his desk. Relaxed and good natured, Morell takes the opportunity to display his now familiar screen traits, fiddling with props almost incessantly and a wry sense of humor. Holding a knife out at new recruit Joyce, Green asks, almost causally, "Could you kill in cold blood?" Later with the same *sang froid*, Morell hands Holden the new "L" pill: "L for lethal," he explains, "painless, instantaneous." Shears learns he is to jump from an airplane without practicing, quipping, "With or without parachute?" Morell's laughter is infectious. In between these scenes Holden manages a brief sojourn at the beach cozying up to British actress Anne Sears (sister of Heather) in an unflattering blonde rinse. Many British reviewers dismissed these scenes as Hollywood schmaltz and went on to condemn the closing action scenes as the final proof that Lean had sold out and made a mainstream movie. There may or may not be some truth in the charge but the whole point of Lean's movie, the stupidity and futility of war, is crystallized into that one single task, the building of a bridge by British prisoners for their Japanese captors. The destruction of this symbol and more significantly the way it is destroyed is the ultimate irony and the triumph of the film remains the portrayal of the opposing colonels, Saito and Nicholson, as no better than each other. Whatever the rights and wrongs of the conflict, the war has become for them a battle of personalities, justified in their minds by the wider issues. It is an intelligent, complex movie, powerfully acted by the principals and supporting cast, and while his role is relatively minor Morell could be more than satisfied with his contribution.

With two completed films awaiting release and a third, *The Bridge on the River Kwai*, in post-production, Morell took the unsurprising decision to spend the summer of 1957 back on the stage. The play he chose was completely unexpected, however, and says a lot about the actor's willingness to tackle the riskiest of subjects. The theatre was the New Arts Theatre in the center of London and the director was an old friend of Morell's, Yvonne Mitchell, who had played the doomed Julia so convincingly in *1984*. The actual storyline of *Less Than Kind* is a little harder to summarize. The complex story centers on the incestuous relationship between a half-Italian aristocrat and his sister, and their deranged mother and her homosexual lover; this potboiler is further complicated by the introduction of an unacknowledged bastard son reduced to acting as a servant to his deviant parents. The play also featured Diane Cliento and Jeremy Burham, the latter better known as a writer who would go on to script *Horror of Frankenstein* (1970). It was heady stuff and a little too much for staid London critics who couldn't resist punning the title in some damning reviews; amongst those jumping on the bandwagon was future Hammer scripter Wolf Mankowitz, who described it as "the worst play ever." *Less Than Kind* opened in June and closed soon afterwards.

Morell could afford to shrug off the disappointment, as he was about to start work on a film that would have a defining influence on his career. The long production saga surrounding *The Bridge on the River Kwai* had rumbled on for over a year and the film was finally scheduled to premiere in London in the early fall. The publicity around Lean's film had reopened some old wounds but in truth the controversy over the Japanese treatment of Allied prisoners was still headline news in Britain and the box-office potential wasn't wasted on James Carreras at Hammer. The company was already sitting pretty in the U.S. Top Ten Box-Office Earners with their first foray into the world of Gothic horror, *The Curse of Frankenstein*. A follow-up, *Horror of Dracula*, was still on the drawing board and in the meantime Hammer's bread and butter remained comedies, thrillers and war movies. James Carreras decided the free publicity presented an opportunity too good to miss and duly announced filming would commence on *The Camp on Blood Island*. Shortly before the film opened, Michael Carreras, the film's executive producer, explained how the project came about:

One morning, a year ago, a man walked into the Wardour Street offices of Hammer Films. He handed me an envelope, explaining its contents consisted of a report of an episode which occurred at a Jap POW camp in Malaya at the end of the war. He said that he had been a prisoner there, and produced documentary proof of this. He felt that the episode he had reported might provide the story of the film. Before he left, the man made one condition: if his story was accepted for filming he must insist, for personal reasons, on remaining anonymous.

It's a great yarn and the press lapped it up—unfortunately Carreras made the whole thing up! The story came from author Jon Manchip White, a veteran of the Burma campaign, whose previous novel had been the basis of *Mask of Dust*. Over lunch with the producer Anthony Nelson Keys, White shared his intention to write a book based on his wartime experiences. The two men chatted about scenarios suitable for filming and by the time they had finished their desserts, they had the core of what would become *The Camp on Blood Island*. White then turned this unlikely dinner conversation into a hard-hitting script, based less on fact and more on shared perceptions of the conflict in the Far East. The story features Allied prisoners as well as the interned civilians, including women and children, who fall under into the brutal custody of Colonel Yamamitsu in two work camps toward the very end of WWII. The senior British officer, Lambert (Morell), and his radio operator, a Dutch planter called Van Elst, are the only ones who know that the Japanese have surrendered and the war is over; they also know that if Yamamitsu finds out his retribution will be terrible. As the Allied forces draw nearer the camps, the prisoners have to endure torture and beatings while arming themselves for the inevitable slaughter.

As always Hammer had one eye on censorship but if the Secretary of the Board of British Film Censors had any reservations about turning such a sensitive subject into a commercial venture, Carreras could only point to David Lean and his crew battling the mosquitoes and heat in the Ceylonese jungle with not dissimilar material. This being Hammer, the Malaysian jungle was recreated at Bray with the weak English sun (and frequent showers) standing in for the blistering tropical heat. Val Guest, who had scored with the company's recent versions of the *Quatermass* television shows, was offered the directing chores for what was clearly going to be a controversial film. Any doubts Guest may have had were quickly dispelled and he later told reporters:

> When I read the draft script of *The Camp on Blood Island* it hit me like a sledgehammer! I knew that this was one I had to make. I'll tell you why. First the story it told was based in fact. Secondly up to that time no one had made a Japanese POW

Morell (right) as Lambert, along with Van Elst (Carl Mohner), knows the war is over in *The Camp on Blood Island.*

picture that didn't pull punches. Thirdly producer Anthony Hinds and executive producer Michael Carreras insisted that this was to be one film which was to be handled without kidgloves.

The story may be fictional but many of the incidents happened: The floggings, executions, starvations and deprivations were all documented fact and certainly there is enough in the script to justify the films on-screen tribute:

> This film is dedicated to the thousands of men and women who, during the last war, suffered unspeakable atrocities in the Far East. This is not just a story; it is based on the brutal truth.

Austrian actor Carl Mohner was cast in role of Van Elst and, although he had assembled a raft of European credits, his best known English language film was for fellow countryman Rudolph Cartier in the latter's big screen debut, *Storm over Jamaica*. American actor Phil Brown, who later appeared in *Star Wars,* plays Bellamy an American soldier, while English actress Barbara Shelley, playing Kate, a prisoner in the woman's camp, was given the unusual opportunity to dispense with makeup and a hairbrush. The sadistic Yamamsitsu is played by British theatre actor Ronald Radd, who would later enjoy a distinguished

CARL MOHNER · ANDRE MORELL · EDWARD UNDERDOWN · WALTER FITZGERALD
in
'THE CAMP ON BLOOD ISLAND' x
also starring PHIL BROWN · BARBARA SHELLEY · MICHAEL GOODLIFFE
A HAMMER FILM PRODUCTION IN MEGASCOPE

career on both Broadway and the West End. Crucial to the success of the picture was the casting of Lambert; this was no mere stiff-upper lip British officer and initially at least Guest was not convinced that Morell was right for the role. With the permission of David Lean, Morell arranged a special screening of his scenes from *The Bridge on the River Kwai* and impressed Guest enough to cast him. Given his own military experiences, one would have forgiven the actor for staying well away from the part; although he had never been a prisoner of war, Morell was all too familiar with the suffering of the Allied troops and civilians in the Far East. Morell gives a memorable rendition of a decent man pushed to the limits of intolerance and suffering and yet determined to maintain his dignity and self respect. It is a powerful film all the more so because of Guest's unfussy and uncompromising direction. Forty years after its release, Guest told the authors of *Hammer Films: An Exhaustive Filmography*:

> There is nothing in my film that didn't really happen— and a lot of worse things did happen that we didn't show. ...The Government wanted to get things back to normal economically—then here comes Hammer with this POW picture! We had a great cast—especially Andre Morell—and I stand by the picture.

In the same tome Len Harris, who was a camera operator, says, "I particularly enjoyed working with André Morell. Hammer was fortunate to have fine actors—and fine gentlemen—like André."

Until the opening of the picture James Carreras was anxious to tread the fine line between good taste and exploitation; the press releases went to great lengths to stress the producer's commitment to reality, insisting that the script had been "authenticated by the very few who survived the massacre." To prove the point, two-dozen former prisoners of war attended the April 18, 1958 premiere. Carreras, with just the tiniest of glints in his eye, confirmed, "This is an expose of what really did happen to British soldiers in Jap prison camps." By the time the film was ready for national release the old Hammer formula was back with a vengeance and an explicit blood-red banner boasted, "JAP WAR CRIMES EXPOSED!" The *Cinema Today* hailed the film as "a prestige picture, one that the trade, critics and public will remember." But not everyone agreed; the chairman of the Motion Picture Production Association of Japan, concerned at the poor light being cast on his country, requested that the film be banned from release in the U.S. The mainstream press reviews read like the very best (and worst) of Hammer's horror movies: "an orgy of atrocities" according to the *Daily Herald*, while *The Observer* branded the film "an abomination." The *Daily Herald* summed it up with "stomach churning." Needless to say it was a huge box-office success and featured prominently in the British Box Office Charts for 1958.

Despite being second billed to Mohner, *The Camp of Blood Island* was a tour de force for Morell, who is haunted but resolute in the face of overwhelming atrocities. The quality of the performance was widely recognized by the critics: "André Morell gives a dauntless performance," said *The Sunday Times*, while the *Financial Times* commented, "despite the efforts of André Morell, the film leaves a distinctly nasty taste in the mouth."

The Camp on Blood Island is rarely revived now, possibly due to the influence of politically correct distributors on a film, which casts mainly Western actors in the principal Japanese roles. A curious decision justified at the time by the lack of Asian actors available in Britain but it led to the bizarre sight of Michael Ripper playing a Japanese soldier. No such sensitivities applied in 1958 and the film became one of Hammer's biggest hits—outside of their horror films—and a paperback tie-in went on to enjoy a life of its own and stayed in print for nearly 30 years.

The success of his film projects put Morell in that most desirable position of struggling to find time for all his commitments. Over the next few years his appearances on stage would take second place to the much more lucrative work available in films and increasingly on television. By the end of the year he had gone from respected stage actor to one of the most familiar faces in British entertainment; predictably it was through television that he achieved his most high profile success and equally predictably it was under the guiding influence of Rudolph Cartier.

After the fuss over *1984* died down, the Cartier-Kneale partnership went into preparation on the second of their *Quatermass* series—unimaginatively titled *Quatermass II*. Reginald Tate, who created the role originally, had been scheduled to reappear in the second series but died of a heart attack shortly before pre-production began. Morell was approached but was committed to a play, so the television actor John Robinson was cast. *Quatermass II* is better directed and constructed than its predecessor, with Kneale providing a much tighter and genuinely shocking script. Once again Quatermass found himself confronting an alien intelligence preparing for a full-scale invasion of Earth, this time operating within the upper echelons of the Establishment. Despite the ratings success, Robinson proved a disappointment as Quatermass and never looked comfortable in the title role, so when the BBC commissioned a third installment, Cartier decided to drop the actor's option. In the meantime Hammer had enjoyed a box-office hit with a truncated film version of the first series directed by Val Guest and starring American Brian Donlevy as an aggressive version of Kneale's studious scientist. A second film also starring Donlevy would follow but neither Cartier nor Kneale were impressed with the big screen incarnation of their leading character and as pre-production started in earnest the role was offered to André Morell.

Nigel Kneale's contract with the BBC had expired and he was happily working as a freelance writer but returned to the Corporation to craft what would be the most ambitious film of the trilogy. Kneale's specialty, demonstrated to chilling effect in the both of the early series, had been the juxtaposition of something very contemporary and recognizable with a threat so outlandish as to be inconceivable—a gigantic alien growth swamping Westminster Abbey for example. *Quatermass and the Pit* would continue this theme to even more alarming ends. Using a backdrop of race riots and social unrest in Britain's inner cities, Kneale's story opens on a building site in the centre of London where workmen unearth the skull of what appears to be an apeman. Before long the find has escalated from an archaeological curiosity to an unexploded bomb and on to an alien invasion.

The first scientist on the scene is Dr. Mathew Roney, a Canadian paleontologist played by Cec Linder who later found fame as Felix Leiter in *Goldfinger*. When Roney is unable to convince the bomb disposal unit under Captain Potter to take the archeological value seriously, he enlists the help of old friend Bernard Quatermass of the Rocket Group. Quatermass, more out of a sense of mischief than social conscience, invites his colleague Colonel Breen to investigate, only to have his own curiosity get the better of him as he delves deeper and deeper into the mystery. Anthony Bushell, who had appeared in *The Black Knight* and *The Black Tent*, plays the martinet Breen. Morell had suggested Michael Gough for Captain Potter before the role was handed to John Stratton. Also amongst the supporting cast is Michael Ripper playing a chirpy British squaddie.

Anyone only familiar with the Hammer films and Brian Donlevy's bombastic Quatermass will find Morell's version a pleasant surprise. He approaches the role with quiet authority and humor and, while not afraid of action, Morell's Quatermass prefers to use intellectual argument and charm to win people over. There is no room for Donlevy's bullying; and for Morell, not knowing the answer is not seen as a sign of weakness—providing one does not make idiotic guesses. This charismatic and fiercely

intelligent Quatermass does not suffer fools gladly but remains a natural leader. This inclination to take charge brings him into direct confrontation with Breen, his appointed superior in the Rocket Group. Quatermass controls his temper with some difficulty throughout the series but the only time he actually gets angry is when he is told that his Group has been taken over by the Ministry of War. Breen then declares, much to Quatermass' chagrin, that the Group will make military bases on the moon "a certainty in the next five years." Breen ominously describes the plan as "a dead man's deterrent." Far more mentally nimble than Breen, Morell enjoys the opportunity to play games and baits the soldier constantly; the humorless Breen remains stoically immune to his wit.

The series begins with Quatermass in a supporting role, on the sidelines, hands thrust deep in his pockets and merely observing the action. By episode two Quatermass has turned investigator; he is the first to show an interest in the haunted house, prowling around in the dark and later interviewing surviving witnesses. It is the open-minded Quatermass who pieces together the occult history of Hobb's Lane. Interestingly Kneale presents Quatermass as all too fallible and at one point he puts himself and others at risk by drilling into the

Morell as Quatermass

hatch of the space ship. But it is Quatermass who constructs the theory that warlike Martians colonized the Earth five million years earlier and modern man is the result of their genetic engineering. Morell's assured delivery manages to make the most crackpot theories sound plausible, though when challenged he shrugs, "I said it was a guess." The man from the Ministry of War is far from convinced: "Do you know what you're implying?" he rants, "That we owe our human condition to the intervention of insects!" In the time-honored tradition of small-minded bureaucrats, the Minister opts for the patently untrue but far more mundane theory that the "space ship" and its contents were a German experimental V-weapon flown into war-torn London to cause widespread panic. The Minister likes the commonsense of that; "it feels right" he enthuses, adding that it is just the sort of thing the "Hun" would do. Quatermass can only frown at the stupidity of his political masters. The inherent self destruction in human nature takes hold as law and order deteriorates and the true nature of the alien invasion is revealed. It isn't the military but the scientists who save the day and the series signs off with some heavy handed if well-intentioned moralizing that "every war crisis, witch hunt, race riot, purge is a reminder and a warning. We are the Martians. If we cannot control the inheritance within us this will be their second dead planet."

The BBC once again demonstrated its faith in Cartier and *Quatermass and the Pit* was seen very much as *the* prestige production of the season. It was promoted heavily in their listings magazines and in the national press long before screenings. Even as Cartier moved into production during September at the BBC studios in Ealing (former home to Ealing Films), anticipation was running high amongst public and critics. To add to the excitement, Hammer's second big screen outing *Enemy from Space* (*Quatermass II* in the UK) had opened and proved every bit as popular as its predecessor. The BBC allocated a budget of $62,000, with Morell earning the princely sum of $3,927 for six episodes including rehearsals and repeat broadcasts. The approach would be the same as before: a mixture of studio work to be broadcast live from the Riverside Studios in Hammersmith with recorded inserts of location and action sequences shot on 35mm film. The first episode was aired on December 22, 1958; and proved staggeringly successful; audience figures were 11 million, with the press once again delighting at the downswing in the crime statistics and recording complaints from pub landlords and bingo hall managers. The subsequent episodes built on this success. Luckily the BBC recorded *Quatermass and the Pit* for posterity and the series has enjoyed several screenings since that early broadcast. Viewed today it compares very favorably with the later and better known Hammer version released in the U.S. as *Five Million Years to Earth*.

Technically Hammer's film looks better, benefiting from higher production values, technical expertise and the use of color, which gives director Roy Ward Baker's work a gloss that Cartier can't match. On nearly every other level the BBC version is superior: Kneale's intelligent script is given full justice with the expanded running time, more subtle ideas and concepts given time to evolve, and a gradual turn of the screw as opposed to Hammer cramming everything in for shock effect. With the additional time peripheral characters are used to add texture and depth, many of whom would be telescoped or eliminated for the film. Cartier's direction has much more edge than Baker's stately approach, and on the whole the acting is superior, in particular Cec Linder who invests Ronay with a nervous enthusiasm totally absent from James Donald's stoic underplaying. As Quatermass, Morell has both wisdom and credibility as he moves effortlessly from elder statesman to trusted friend and colleague while still humanizing an enigmatic character.

Morell and Cec Linder in *Quatermas and the Pit*

And of course neither Andrew Keir nor Brian Donlevy can match Morell for charm and dignity, though perhaps both offer a more energetic and brusque character more in keeping with the big screen's truncated requirements.

Hammer snapped up the rights to the third series, placing Morell on their shortlist (which also included Peter Cushing and Kenneth Moore). *Quatermass and the Pit* was originally slated to shoot in 1961 but remained resolutely on the drawing board. The Dracula and Frankenstein franchises offered far more lucrative box-office prospects in the U.S. and Hammer shelved the project in favor of their Gothic cash cows. By the time the company returned to the character in 1967, Morell was considered too old for the role and the silver screen lost out on its best Quatermass. He probably regarded it as a blessing. The success of *Quatermass and the Pit* solidified André Morell's identity in the role for a generation of Britons. He later recalled being stuck in a cab, besieged by fans after someone shouted, "Look, it's Quatermass!" The newspapers, irrespective of the context, took to identifying him as André "Quatermass" Morell. For an actor who spoke on more than one occasion about the dangers of typecasting it seemed that he may have created a millstone around his neck. Certainly it led indirectly to a film that Morell would describe (when he could bear to talk about it) as the "worst of his career"—*The Giant Behemoth*.

If *Seven Days Till Noon* offered cinemagoers an intelligent take on the dangers of the nuclear age, *The Giant Behemoth* presented the same theme in a kiddy matinee format. Morell was handed the honor of saving London again, this time in the guise of Professor James Bickford, a poor man's Quatermass running Britain's Atomic Energy Commission rather than the Rocket Group. With the producers promising, "The Biggest Thing since Creation!" the money was actually coming from Artists Alliance, a cheapjack British company and the people behind the camp classic *Blood of the Vampire*. Predictably the publicity department would completely ignore the reality of the film's budget when it came to setting public expectations:

> SEE the Beast that shakes the Earth! LIVE in a world gone mad! WATCH the chaos of a smashed civilization! FLEE from the mightiest fright on the screen! NOTHING so Big as Behemoth!

The film's writer-director at least had some credibility: Eugene Lourie could boast an impressive pedigree including the definitive monster movie and late-show favorite, *The Beast from 20,000 Fathoms*. Allegedly Lourie's first draft for *The Giant Behemoth* required a completely invisible monster, which would have been an interesting challenge for the special effects team and offered a novel approach to a theme that was, even in 1959, looking old hat. At least Artists Alliance recognized the limitations of their wallets and, on financial rather than artistic grounds, Lourie was instructed to rewrite his concept into a more conventional monster; in doing so it became a more or less straight remake of Lourie's earlier film.

The film opens with some inexplicable disappearances off the coast of Cornwall: lots of rumors, muttering fishermen and wreckage but nothing very tangible. As luck would have it, at the same time the creature is making its presence felt off the south coast of England, American marine biologist Steven Karnes is addressing a seminar in London on the dangers of nuclear testing and disposal of the waste. Prominent in the audience is Professor Bickford, who invites the American to comment on the growing number of incidents involving dead fish, mysterious burns and radiation leakage. It isn't too long before the truth has been successfully diagnosed, even if the scale isn't fully appreciated until later. (The evocative title incidentally comes from the creature's early

encounter with a Cornish fisherman who opts for a cryptic Biblical description when, as one critic pointed out, a more literal description would have saved the authorities a lot of time!) The movie staggers towards its climax with the titular creature leveling London and leaving a trail of destruction in its wake. Karnes, in the time honored fashion of square-jawed heroes, sets out to vanquish his nemesis face to face, or least as near as one can get in a mini submarine, while, from the sidelines, Bickford looks concerned.

In a movie like this, the human cast is always going to play second fiddle to the monster but given the circumstances they do reasonably well, particularly in the early sequences when Lourie is in detective mode and *The Giant Behemoth* could pass as an acceptable mystery thriller. Karnes is played by Gene Evans, the Arizona-born actor who had appeared in *Donovan's Brain,* who comes across as a likeable hero while Morell offers a nice line in bureaucratic skepticism while wryly observing his heroics. Once again Morell proves his value by delivering the usual pseudoscientific mumbo jumbo with convincing gravitas and credibility; and the interplay between Karnes and Bickford, as well as the careful build up, gives the film more than a passing similarity to the Quatermass series. But Lourie's efforts to overcome the budgetary shortcomings with omnipresent banks of fog and moonlit shadows could only go so far; when the creature emerges from the depths, the carefully worked tension dissipates entirely. The "mightiest fright on screen" looks no more convincing than a child's toy and is undermined further by the need to reuse certain shots to try and save money. This the most disappointing aspect of the film; Artists Alliance hired an experienced effects team and then failed to give the time and budget to do even a halfway decent job. The principal team included Jack Rabin, Irving Block and Louis DeWitt who could count *The Night of the Hunter* and *The Atomic Submarine* in their collective filmographies. Also involved in the animation sequences was the legendary Willis O'Brien who had worked on the original *King Kong* and, along with his assistant Pete Peterson, shared the credit for the title character in *Mighty Joe Young*. Sadly their combined efforts are largely wasted here; rather than enhancing the film, the effects reduce it to a comedic standard.

The Giant Behemoth came lumbering into cinemas at the end of the "monster on the loose" cycle by which time it had all been seen before and considerably better. *Variety* called it a "modestly made, routine science-fiction yarn which cannot be regarded as more than a useful dualer for average audiences," but at least noted that "Gene Evans, Andre Morell...are among those who conscientiously do their thesping stints with as much serious intent as if they were all in line for Oscars." Morell himself hated being involved, as he told David Soren in *Little Shoppe of Horrors*:

> That Behemoth thing, I never saw it and I was ashamed of it, ashamed of being seen in that kind of film. And Gene Lourie, the director, had a time with me because I kept turning my back to the camera trying to hide and he'd say, "Don't play your scenes with your back to the camera!"

While the embarrassed Morell was saving civilization as we know it, his erstwhile employers, Hammer, had consolidated their position as the world's premier supplier of Gothic horror films and were about to embark on an adaptation of a more mainstream Victorian novel, *The Hound of the Baskervilles*. At first glance there seems to be a natural association between Hammer and Sherlock Holmes if only because the British company had been working their way through Universal's back catalogue, which included the best known Holmes series starring Basil Rathbone. In fact the most famous version of the story, starring Rathbone and Nigel Bruce as Dr. Watson, was filmed by 20th Century-Fox in 1939. Fox made one sequel before Universal picked up the rights and made a further 12 films with Rathbone and Bruce. In truth, Universal had nothing to do with the Hammer project; the British company had been approached by Kenneth Hyman at Seven Arts, who had bought the rights from the Conan Doyle estate, and agreed to partial financing through United Artists. James Carreras and Tony Hinds saw the film, and the potential series it would spawn, as an ideal running mate for the successful Dracula and Frankenstein franchises. Naturally Peter

Holmes (Cushing) and Watson (Morell) breakfast together in *The Hound of the Baskervilles*.

Cushing, who was very much the star in residence at Hammer, was part of the funding package and, with a passing resemblance to Holmes, was an obvious choice to play the lead. Cushing was a great admirer of Conan Doyle's work and delighted at the chance to move away from horror movies.

To stay true to its successful formula Hammer found a role for another resident ghoul, Christopher Lee, and he was shoehorned, rather inappropriately, into the romantic lead, Sir Henry Baskerville. Both men were announced to the press on August 1, 1958; a week later Terence Fisher was added to the recipe but it wasn't until the September 3—five days before shooting was to begin—that Hammer announced that Andre Morell had been cast as Dr. Watson. The film was officially unveiled to the press at a launch party in the Sherlock Holmes pub in London, appropriately enough the site of the old Northumberland Hotel where the fictional Holmes and Watson first meet Sir Henry. Speaking to the press, Tony Hinds sought to reassure any skeptics by insisting, "this will be authentic—the definitive version." James Carreras on the other hand saw *The Hound of the Baskervilles* as a continuation of Hammer's proven formula both in terms of cast and content and was keen to ensure things had a familiar look behind the camera. Apart from Fisher, the veterans from Hammer's horrors included cinematographer Jack Asher, composer James Bernard and production designer Bernard Robinson. Only screenwriter Jimmy Sangster was busy elsewhere, so the script chores were handed to Tony Hinds' good friend Peter Bryan. On September 8, *The Hound of the Baskervilles* began shooting.

The story opens with a suitably Hammer-esque introduction told in flashback by Dr. Mortimer in his best undertaker tone:

> Know then the legend of the Hound of the Baskervilles. Know then, that the great hall of Baskervilles was once held by Sir Hugo of that name: a wild, profane, and godless man. An evil, in truth, for there was with him a certain ugly and cruel humor that made his name a by-word in the county...

Immediately *The Hound of the Baskervilles* is off and running, looking more

like Hammer than Conan Doyle with Fisher reveling in scenes of tortured servants, despoiled maidens and a frantic chase across the moonlit moor—all acting as a lurid prelude to the (off-camera) introduction of the beast itself. From there the scene switches to the Baker Street apartment of Holmes and Watson and the attempt by Dr. Mortimer to engage the detectives as bodyguards for the last of the Baskerville line, Sir Henry, newly arrived from South Africa. The chase soon leads to Dartmoor where Watson, and later Holmes, begins to unravel the mystery and protect Sir Henry from the "Hound of Hell." Hammer made much of the hound in their publicity and Fisher carefully builds up the tension toward its first appearance. Depicting the animal would prove something of a challenge even for the most creative of Hammer's team. In chapter 14 of Conan Doyle's novel, Watson describes his encounter with the creature:

Perkins (Sam Kidd) is clearly not to be trusted by Watson.

A hound it was, an enormous coal-black hound, but not such a hound as mortal eyes have ever seen. Fire burst from its open mouth, its eyes glowed with a smoldering glare, its muzzle and hackles and dewlap were outlined in the flickering flame. Never in the delirious dream of a disordered brain could more savage, more appalling, and more hellish be conceived than that dark form and savage face…

Hammer's hound was an affable Great Dane called Colonel; a mask designed and fitted by Margaret Carte and made from rabbit fur failed to suggest any menace about the friendly animal more inclined to lick than bite its victims. It was time for something more extreme, as Peter Cushing remembered in his autobiography:

> The production team endeavoring to create an illusion of the dog's massive proportions, hit upon the idea of employing three young boys corresponding in relative size to Andre Morell, Christopher Lee and myself… On the following day the rushes were viewed and disappointment deflated all

concerned. We saw three small boys, dressed up as if playing charades, foggy toy scenery, and a wet, hungry dog in the middle.

It was a problem that Fisher never really resolved satisfactorily. The Hound would prove a disappointment in the finished film, only one of the problems experienced by the filmmakers. Conan Doyle's tale is heavy on atmosphere and short on action: Peter Bryan's script had to reverse that ratio and, with much of screen time falling to Watson, it was decided that the bumbling character played by Nigel Bruce in the earlier films would not be able to carry the movie. Fisher and Bryan were adamant that Cushing would be graced with a partner who, if not his intellectual equal, would certainly be a worthy friend and confidante. The new Watson is a thoughtful and occasionally dynamic man, a capable and energetic character in his own right. Casting Morell ensured that Watson had not only intelligence but humor, and it's obvious that the doctor is now a valued colleague rather than a tolerated friend. Both Cushing and Morell are at home with their characters, with Watson happily swirling a brandy glass, chewing on a cigar or fiddling with his pipe as the perfect foil for Holmes' nervous energy. Morell was very much in his element and his characterization is underlined with a host of little touches: pulling out and replacing a pocket watch while talking to Holmes, then just as casually producing a handkerchief from his sleeve and wiping his nose, without missing a beat. That watch would appear and reappear later on from different pockets.

Christopher Lee is not well-served by the script: Sir Henry is a supporting character who doesn't sit well with the actor's commanding screen presence, and he struggles to make the role credible, certainly a flaw at the centre of the film. Lee is too clever an actor not to be aware of the miscasting and his discomfort showed both during production and on screen—aggravated no doubt by his final billing, third behind both Cushing and Morell. Fifty years later Lee is still reluctant to talk about his costar though concedes, without elaborating the reasons, that he and Morell did not get on. It is telling that, in his autobiography and various interviews over the years, he makes frequent mention of the film and his costars, including the minor character parts, but never makes reference to Dr. Watson. Morell for his part couldn't be drawn to comment on Lee, beyond an observation made to his family that he was a "dull actor."

For once Hammer's approach wasn't entirely successful. Bryan's script takes a number of liberties with Conan Doyle's work, not all of them for obvious reasons; for example, the main suspect, Stapleton, is now inexplicably deformed, presumably to make him even more suspicious, and the villain of the piece undergoes a sex change to become the dark-eyed Cecile, played with delicious wickedness by former model Marla Landi. Bryan struggled with the complicated character of Holmes, who comes across as a curiously underwhelm-

ing figure, physically diminished by sharing the screen with the huge frames of not only Lee but also the gigantic Francis de Wolff as Mortimer. Significantly Holmes is twice mistaken for minor officials (Sir Henry thinks he is the hotel manager and Miles Malleson's comic bishop takes him for a repairman). It is probably not coincidental that Holmes has echoes of Van Helsing, particularly when he says, "the powers of evil can take many forms...do as the legend tells and avoid the moor when the forces of darkness are exalted." Bryan's failings are all too obvious and Cushing's performance suffers accordingly; the actor was much better when he played the role in the BBC version with Nigel Stock as Watson. Fisher's direction is, as always, restrained but he is handicapped by the poor use of location; the moor, which should have lent the film an air of menace and foreboding, is never adequately recreated on the army training fields at Chobham Common and at Frensham Pond, some 40 miles from London. There was some second unit footage shot at Dartmoor but so ill-used that it was hardly worth the trip. The film does have impressive cinematography by Jack Asher, excellent sets from Bernard Robinson, and an impressive Morell moustache, one of the many remarkable makeup creations of Roy Ashton. But James Bernard's score is merely adequate; to cope with budget restrictions he fleshed out the music with excerpts from *Horror of Dracula*. Nevertheless James Carreras was pleased enough to tell the *Daily Cinema*, "The fact that the

Sherlock Holmes Society in London rate it the greatest Sherlock Holmes film ever made supports all our own high claims for it."

The critics were less impressed: *The Observer* noted, "It would seem hard to make a dull picture of *The Hound of the Baskervilles* but Hammer Films have done it." The reviewer also found fault with Cushing, claiming he "seems fussy, finicky and indeterminate." By comparison Morell's Watson was received almost kindly: "He works hard to avoid the buffoonery of the part." The *New York Herald Tribune* was a little more sanguine, calling the film a "sound version, nicely photographed and should be a pleasant introduction to the adventure." Morell was singled out by the *Daily Telegraph*: "André Morell who cannot act badly plays Watson very well." The *Daily Herald* opined, "The hound is a bit of a disappointment, but Peter Cushing is accurately irritable, precise and prissy as Holmes, and Andre Morell is the perfect Watson." Many years later Cushing, in a television documentary, summed up Morell's contribution with a succinct "André Morell, well you can't get much better, can you?"

The closing sequence as Holmes and Watson share muffins in their Baker Street apartment suggests that a sequel be forthcoming but the film appealed to neither horror buffs nor Conan Doyle fans (of which, as later films proved, there are conspicuously fewer than you might think!). The lackluster box-office performance led to James Carreras canceling plans for a series.

Cushing and Morell were reunited in March 1960 but under very different circumstances. *Trouble in the Sky* is a modest little thriller about investigators struggling to resolve the mystery behind an air crash. The British title, *Cone of Silence*, refers to the area of radar blackout which pilots must find when flying blind. The phrase also has connotations of a cover-up, in this case involving the crash of an experimental aircraft. Bernard Lee is the pilot suspected of incompetence, with the non-flying sequences enlivened with some familiar faces including Noel Willman and George Sanders, with Morell contributing a reliable if unspectacular turn as a pensive airline boss. Cushing, taking a break from horror movies, seems happy enough in a supporting roll as a duplicitous pilot but the whole thing is too mannered and talky to appeal to a wide audience. The movie did very little business on either side of the Atlantic.

By this stage in his career Morell had appeared in his fair share of big budget movies but the word "epic" doesn't quite do justice to the film he made for veteran director William Wyler. There is a unwritten rule somewhere in Hollywood that says Britons make the best Romans and this was to serve the UK's acting fraternity particularly well on MGM's sprawling $15 million remake of *Ben-Hur*. Morell was cast as Sextus, the outgoing tribune of Judea, who appears in the film's opening sequences to impart a sense of foreboding and also suggest that not all Romans are as bad as they were later painted. Wyler needed an actor who could portray the dignity and wisdom of Rome, in contrast with the hotheaded intolerance of his successor, Messala, and Morell fitted the bill perfectly. In these early scenes Sextus tries to warn Messala that the days of Roman dictatorship are coming to an end:

> I think you'll find the people changed since you were a boy... won't pay their taxes, an irrational resentment of Rome...then there's religion. I'll tell you, they're drunk with religion, smash the statues of our gods, even those of the Emperor.

It is Morell who sums up in one line the entire ethos of the movie: "You can break a man's skull. You can arrest him. You can throw him into a dungeon but how do you control what's up here. How do you fight an idea?" The words are wasted on a clearly disinterested Messala (Stephen Boyd), who reveals he intends to deal with the new religion as he would any "rabble rousers" with direct and ruthless action. The younger Roman makes no distinction for childhood friendships, so naturally when Judah Ben-Hur, his boyhood friend, doesn't wholly commit to this plan he is labeled an enemy and treated accordingly. The trials and humiliations heaped on Charlton Heston's Ben-Hur and his rise to take his vengeance form the crux of the rest of the movie. Famous for its spectacular set pieces and in particular the climactic chariot race, *Ben-Hur* also has a number of memorable performances by Jack Hawkins, Hugh Griffiths and

Morell as Sextus in *Ben-Hur*

Finlay Currie. Morell enjoyed the trip to Italy for the filming and he also liked working with Wyler, whose best work includes *Wuthering Heights* and *Roman Holiday*, and who insisted, much to the delight of his English cast, on extensive rehearsals before scenes were shot. Sadly Morell's involvement is limited to the first part of the film, and the ballyhoo surrounding the subsequent scenes made certain that this quiet but dignified moment remained all but ignored by critics and filmgoers. The film went on to win a staggering 11 Academy Awards, including Best Picture, Best Director and Best Cinematography.

Despite his screen success Morell maintained he was only a reluctant film star. "Income Tax drives me into films," he confided to the *Evening News*, "I must do film work to pay my tax. I would like to go back to theatre work." Morell went on to assure the interviewer that he will continue to pursue leading roles in the theatre but preferred only provincial shows, explaining, "These smaller theatres have only short seasons which allows more time for films." He was being modest; amongst these "smaller" efforts at the time was *Hedda Gabler* at the Oxford Playhouse opposite Joan Greenwood and a return to *The Master Builder* in Nottingham—both significant events in the theatrical calendar for

Joan Greenwood, Andre Morell wed in Jamaica

NEW YORK, May 24 (Reuter): British stage and screen star, Joan Greenwood and television actor Andre Morell were married quietly at the home of friends at Discovery Bay, Jamaica, on May 16, according to John Wulff, her New York agent.

He said Miss Greenwood had told him this last week. Their brief honeymoon, he said, was spent at a Manhattan hotel. It was the first marriage for both.

Miss Greenwood, who is 39, and her 50-year-old husband were preparing here tonight to fly to London after their secret marriage and honeymoon.

Miss Greenwood has appeared in such films as "Kind Hearts and Coronets" and "Stagestruck". Morell was Professor Quatermass in the British television horror serial "Quatermass and the Pitt".

Gleaner Northcoast Cor. ST. ANN'S BAY: JOAN GREENWOOD, English actress, and Andre Morell, actor, were married on May 16 by the Rev. Fr. Harrison here, in a quiet ceremony attended only by their servants. The actress and Mr. Morell had been holidaying at Bean Bird Lodge, Discovery Bay, part of Panorama Development.

According to Mr. Albert Brietang, head of the development, he kept their presence quiet at the request of the actress. The couple enjoyed snorkelling at Discovery Bay and the scotsmen afforded them by the other residents.

They left Jamaica on Tuesday, May 17, for five days in New York and arrived in London on the 22nd, having cabled a few friends of their marriage, according to Mr. Brietung.

their respective years. Morell's position as a formidable stage actor was further evidenced in 1962 when he was invited by the artistic director, Laurence Olivier, to join the inaugural season of the prestigious Chichester Festival Theatre, playing in *Uncle Vanya* opposite John Neville, Michael Redgrave, Joan Plowright, and Sybil Thorndyke. Also in the cast was Joan Greenwood who on the May 16, 1960, had become Mrs. Morell, or as the *Daily Mail,* one of Britain's largest circulation broadsheets, had headlined, "The Bride of Quatermass." Though you wouldn't have known it from the press reaction, the wedding had actually come as something of a surprise even to close friends of the couple. Only a few years earlier Morell seemed to have accepted, albeit reluctantly, his bachelor status, bemoaning, "Men of my age are automatically cast by eligible women as wolves." It was such a well kept secret that Joan's mother was under the impression her daughter was holidaying in Europe with a friend!

London-born Greenwood was one of the most striking actresses of her generation (40 years later *Empire* magazine included her in their list of *100 Sexiest Stars of All Time*). She was a revelation in the thriller *Latin Quarter* and, signing on at Rank soon afterwards, went on to star in some of the studio's best films, including *Kind Hearts and Coronets*. Her track record in British films is probably unequalled and includes the classic Ealing comedies *Whisky Galore!* and *The Man in the White Suit*, as well as the romantic tragedy *Saraband*. Amazingly, given she was one of the most recognizable actresses of her generation and Morell was a household name, the couple managed to keep their relationship secret from the press. They married in a private ceremony at Discovery

Morell and Greenwood had appeared together in *Flesh and Blood* in 1951.

Bay in Jamaica and it was only during the stop over in New York on the way home that the news slipped out. The event may have been front page news in England but in the U.S. it went practically unnoticed; *The New York Times* carried a small paragraph headed,

> Joan Greenwood, the British stage and screen star, is honeymooning in N. Y., with Andre Morell, after their marriage in Jamaica. Morell played the blackmailing Judge Brack to Miss Greenwood's Hedda Gabler . . . In discussing their stage plans the groom said: "Oh, we can't do 'Hedda Gabler' again—at least not with me playing Brack. We'd giggle ourselves silly."

"Joan Greenwood Wed" and recorded that she had married "Andre Morell, an actor." Morell was 50, Joan was 38 and their marriage relatively late in their lives was followed in 1962 by the birth of their son Jason. Forty years later Jason offered a revealing insight into their relationship:

> They met just after my mother left RADA in 1938 and my father was at the Old Vic; he was a leading man at the time and he was visiting his agent while she was sitting outside the office. He asked who she was and his agent said, "That's Joan Greenwood and she's only 17 so you keep your hands off of her!" As he left the office he flashed his most charming smile, my mother said she thought, "what a disgustingly over good-looking, over confident young man." He pursued her on and off throughout the 1950s, they met in various places around the world, exchanged cards and letters and so on.

Morell and Greenwood enjoyed a huge success in *Hedda Gabler* after which they decided to take that secret holiday:

> My grandmother was very proper and would never hear of such a thing so my mother had to pretend she was going to Switzerland for a rest cure. She packed all her cotton and linens in the bottom of her suitcase and all her tweeds in the top and then flew to New York were she met up with my father. She was actually late; my grandmother had come to see her off so she couldn't get on the plane immediately. My father was fuming and saying he would never be stood up by a woman again. Anyway they made it to Jamaica, had the time of their lives, spent a month in the sun, resting, swimming and presumably having great sex; they never really talked about marriage, it just seemed to evolve.

The ceremony itself took place at the Governor's residence with the handyman acting as a witness; the whole thing was so last minute that the only ring they

Joan Greenwood

had was a brass stage prop from *Hedda Gabler,* which Morell later had plated in gold.

A year earlier Morell had told the press that he wanted to reduce his work rate on television, "largely to avoid being typecast as a rat." The arrival of Jason in their lives changed that and he would, over the next decade or so, take advantage of the shorter production schedules on television to spend more time with his family. Amongst the one-off dramas, he appeared in *Musical Chairs* with Barbara Shelley, *The Tomb of Tutankhamen* as Howard Carter; and in guest slots in peak time series like *The Avengers* and *International Detective.* His film commitments changed too; his domestic arrangements took precedence now and in an increasingly rare press interview he revealed, "My own childhood was colored by my parent's inability to adjust to each other. Eventually it resulted in divorce." This was one of the very few times Morell talked about his early childhood; even at home the matter was seldom discussed. Jason remembers the day he discovered he had an aunt:

> She and my father didn't get on, I am not sure why but I think it might have been to do with money. I remember as a small boy getting a birthday card from "Aunt Rosa" which was a bolt from the blue and I asked my father if I had an Aunt Rosa, he took the card looked at it and ripped it up with a curt, "No!"

By the time he was old enough Jason was sent to Hill House School in Knightsbridge, just round the corner from the family home (it counted Prince Charles amongst its ex-pupils) and later Westminster School, again in the centre of London close to the Morells' Chelsea apartment. In contrast to the 1950s, when the actor would be jetting round the globe from one exotic location to another, Morell now decided to limit his screen work to the UK and almost exclusively to Hammer, whose Bray studio was a convenient commute from the centre of London.

Surprisingly perhaps for such a confirmed bachelor Morell adjusted easily to married life; he and Joan were devoted to each other and wrote long and passionate letters whenever work forced them apart. Even at the height of his television fame, Morell was never a party animal and seldom appeared at premieres or showbiz parties; like Peter Cushing he was interested in model making and once constructed an elaborate scale model of a Shakespearean theatre but it was never a passion with him. His real love was Elizabethan theatre and he consumed any and every book on the subject; he enjoyed sitting in his favorite armchair and tackling *The Times* crossword and spending the afternoon shopping with Jason at the local supermarket because Joan was invariably committed to the stage. Morell, who after all had been raised with Victorian values, was a loving father who wanted the very best for his son and found it difficult to compromise his standards. He was all too aware of his weaknesses as Jason remembers:

> He once got very angry with me when he was trying to teach me math and he just exploded. Later he called me to him and said he was very sorry, he had hand written all the tables on a massive grid with different colored inks just to help me. He said if I ever saw him losing his temper again I should hold up my finger and say, "Just count to 10, Papa."

As the 1960s rolled on tastes changed on both the big and small screens; the days when a leading man could wear a tweed suit and smoke a pipe were slipping away and increasingly Morell was cast in supporting roles or in lower budget movies. His first Hammer film in the new decade was one with a quaintly old fashioned feel to it, *Shadow of the Cat*, a project that had come about almost by accident. John Gilling had been writing and directing second features since 1933 but his first horror film, in the literal sense of the word, was the lamentable Bela Lugosi vehicle *Old Mother Riley Meets the Vampire*. Gilling had been engaged by Hammer to direct *The Inquisitor* based on the Spanish Inquisition but the company pulled the plug practically at the 11th hour. *The Curse of the Werewolf* would be slammed into production to utilize the already constructed sets while Gilling was re-routed to the modest little thriller hurriedly prepared to form the lower part of a double bill, *Shadow of the Cat*. The script came from George Baxt who had earlier credits for *Circus of Horrors* and *City of the Dead*, and revolves around the decrepit Ella Venable who is forced by her

Vanda Godsell and Morell in *Shadow of the Cat*

scheming husband, Walter, to rewrite her will in his favor. The unfortunate woman is promptly murdered by Walter and his cronies and buried in the woods for her trouble. The murderers develop a preoccupation with the old woman's cat—the only living witness to the murder—but despite their increasingly desperate efforts they can't force a solution to this loose end. Baxt's script called for subtlety, with the cat seen as a manifestation of the murderers' guilt, a la Val Lewton, and only ever seen in shadows. Gilling, never one for restraint, opted for more literal approach and has the murderers picked off one by one as they attempt to dispose of the cat, including drowning in swamps and falling from roofs. Morell was cast as the nefarious Walter Venable, ringleader of the gang, whose efforts to capture the feline induces a heart attack that later claims his life. In the end the cat oversees justice dispensed to all the wrongdoers and the only survivor is the innocent Elizabeth who is free to inherit.

Catherine Lacy plays Ella, with Freda Jackson chewing the scenery as the evil maid Clara, and Barbara Shelley, sadly underused, as the virginal niece Elizabeth. The cast is excellent, particularly Morell who plays the wicked uncle role with considerable relish, exuding a duplicitous charm as well as menace. *Shadow of the Cat* was actually made by BHP productions, an independent company formed by George Baxt, Richard Hatton and Jon Pennington, under commission from Hammer, sparking a running debate ever since whether this is or isn't a Hammer film. In fact this arrangement isn't uncommon. Hammer would use it again with Fantale and *The Vampire Lovers*. Gilling's interpretation may have been less atmospheric but it was in line with Hammer's limited ambitions for the project. *Shadow of the Cat* was a B picture, shot cheaply and intended purely as a support feature. Despite some respectable notices the double bill failed to fire the imagination of audiences who liked their horror bloodier and full bodied.

About this time Morell was asked what he looked for in a script: "Any zonking good part," he said, before adding, "I would like to play a comedy part—from my point of view it seems very desirable to get away from all of these existentialist roles." Hammer films didn't have any comedies in mind for him but did have a "zonking good part."

Despite their reputation for horror movies, Hammer's schedule at the time was devoted to comedies and thrillers with only one film that could conceivably be called horrific, *Terror of the Tongs*. Peter Cushing was still the studio's biggest star and was pressing for more non-horror roles, so Hammer responded by purchasing the rights to a project that seemed tailor-made for him, *Cash on Demand*. In fact the project started out as a television play called *The Gold Inside Mr. Fordyce*, which was broadcast on the ATV network in September 1960. Richard Warner had starred as a finicky, small-minded bank manager called Fordyce who learns the true meaning of Christmas when he is confronted by a suave but ruthless bank robber. André Morell played Colonel Gore-Hepburn, the smoothest of villains, in what was a simple updating of Dickens' *Christmas Carol* with Fordyce's Scrooge redeemed through a thoroughly unpleasant experience. The play was a modest affair but attracted some good notices particularly for its leading performers. For the big screen adaptation Hammer cast Cushing as Fordyce and handed Morell the opportunity to recreate his Gore-Hepburn character—inadvertently recasting the two men as torturer and victim. There is certainly more than a touch of *1984* about Gore-Hepburn's tormenting of the uptight Fordyce with the news that his wife and son are being held captive:

> There are two men at your house. At this moment your wife has an electrode attached to each side of her head. If you fail to cooperate with us in any way whatsoever they will pass a charge through the circuit. It is extremely painful and I'm afraid the effects of it are permanent. She would never recover her wits.

This time around Morell was allowed to edge his cruelty with slippery charm and humor. "What do you want?" demands Fordyce. "Just some money," the Colonel replies nonchalantly. Then as the drama unfolds the Colonel develops a bond with Fordyce; he is fascinated by the bank manager's pettiness and his condescending attitude to his employees and becomes as interested in

Morell as villain Col. Gore-Hepburn in *Cash on Demand*

the man's character flaws as he is in the loot. The whole thing is an elaborate bluff: Gore-Hepburn is working alone and the robbery goes wrong when one of Fordyce's employees intervenes. The stress and fear induced by the robbery persuade Fordyce to change his ways and, in a true Dickensian moment, he becomes a "nice guy."

Competently directed in black and white by Quentin Lawrence who had also shot the ATV version, *Cash on Demand* was filmed almost like a television production in a mere 15 days for only slightly over $135,000 with limited sets and a small cast. The film is an engaging thriller relying totally on tension rather than action and the menace all stems from the verbal game between the two leading men, both of whom offer splendid performances, though neither is really being pushed into uncharted territory by their respective roles. In Morell's case the pressbook sums up his entire screen repertoire in one sentence:

> Andre Morell could very easily sit for a portrait for the advertising world's man of distinction and casting directors have recognized this by having him portray leaders in the business world, politics and the military.

It is interesting to think that either actor could have successfully played either role; reversing the parts might have proved an even more entertaining experience. Sadly, James Carreras had little idea what to do with the film; in England it sat on the shelf for two years before limping out shorn of almost 20 minutes. In the U.S. it faired slightly better, released on the lower half of a double bill supporting the Laurence Harvey-Capucine melodrama *Walk on the Wild Side*; though filmgoers might have been mislead by Columbia's description of Morell as "The Most Daring Bank Robber Who Ever Broke into a Vault!" The reviews were generally favorable and most critics enjoyed the sparring between two accomplished screen performers while accepting the modest ambitions of the movie.

It is a shame Hammer couldn't have found more enthusiasm for the film in Britain where it might have gone some way to restore the company's tarnished reputation as purveyors of worthless exploitation. By December 1964 the company's image was so bad that respectable critics had to be pressganged in attending a gala luncheon hosted by James Carreras, nominally to celebrate 10 years of Hammer Horror. Amongst the industry executives and stars who gathered was noted film reviewer Nina Hibbin of the *Daily Worker*, who was unmoved either by what she saw or the free lunch:

> It was sad to look around at the bright and intelligent faces of present and former horror players—like Peter Cushing, Andre Morell, Charles Tingwell, Heather Sears and Oliver Reed—and to dwell upon that prodigious waste of talent. Saddest of them all was the contemplation of the Hammer Company's spectacular rise to power and prosperity through 10 years of trading in morbidity, putrefaction and pain.

James Carreras was never unduly perturbed by his critics. Hammer's exercises in "morbidity" regularly proved box-office winners and, unlike many of its more worthy contemporaries, found a ready audience in Britain and throughout the world.

Morell's next film for the company did indicate that they were beginning to raise the standard of their game—at least a little. *She* was easily the company's most expensive and ambitious film to date. As early as 1962 Kenneth Hyman, who was in charge of European production for Seven Arts and a close friend of James Carreras, had suggested that the companies collaborate on an adaptation of H. Rider Haggard's novel. Published in 1887, Haggard's book had sold in excess of 80 million copies and tells the story of Major Holly leading a small expedition across central Africa to find the lost kingdom of Ayesha, "She-who-must-be-obeyed." It previously had been adapted for the screen, most notably by RKO in 1935, but its cinematic potential had been overshadowed by Haggard's better-known *King Solomon's Mines*. The Hammer-Seven Arts version made painfully slow progress to the screen, as the script went through a number of

Haumeid (Morell) and his daughter Ustane (Rosenda Monteros) try to help Holly (Cushing) and Job (Bernard Cribbins) in *She*.

drafts in the hands of John Temple Smith, Berkeley Mather, Robert Day and finally David T. Chandler, who had previously adapted *Cash on Demand* for Hammer and who retains the sole credit on the final film. Over the course of the various revisions the story had moved away from Rider's dark and violent fantasy into a family action-adventure yarn, the centerpiece of which is the immortal Ayesha love/obsession with Leo, an impressionable Englishman adrift in the Middle East. Ayesha believes Leo to be the reincarnation of her lost love, Killikrates, and intends him to rule the lost Kingdom of Kuma at her side—after he has been induced to enter the flame of eternal life.

Leo and his friends, Major Holly and Job, are lured across the desert, braving the elements and hostile locals before arriving to the initially reassuring protection of the beautiful Ustane, a servant of Ayesha. Their arrival is also witnessed by Billali, the High Priest, who has his own reasons to resent the Englishman, and the statuesque Ayesha, who soon reveals the extent of her own cruelty and rage. Confronted by the truly wicked woman, Holly is repulsed and plans to leave but Leo remains entranced and vows to stay. Just as the friends prepare to go their separate ways a rebellion breaks out amongst the slaves, leading to the climactic showdown between Billali, Leo and Ayesha. This is rip-roaring stuff with elements of a classic action-adventure, supplemented by Hammer's Peter Cushing as Holly and Christopher Lee as the brooding Billali. The film seemed destined for great things; certainly MGM thought so when contributing to the £312,000 budget as well as freeing up space at their British base, Elstree, for the interiors. The U.S. dollars guaranteed the cooperation of the spectacular Ursula Andress in the title role, which in turn generated the much needed acres of newspaper coverage, but by all accounts the former Bond girl was less than enamored with the project—and it shows in her performance.

One of the innovations introduced by David T. Chandler was the character of Haumeid, Ustane's father and the appointed leader of the oppressed slaves, the Amahagger. Morell was well cast as this former soldier of Ayesha who reluctantly accepts his role as father figure to her minions and holds them in check by shear force of personality. Certainly the actor cuts a dignified figure, bare-chested and bronzed with a clear love and respect for the slaves under his charge. Morell manages to bring both solemnity and melancholy to some leaden dialogue:

> Her wisdom is limitless, her anger boundless. Perhaps one day that will change for hate is festering in the bosom of this people. Hate which could become strong enough to defy the hate they live with.

After Ustane is murdered by Ayesha in a jealous rage, her ashes are returned to her father by a centurion, who informs him, "She-who-must-be-obeyed returns your daughter to you as a warning to all who displease her." He proceeds to empty her ashes on the ground, and Morell, in only a few moments of screen time, conveys all of the despair of a father and pent-up anger of an abused servant. This one moment of casual cruelty from Ayesha sparks the revolt than ultimately brings about her downfall; unfortunately it also marks the end of Morell's involvement in the film.

The direction of *She* was entrusted to Robert Day, who had directed Richard Gordon's Gothic horrors *The Haunted Strangler* and *Corridors of Blood* but his credentials for Hammer undoubtedly rested on his handling of the action pictures *Tarzan the Magnificent* and *Tarzan's Three Challenges* (starring Gordon Scott and Jock Maloney, respectively). Shooting began on August 24, 1964, with Day, cast and crew enduring arduous conditions on location in Israel. Morell was spared that discomfort and joined the production a few weeks later when they returned to Elstree for the interiors. Day, speaking to authors Tom Johnson and Deborah Del Vecchio, said:

> André Morell was another marvelous actor. Like many British actors he was able to go back and forth between big and small films. Like Peter Cushing he came from a school of acting with too few students today. When an actor of Morell's quality has seventh billing it speaks well of any film.

Day was being diplomatic because, despite his enthusiasm for the project, the acting in *She* can best be described as variable. Cushing and Lee acquit themselves well but Andress sleepwalks through the film, offering little beyond her extravagant cleavage. The romantic leads, John Richardson as Leo and

Rosenda Monteros as Ustane, are both very poor—the latter had the admittedly thankless task of trying to upstage Andress. Morell is excellent in an underwritten part, but Day decided his accent wasn't "ethnic" enough, so his voice was dubbed by Hammer veteran George Pastell.

While *She* was shooting at Elstree, Quentin Lawrence was putting the finishing touches on *The Secret of Blood Island* for Hammer at Bray, with Barbara Shelley once again behind the barbed wire. This shift away from horror movies certainly pleased Michael Carreras, heir apparent to his father, who took the opportunity to tell the British trade paper *Kine Weekly*, "There's no doubt the future lies with bigger productions." Hammer's subsequent involvement with another RKO remake, *One Million Years B.C.*, seemed to signal a move in that general direction. Unfortunately the budget for *She*, generous by Hammer's standards, was clearly inadequate for the "epic" proportions required and it shows; in many sequences the film looks distinctly low rent. This lack of style, old-fashioned pacing and simplistic narrative irritated the critics but the film did respectable business and *She* would count amongst the top earners for the year in England—a position repeated throughout the world.

Morell portrayed the yacht captain in the *Moon-Spinners* before working on *She*.

Despite the success Hammer would always be at a financial disadvantage with this type of production and the company was soon retreating back to more familiar fare. James Carreras in a press release announced:

> We shall make four pictures, the titles have not yet been decided, but the pictures will be made back-to-back, in pairs and released as two of the greatest all-horror programmes seen in years!

The four pictures he had in mind were *Dracula Prince of Darkness*, *Rasputin the Mad Monk*, *The Reptile* and, for Morell, a leading role in an unusual horror film, *The Plague of the Zombies*. A decade later he told David Soren how he became involved in this "all horror programme":

I went on holiday to Elba and Hammer wanted me to come back in three weeks. My agent rang me and said come back and do this Hammer film for good money. What is it, I asked? He stammered out that it is a...uh...costume drama. But I asked him what it was called and he said, *"The Plague of the Zombies."*

Hammer's "costume drama" first surfaced in 1963 as *The Zombie* with a script by Peter Bryan; the project sat on the shelf for a while before resurfacing as *Horror of the Zombies* sporting a script by John Elder, aka Tony Hinds, and this time got as far as a typically Hammer press announcement:

FRIGHTENING! HORRIFYING! SHOCK-LOADED! A ZOMBIE ARMY...AN ARMY OF "THE WALKING DEAD" RISES FROM THE GRAVE, AS IT SETS OUT ON A MURDER RAMPAGE AT DEAD OF NIGHT...HORROR TERROR AND SCREAMING PANIC SWEEP THE ENGLISH COUNTRYSIDE!

This description is rather at odds with producer Anthony Nelson Keys' contention to the *Daily Cinema* that:

People have to remember that these are morality tales, not unlike Greek heroes crusading against evil. Surely it's far better to make costumed horror films, rather than those modern sadistic and neurotic films where there are definite everyday associations and messages.

The British Board of Film Censors wasn't too impressed with the Elder-Hinds effort and described the script as "insane rubbish." Director John Gilling disagreed, having been allocated the two supporting features. He rewrote *The Reptile* with a vengeance but left *The Plague of the Zombies* largely intact. A mere eight days after Terence Fisher wrapped *Rasputin*, Gilling was on the same soundstages shooting the first set-ups. Rasputin's frozen river now was transformed, care of Bernard Robinson, into a sunken graveyard in a Cornish village. *The Plague of Zombies* opens with the village in the grip of a virulent disease and the local doctor, Peter Thompson, pleading for help from old mentor Sir James Forbes (Morell). Sir James arrives with his daughter Sylvia and, intent on performing an illegal autopsy, digs up some recent graves only to find them empty. In the meantime Alice, Thompson's wife, is displaying the same symptoms; all the clues point to local decadent aristocrat—this is a Hammer film after all—one Clive Hamilton (John Carson), who picked up some interesting habits during a recent sojourn in Haiti and now uses reanimated corpses as cheap labor in his tin mine. Carson's velvet-voiced heavy is a strictly-by-the-numbers villain, right down to his large and grotesque signet ring, but Carson plays it with such knowing perfidy that you can't help but enjoy the melodrama. Brook Williams is barely adequate as the befuddled Peter Thompson but he and Morell bonded both on and off the screen and they never let the absurdity of the situation get the better of them. Morrell remembered:

> I absolutely loved it. I had a lot of scenes with Brook Williams, son of Evelyn Williams, and we had great fun. To make a film like this of course one doesn't believe in zombies, but one says it and does it seriously.

Diane Clare who had been very good the previous year in *Witchcraft* made a vacuous Sylvia, but her performance was not helped in post-production by poor dubbing. On the set Morell was less than impressed with this costar, as confirmed by Brook Williams:

> André was a marvelous, witty and generous man but he and Diane didn't get on. I don't think it was personal, in fact I know it wasn't personal; he just felt that her inexperience was letting the side down a little bit. André would never have put it in stronger terms than that. I'm not sure what Diane might say but I thought he was far too professional to even let it show though. I have to say he seemed to be having a good time on that film.

Whatever was going on behind the camera, the witty interplay between Sir James and his daughter adds a welcome dose of humor to a film otherwise best known for its gruesome makeup. Jacqueline Pearce, who plays a suitably wan and haunted Alice, had to endure not only the discomfort of Roy Ashton's make up but the justly famous beheading sequence. This particular scene has Sir James and Peter hiding in a graveyard only to be set upon by the undead clawing their way out of graves. Gilling's strong visual sense provides the film with something of a *cause celebre*; not only is the scene superbly staged, it is also genuinely chilling—features all too rare in many of the later Hammer Horrors. Partly as a result of this scene *The Plague of the Zombies* has an enduring reputation far beyond what one expects for a low budget B and is all the more remarkable given it doesn't feature any of the main talents normally associated with Hammer: Cushing, Lee or Fisher. Gilling's ability to stage visually striking scenes played a significant role in the success of the film and amongst the highlights is a coffin tipped over by the fox hunt and the sudden appearance of the zombie, with girl in arms, at the tin mine.

Morell and Williams take a break on the set of *The Plague of the Zombies*.

Morell was the perfect actor for Gilling; his natural charisma and innate ease with props perfectly complement the director's staging. The scene where Sir James and Peter resolve to perform an impromptu autopsy is a good example of excellent screen acting and creative presentation. "We must have a body to examine," Sir James warbles happily:

> We can't possibly work with out one, we will dig one up. That lad they buried today will do, nice and fresh, and then we might learn something. Do it tonight, there's a full moon, couldn't be better. We'll start off about midnight.

This grisly exchange takes place while the two men are up to their elbows in soap bubbles washing the dishes!

Morell had never looked so relaxed and comfortable in a role for Hammer; he plays the crusty professor with a twinkle in his eye and a spring in his step. Even the redoubtable Dr. Watson wasn't as energetic or commanding as Sir James, and the scenes where he confronts the Squire and his henchmen positively bristle with excitement. Morell threw himself into the fiery climax with such enthusiasm that he was promptly dispatched to Bray Studios' first-aid officer, suffering from singed hair and eyebrows as well as a sore throat. John

Sir James Forbes (Morell) tries to stop the horror of *The Plague of the Zombies*.

Carson was the perfect foil, and the physical and intellectual contest between good and evil matches anything that Cushing and Lee achieved in their better-known encounters. Like so many of his colleagues, Carson has nothing but respect for his costar even if he did lean towards eccentric footwear! "I've always admired André Morell," he told the *Little Shoppe of Horrors*:

> He had the intelligence and authority which always gives a marvelous ballast and believability to a show. He had that top weight which anchors a show down. He always wore red socks. The reason he gave was that if he lost one, it didn't matter. He was always losing socks.

Tony Hinds may not be the most creative writer ever employed by Hammer but the script offers a number of intriguing ideas, including the unusual juxtaposition of theme and location (voodoo rituals in rural Cornwall) or confrontation between science and hedonism. The script's real failings are the lack of depth in his characterizations and the curiously downbeat ending. Eschewing Hammer's normal practice, the lovers do not walk off into the sunset; instead Peter is left a widower and Sir James and Sylvia are looking spent and exhausted rather than victorious. Of course, evil is vanquished and the village is free from the titular plague all in the space of a compact 90 minutes.

Just how impressive Gilling's achievement was can be underlined by a glance at the production accounts. The film came in at marginally over $357,000. Morell earned $8,568, three times the next highest salary, which went to John Carson. Gilling picked up $10,710 for directing and touching up the script, while the special effects were recorded at slightly over $6,000!

The critics for once approved: *Time Out* called it "highly atmospheric, often imaginatively directed and boasting classy photography," while the respected British magazine *Films and Filming*, usually notoriously intolerant of Hammer, noted, "the spell cast of *The Plague of the Zombies* is quite a potent one."

The gimmicky nature of the whole four film arrangement carried forward in to the marketing, particularly in the U.S. where 20th Century-Fox promoted the double bill with *Dracula Prince of Darkness* by

offering vampire fangs to boys in the foyers while young ladies could startle their dates with "zombie eyes." If that wasn't enticement enough, cinemagoers were promised "The Greatest All New Fright Show in Town" and creatures so terrifying that "Only the Lord of the Dead Could Unleash Them!"

Morell and Gilling were reunited at Hammer a year later for *The Mummy's Shroud*, the third entry in the studio's Mummy series, very much a poor relation to their Dracula and Frankenstein films. The film, announced as *Shroud of the Mummy*, was conceived as a supporting feature for *Frankenstein Created Woman*—hardly an A film—and Gilling was openly contemptuous of the John Elder script, deciding it was "going nowhere...another worn out theme." Denied the time to do a complete re-write, Gilling hoped he could tweak the script into something more satisfactory and then rely on his skills as a director to rescue the project. Visually the concept offered Gilling some room for maneuvering, and the mummy he envisaged would be a dry skinned but recognizably human creature, not unlike Karloff in Universal's original. Gilling's script describes the creature as "the perfect semblance of a human face and body, skin, hair...is intact yet so opaque in appearance that one might suspect it could crumble if breathed upon." Sadly most of Gilling's innovations were abandoned in the name of economy, leaving the disgruntled director adrift with a rather routine script.

Morell had no such reservations; he liked Gilling and enjoyed the convivial atmosphere at Bray, so he happily signed on for the role of Sir Basil Walden, leading an expedition across the Surrey sandpits in search of the tomb of Kah-to-Bey. Our hapless explorers have to endure the twin terrors of the obligatory curse and opportunist financier Stanley Preston, gleefully played by John Phillips, who is intent on hijacking their find to further his own financial gain. Having found the tomb, Sir Basil falls afoul of Preston's conniving and is institutionalized as insane, which leaves villain Hasmid Ali (Roger Delgado) free to resurrect the long dead mummy and extract revenge on the desecrators.

Struggling to wring some entertainment out of the tired concept, Gilling made the tactical error of killing Sir Basil off early, sparing Morell's dignity but robbing the film of its most effective character. The director went some way to make amends during the mummy's shuffling rampage and arranged some effectively staged set pieces, in particular the slaughter of the pathetic Longbarrow (Hammer stalwart Michael Ripper). Morell's death scene is also a highlight, with Catherine Lacy's haggard soothsayer distracting Walden while the mummy attacks him from behind. Judicious editing and sickening sound effects create a memorable sequence but it's hardly enough to save the movie. After Morell's gory departure the acting is decidedly second rate. The buxom Maggie Kimberly, who falls out of her costume better than most, provides the glamour but struggles to make anything of her character. The hero originally slated for John Richardson is played by David Buck who continued a long line of colorless Hammer leading men. (Buck had earlier appeared in a remake of *1984* made by the BBC with Joseph O'Conor playing O'Brien).

The typically outspoken Gilling had no enthusiasm for the project and readily conceded he accepted the assignment only to break away from television; years later he confessed, "I wasn't very proud of *The Mummy's Shroud*. In fact I thought it one of my worst"—quite an indictment from the man who made *Old Mother Riley Meets the Vampire*! Relegated to supporting one of Hammer's weakest series efforts, *Frankenstein Created Woman*, *The Mummy's Shroud* is probably best remembered today for the ludicrous ad line "Beware the Beat of the Cloth Wrapped Feet!"

This was Gilling's ninth and last film for Hammer; Morell however would have one last outing for the company he had served faithfully since 1951. The "golden age," if Hammer ever had such a thing, was now drawing to an end. The company was tied to a number of distribution deals with major studios—a prerequisite of which was the use of their soundstages, so Hammer made the decision abandon Bray to set up a production office at Elstree. The move is generally seen as a watershed for Hammer but its films had been in decline for some time. Morell's next project would mark another low for the company.

James Carreras had started the ball rolling on a sequel to *She* almost as soon as the cash registers started ringing. Originally titled "Ayesha—Daughter of She," with Ursula Andress, much to her annoyance, contractually obliged to repeat her starring role. It resurfaced again on the company's 1966 schedule as "The Return of She" by which time Andress' contract had expired and she showed no inclination toward generosity. By the time Hammer started serious pre-production, Susan Denberg, star of *Frankenstein Created Woman*, was being primed for the role but the former Playmate of the Year would lose out to another *Playboy* discovery, Czechoslovakian model and Andress look-alike Olinka Berova. Television director Cliff Owen was engaged to helm a script by pulp novelist Peter O'Donnell, a thinly disguised retread of the first film. This time it is Killikrates pining for his lost Queen and scouring the globe for her reincarnation.

The Vengeance of She opens with Carol (Berova) clearly confused and wandering somewhere in the South of France, where she is accosted by a particularly grubby truck driver whose amorous intentions come to an untimely halt when he is run over by his own truck! This sets the pattern for the movie, with Berova a disinterested observer to a series of mishaps befalling those around her. To distract attention from the paper-thin plot and dreadful acting, Owen had his star strip to her underwear and stow away on a yacht to North Africa. On board she is drawn to something she can't describe, and we meet the nominal hero (Edward Judd) and learn that Carol may or may not be Scandinavian and an amnesiac. Parallel to all this we are reintroduced to Killikrates (John Richardson), who in the intervening years has lost his bouffant haircut and grown amazingly bad tempered. He also has enlisted the black magicians of the Magi to compel Carol, whom he believes is the reincarnation of Ayesha, to come to Kuma, where she will enter the flame of eternal life. Predictably the Magi, led by the splendidly wicked Men-Hari (Derek Godfrey), aren't acting on altogether altruistic motives.

Well into the film's seemingly interminable running time Morell pops up as the mysterious Kassim, resplendent in Arab robes and mumbling that he has "certain psychic ability." Kassim is a "scholar and a mystic" but (in line with the overall lazy scripting) exactly who he is or why he should be so interested in helping Carol isn't explained. After treating Carol to dinner he divines the forces controlling her:

> This man who calls you Ayesha is protected by a black shield, not on the physical plain but the astral. He is immortal—he will never die. And he is drawing you to him...I had thought such power was lost to mankind long ages ago but they are masters of it. Their skill lies in the understanding and use of the human mind's deepest powers magnified by rituals and symbols into a real living force.

Morell manages to make the trite dialogue sound credible and the film briefly looks like it may develop into something interesting—or at least worth watching. Kassim, rather naively, resolves to assist Carol: "I have not studied the occult all my life without gaining some small skill...but first I must remove your mind from the conflict. It will be safer."

The Magi are rallying their numbers to do battle with the magician in a distinctly one-sided contest. In a set up vaguely reminiscent of Hammer's *The Devil Rides Out* (coincidentally shooting simultaneously at Elstree), pentacles are drawn, sacrifices prepared and chanting begun. With Carol's mind presumably in a safe place, Kassim dons his best black magic robes and, in the best sequence in a dire film, locks metaphorical horns with Men-Hari across the astral divide. After all the careful build-up, the battle of wills turns out to be a bit of a damp squib and the Magi sweep Kassim aside quite literally, as a diabolical wind sends Morell over his balcony onto rocks below. Carol is once again cast into the desert.

Morell didn't join the production until late August (when Owen already had filmed most of the interiors at Elstree) and his scenes were shot at Almeria, Spain. Sadly by then the damage was already done. Owen had slipped a disc early in shooting and was forced to work from a horizontal position, which may account for his lifeless direction. The turgid script, dreadful muzak soundtrack and monumentally bad performance from Olinka Berova don't help, either. The best thing about Berova is her spectacular looks, and the cleavage-hugging gowns by Carl Tom are a special effect on their own. Only the black magic sequences suggest there might be a better film struggling to get out; otherwise the venture is completely forgettable. *The Vengeance of She* proved a waste of everyone's time, and it was the last and least of Morell's Hammer movies. The company would soon be in terminal decline. Tony Hinds left and James Carreras began his search for newer, usually sexier, subjects in a vain attempt to pump new blood into tired formulas. Peter Cushing and Christopher Lee would still prop up the increasingly lame efforts but the familiar reparatory company that was so much a feature of the company gradually dispersed, and with it much of the unique quality

of the films. Unlike many of Hammer's actors, Morell enjoyed the work; in the 1970s he told David Soren, "I loved doing those Hammer films and I'd do more if they asked." His son Jason confirmed this view:

> He thought of himself as a classical actor and these were essentially B pictures; I think every one who did the Hammer films thought that. He wasn't ashamed of them or anything like that; he did them I suppose to pay the school fees. I know that he tried to stop my mother seeing *Plague of the Zombies* but she sneaked into a cinema on a wet afternoon and watched it. I think she rather liked it. I also know he was very proud of his Dr. Watson and I think he probably enjoyed most if not all of them.

Morell's last film of the decade, MGM's bloated action-adventure *Dark of the Sun*, showed only a marginal improvement over *The Vengeance of She*. *The Mercenaries* (as it was known in its native England) is a big, noisy, simplistic movie set against the backdrop of a very complex civil war in the Congo.

The extent to which the filmmakers simplified the conflict is illustrated by the tagline "You don't kill for women. You don't kill for diamonds. You kill because you are paid for it!" Filmed in the more relaxing environment of Jamaica, the film features an interesting cast including Rod Taylor, Yvette Mimieux and Jim Brown, all of whom struggled through the mud and bullets, with Kenneth More and Morell offering what they could from the sidelines. It is an uninspired affair and disappointing for the few who managed to see it.

Having spent most of his career in character parts Morell now looked far older than his actual 60 years and, with the general decline in film production in England, his film appearances became restricted to cameos or minor supporting roles. Despite his age Morell wasn't afraid of challenges and in the summer of 1969 he proved he was still a force on the English stage when he appeared in the inaugural production at the Thorndyke Theatre in Leatherhead, just outside London. The play chosen was *The Lion in Winter,* already a celebrated film starring Peter O'Toole and Katherine Hepburn. Morell took the title role of King Henry II and played opposite the formidable Ursula Howells as Queen Eleanor. Premiered for Princess Margaret and her husband Lord Snowdon, the play was a popular hit with the public as well as the critics who recognized the powerful presence they had in their midst. The *Surrey Advertiser and County Times* wrote, "Andre Morell can count his performance as one of the most outstanding in over 30 years of solid success on the English stage."

This wasn't Morell's last appearance on the stage but during the last decade of his life his best work was probably on television, including appearances in several prestigious productions, notably Granada's historical drama *The Cae-*

sars. First broadcast in 1968, *The Caesars* offered a racier take on the Romans than the more stately BBC dramas and by the end of the series even the most casual viewer knew Roman royalty was a byword for sex, murder and madness on a grand scale. The starry cast list included Ralph Bates, Freddie Jones and Ronald Culver, with Morell appearing in the third of the six episodes as the aged Tiberius, whose increasing depression and paranoia made him one of the most unpopular Emperors. The segment was aired on October 6, 1968, and Morell fully merited the good notices he received; the series proved popular entertainment and spawned a number of look-alike historical exposés on British television.

Morell kept the robe and sandals to play Cicero in Charlton Heston's overblown version of Shakespeare's *Julius Caesar*. Christopher Lee and old friend Michael Gough also were featured in an eccentric cast that included Robert Vaughan, Richard Chamberlain and John Gielgud. American audiences had to wait for a year after the British release but critics and cinemagoers on both sides of the Atlantic failed to take to the production. Even with exploitation giants AIP behind the North American release it failed to find an audience. Much more rewarding was the BBC play *The Expert*, a one-off effort under the weekly *Play for Today* banner, with Morell cast as a cantankerous and bitter old man crippled by arthritis and unable to come to terms with the burden it places on his family. The play also starred Marius Goring whom Morell first worked with on the London stage in 1936. The small screen continued to recognize his star appeal with the role of George Joyce in the BBC's adaptation of Somerset Maugham's *The Letter*, and then as a beleaguered aristocrat confronted by the title character in *Hell's Angel*, in which Michael Kitten and Angharad Rees also appeared.

Then there was *Spyder's Web*, a sort of poor man's version of *The Avengers*, dealing with supernatural subjects but keeping the same quirky tone. Morell guest starred in one of the more intriguing segments, "The Executioners", as

Morell as Judge Lewis in *10 Rillington Place*

crusty aristocrat Lord Rushmore, who presides over a modern-day version of the Hellfire Club. Directed by Roy Ward Baker, it also featured Veronica Carlson. It seemed whenever television producers needed an authority figure they would send for Morell, who popped up as the 19th century Prime Minster Lord Palmerston in the celebrated miniseries *Edward the King*, and donned a doublet and ruffle opposite Tim Curry's randy Bard in *The Life of Shakespeare*.

On the big screen Morell was in a more somber mood for Richard Fleisher's gloomy retelling of the life and death of English serial killer John Christie, *10 Rillington Place*. Richard Attenborough gave an uncharacteristically subtle performance as the dome-headed strangler Christie whose heartless slaughter of a young woman and her child led directly to the wrongful execution of her simple-minded husband, Timothy Evans (John Hurt). Christie's crimes were later proved to extend to the murder and rape of a number of women over a period of time, with their rotting cadavers hidden under the floorboards and behind the walls of his terraced house in Rillington Place. To add a chilling realism, Fleisher shot the film partly at the site of the murders but Morell was probably relieved to have all his scenes staged at Shepperton Studios where a recreation of the imposing Old Bailey courtroom was constructed. Morell played Judge Lewis, who presided over the trial of Evans for the alleged murder of his wife (Judy Geeson). Also appearing in the courtroom scenes was Robert Hardy as the defense barrister. Bedecked in luxurious red robes and wig, Morell cuts an imposing figure, particularly when he dons the black cap to pronounce Evans' death sentence. Fleisher's sober reconstructions make *10 Rillington Place* a difficult film to like but an absorbing one to watch. The acting is of a high standard though the power of the courtroom sequences can't compete with the growing horror of Christie's crimes

In 1972 Morell had his last brush with the fantasy genre when he appeared as a decidedly creepy Victorian doctor in the short film *The Man and the Snake*. John Fraser plays the very proper school teacher invited to spend the evening with Dr. Druring and his family, learning, much to his dismay, of his host's penchant for poisonous snakes, some of which are prone to escape from the cages from time to time. Based on a story by Ambrose Bierce and directed by Sture Rydman, *The Man and the Snake* runs a mere 26 minutes and thus enjoyed only a limited shelf life. It did, however, attract the attention of critical publications, including *Films and Filming*, which described "an atmospheric period piece, an immaculate exercise in turning the screw of suspense."

Morell continued to play cameos in ambitious movies, including *Pope Joan*, *The Message* and *The Slipper and the Rose*, none of which could be considered successful in box-office terms. He also made an appearance in one film, which, although a disappointment at the cash registers, merits more than a footnote in cinema history. The film was *Barry Lyndon* directed by Stanley Kubrick from *The Luck of Barry Lyndon* by William Makepeace Thackeray. Ryan O'Neill plays the title role, a scoundrel who lies and manipulates his way from humble roots in Ireland through the British army to the very top of society.

What could, and perhaps should, have been a bawdy romp, becomes in Kubrick's hands a downbeat and tedious trudge through the social, sexual and political life of the 18th Century, albeit stunningly recreated and beautifully photographed (an Oscar for John Alcott). The movie is neatly divided into two halves plotting Lyndon's rise to fame and fortune and then his slow—very slow—decline. Morell is prominent amongst a veritable army of British supporting players including Patrick Magee, Leonard Rossiter, Anthony Sharp and

Ryan O'Neal, Marisa Berenson and Morell in *Barry Lyndon*

Steven Berkoff. Morell doesn't appear until well into the film's three-hour running time and his arrival is heralded by the question, "Do you happen to know Gustavus Adolphus, the 13th Earl of Wendover?" The very name of the character may be an in-joke by Kubrick: Gustavas Adolphus, the name of a famous Swedish King from the 16th Century, is mentioned only once. Assured that the Earl is on intimate terms with the King of England and is therefore in a position to assist in social advancement, Lyndon makes sure he seeks out the older man's company. Morell's Wendover comes complete with pancake makeup and elaborate wig and, sherry in hand, assures Lyndon that he will smooth his elevation to the peerage. In the montage of scenes that follows, Wendover eases Lyndon into the top echelons of society and secures an introduction to the King, but his efforts result in the frittering away of Lyndon's considerable fortune. Wendover is also on hand to witness Lyndon's humiliation when he brutally beats his stepson, a violent over-reaction which leads to the Irishman's social exile. Morell is last seen politely declining an invitation to dine with the outcast.

It was an interesting cameo appearance for the actor, one allowing him an unexpected influence on his celebrated director. Relaxing between set-ups, Morell told Kubrick a story of how he had been shopping in the local supermarket—with Jason in tow—and had been accosted by a complete stranger who had demanded to know if "Andre Morell was dead or alive?" Temporarily lost for words, the actor could only stumble out "why, he's dead." The stranger then responded, "that's what I have heard" and left content with this information. Kubrick liked the story so much he had Morell, in character as the stuffy Wendover, retell the same anecdote—a rare moment of humor in an otherwise cold movie. *Barry Lyndon* wasn't popular with critics at the time of its release and, while most appreciated its artistry, it was deemed overly long and ponderous. The film has enjoyed something of a re-evaluation in recent years but it remains one of Kubrick's least accessible projects.

In 1978 Morell lent his considerable vocal talents to the animated feature *Lord of the Rings*, Ralph Bakshi's multi-award winning version of Tolkien's classic work. Bakshi became something of a cult figure after his outrageous adult cartoon *Fritz the Cat* in 1972 and was only one of a number of filmmakers struggling to bring Tolkien's supposedly "un-filmable" book to the screen. Despite the title, Bakshi's work accounts for little more than half of Tolkien's epic, though he makes a fairly decent stab at the story even if some of the animation is a little too amateurish. He assembled an impressive list of vocal talents including John Hurt as Aragon and Anthony Daniels as Legolas. Peter Woodthrope, an actor known almost exclusively for Professor Zoltan in *The Evil of Frankenstein*, renders an excellent Gollum. Morell voices the elf Elrond, the role later played by Hugo Weaving in the Peter Jackson version, which has now sadly eclipsed this rather charming if uneven effort.

Morell voiced Elrond in *Lord of the Rings*, 1978

When Morell wasn't working, he devoted his time to the British arm of Equity, the actor's union, and served as president for two years, following four years as vice president. This was a far from ceremonial position and he spent exhausting hours serving on committees, ruling on decisions and debating policies on behalf of the union. While he could not have been considered a political man—in Jason's view he may have been a socialist in his earlier years but mellowed as he aged—Morell took his role in Equity very seriously. Jason remembered one particular occasion:

> I said to him that the 1920s seemed such a marvelous time, he told me about the hunger and queues of men looking for work, he remembered all of that misery and I think it affected him. In the 1960s the trade unions seemed to take over and he was terrified that Equity would be taken over by Trotskyites and that actors would suffer a backlash. He worked endlessly against that.

Then of course there was his family. Morell was devoted to Joan and his son and wasn't slow to show his lighter side. Jason remembered, "My mother always said he made her laugh so much, she would cry. He was very deadpan and had a great sense of the absurd; he could be very funny." The one subject that Morell did not think suitable for amusement was his acting, as Jason witnessed:

> I remember we were watching *Flesh and Blood* where my father had a dodgy accent and the makeup was dreadful. My mother and I teased him about the film and he took it very badly. I think he didn't speak to me for a week after that; he could be very sensitive about his work.

Joan was still working, and her career started to pick up as she aged into character parts, but Morell took his role of provider for his family very seriously. He had lost money in the stock exchange crash in the 1970s and with a teenage son to care for this worried him a lot. He continued working past the age of retirement partly to ensure that Jason and Joan were provided for. David Lean, Jason's godfather, knew how much Morell worried about his son and, honoring his role as godfather, was generous in his support. The two friends had parted company some years earlier over some minor disagreement that neither of them cared to discuss. Jason thought it may have been a word spoken out of turn or a misplaced comment and certainly Morell had been less than enthusiastic about *Doctor Zhivago*. Lean, who was bordering on the paranoid when it came to criticism, may have reacted badly to any negative opinion from a close friend. The two men weren't on speaking terms by the time *Ryan's Daughter* was released to a critical mauling and Lean, convinced he could never make another movie, became something of a gypsy, wandering from one far-flung location to another. By the mid-70s Lean was back at work, wrestling his weighty *Mutiny on the Bounty* project, and the deep mutual respect and friendship between the two men was rekindled. Morell, Joan and Jason were invited to spend four weeks sailing the South Pacific in Lean's yacht as the director chattered happily about his newly rediscovered love of cinema. It was during this sojourn that Lean persuaded Morell, the lifelong smoker, to finally kick his 60-per-day habit. Neither of them knew that it was already too late.

Morell appeared in what would be his last screen role, a judge in the Sean Connery-Donald Sutherland romp *The Great Train Robbery*. It is a fun film, and Morell, despite looking old and frail, still commanded respect in a brief cameo.

He then appeared in an episode of the afternoon soap drama *Crown Court* but he was concerned about his voice, feeling it had lost some of its tone and pitch. In September 1978 he checked into a hospital for what he thought was a few days to clear up a bout of emphysema in time for a family holiday later that month. The doctors drained his lungs but the positive benefits were so short-lived they were compelled to drain them again. This treatment continued at regular intervals until November. By then the X-rays

The Plague of the Zombies

had confirmed that he would never leave the hospital. Joan made the decision not to tell her husband but as he weakened almost daily it is unlikely he really believed in the long promised family break. On November 28, 1978, André Morell passed away at age 69.

Amongst the many obituaries was one from Equity Secretary Peter Plouviez who seemed to sum up everyone's view of the actor:

> An utterly dedicated member of the profession who fought untiringly for the interests of his fellow members. He was deeply respected by those who knew him well…and his death represents a great loss both to the profession and to Equity.

A memorial service was held at St Paul's in London's Covent Garden, the Actor's Church, where a plaque was unveiled in his memory. Morell, who wasn't religious, was cremated at his own request.

Joan Greenwood survived her husband by nine years and continued working on television and films right up until her death; one of her last screen roles was in the Peter Cook-Dudley Moore send-up of *The Hound of the Baskervilles*. She died of a heart attack in her London home on February 27, 1987, at age 66.

Ándre Morell's rich legacy as a screen actor hasn't been entirely lost; in 2006 *The Hound of the Baskervilles* opened a film festival in London's West End, while later the same year *The Plague of the Zombies* played to a paying audience for the first time in decades, in an actual Cornish tin mine! In August 2007 the prestigious National Film Theatre in London honored the actor's centenary with screenings of *Cash on Demand* and *The Camp on Blood Island*. But there is no doubt that the range and power that so impressed theater audiences and critics was never fully exploited by cinema, and Morell's best work has now

been lost. The intriguing playbills, occasional anecdote and yellowing press cuttings are all that remain of a remarkable theatrical career. The actor's charm, good humor and amazing range were luckily captured on television, although sadly many of the tapes have been lost or destroyed. Recent broadcasts of *1984* and *Quatermass and the Pit* on the BBC have proved that those shows have lost none of their power to fascinate and shock, and they offer a rare glimpse at Morell the actor and the man.

Jason Morell, only 15 at the time of his father's death, has gone on to carve a career for himself as an actor, predominately on the stage but also in films such as *Mrs. Brown* and *Wilde*. When asked which role he thought was closest to the man he knew at home, Jason said without hesitation:

> Quatermass—that is where I recognize my father most. He was a very loving father; he absolutely doted on my mother but he had a temper...was an angry man and sometimes— not often— this side of him showed. In *Quatermass and the Pit*, when you see the rage in him boiling up and he is trying to control himself, he knows he is about to lose his temper and is desperately trying to hold it in, that's what I remember. And his explosive good humor, the intelligence, his passion and anger—it's all there in Quatermass.

Dennis Price: The Naked Truth

In a film career that lasted three decades Dennis Price made over 90 films, in the majority of which he was the star or at least had star billing. His rise to fame was meteoritic and at his peak, between 1946 and 1949, Price was one of the most popular and highly paid stars in Britain. By the early 1950s his career was in tatters and he faced financial ruin, divorce and a much-publicized suicide attempt. Instead of breaking his spirit, these "bad times," as he called them, provided the impetus to revive his fortunes and although he never regained his former status, Price worked constantly for the rest of his life. Even in the 1960s, when his brand of smooth villainy and cynical humor was well and truly out of fashion, Price found gainful employment in cameo appearances or propping up low budget films. He spent the last decade of his life almost exclusively in horror and fantasy movies in which he worked for some of the genre's most influential figures including Terrence Fisher, Jimmy Sangster, Jess Franco and Michael Armstrong. Sadly three decades after his death mainstream cinema considers Price to be one of its footnotes and even his signature role, as the scheming murderer in the classic *Kind Hearts and Coronets,* is frequently overlooked in favor of Alec Guinness' vaudeville turn(s) as the doomed d'Ascoynes.

As far as the fantasy genre is concerned Price could hardly be regarded as one of its leading lights, and films like *The Earth Dies Screaming*, *Count Downe* and *Dracula vs. Frankenstein* would get featured in many critics' top 10. Nevertheless the actor always rose above low production values and bad scripts to make even the most fleeting of appearances worth catching. Dennis Price was a complex and sensitive man and he faced many personal demons with dry humor and indefatigable charm. All of his films are better for his involvement, and his contribution to cinema is long overdue for recognition.

If family tradition is anything to go by, Dennis Price should have ended up in the higher echelons of the British army rather than treading the boards as an actor. The second of three children, Denistoun Franklyn John Rose-Price was born into luxury at the family home in Twyford, Berkshire, in 1915. His father was the celebrated soldier Brigadier-General Thomas Caradoc Rose-Price, and his mother, Dorothy Patience, was the daughter of Sir Henry Verey, a referee—a form of judge advocate—at the Supreme Court of Judicature. With a paternal grandfather in the army it was naturally assumed that all the sons of the Brigadier-General would follow in the family footsteps and while his brothers served in the army and air force, it was clear by his teenage years that young Dennis was not cut out for a career in the services. He may have been born into a world of fox hunting, horse riding and shooting weekends in the country but, by the time he enrolled at Worcester College, Oxford, it was obvious he was cut from a different cloth. By then he was studying French

and Latin, a clear sign that the sensitive youth was being groomed for a career in the Church or the Law.

Unfortunately Price wasn't exactly a model student; he was easily distracted and developed a taste for socializing on a scale that his modest allowance would never support. "You see," he confessed to *The Leader* magazine a decade later, "I wasn't any good at my books." Price, or Rose-Price as he then was called, cut a popular figure amongst the students and, generous to the point of extravagance, he was at the center of a social circle that preferred drinking and carousing to studying. Of course his grades suffered and his sojourn at Oxford came to an ignoble end in 1936 when he was "sent down," a polite term for expelled, which effectively ruled out any immediate prospects in the more socially acceptable career options. If his father the General had discussed the prospect of a commission in His Majesty's armed forces then the conversation is lost in the mists of time; but Price, despite having no formal qualifications, remained sanguine about his future—a confidence buoyed by the support of his affluent family. The youngster had already made enquiries about a possible job which he hoped would keep him gainfully employed for the foreseeable future and allow him to put off making any serious career decisions for a few years. There had been one area of university life that had appealed to him: the Oxford University Dramatic Society (OUDS), which not only satisfied his inclination to show off but garnered him awards for both acting and elocution. More importantly he felt far more at home with aesthetic temperaments than he had in the more physical pursuits of his home life.

Although he was not yet 21 years old, Price made up in self confidence what he lacked in formal acting training. He would later enroll at the Embassy Theatre School to refine his craft but even before he formally left Oxford, he was looking for a way to shorten the prolonged learning process. In March 1936 he wrote a letter of introduction to Val Gielgud, elder brother of John, and one of the great pioneers of radio drama in Britain. Val was Head of Drama at the BBC and, having studied journalism at Oxford, retained strong connections with the university. Price wasn't slow to turn this to his advantage and no one could accuse the handwritten letter, which still exits in the BBC's archives, of being demure:

> Dear Mr. Gielgud
>
> Please forgive me writing to you like this, completely from the blue, my only justification being the encouragement of a mutual friend, Charles Finch, now at Radley. I also believe Eric Gillett is not unknown to you. Both would "furnish testimonials."
>
> I leave Oxford in June and want so much to become involved as quickly as possible in some dramatic sphere. Is there I wonder, any opening within your control for which one might begin to compete? For such an opportunity you have, no doubt, handfuls of requests in every post. My only qualifications are entirely amateur; a considerable amount of acting and speaking; Gillett and Finch, would, perhaps, enlarge on these more shrewdly than I can.

> If it were possible to become an active member of a repertory company I'd most gratefully snatch at the offer, and I wondered if you would advise which of the many companies might consider yet another applicant with interest.
>
> It would be very kind indeed of you to consider any of this.
>
> Yours
> D Rose-Price.

Gielgud certainly had it in his power to employ Price but chose instead to offer a diplomatic response:

> I'm afraid I don't know quite how to advise you for the best. Conditions of employment in the world of theatre are at the moment such as to weight the dice heavily against a newcomer with only amateur qualifications, and though I would gladly give you the opportunity of a microphone test here, it would be foolish not to warn you that acting in broadcast plays cannot at present be considered a whole time career. I am, unfortunately not in particular close touch with any of the repertory companies though I would certainly agree with you that membership of one of these would be the best introduction to a dramatic career that under modern conditions you could obtain. It might be worth writing to Mr. William Armstrong at Liverpool or Mr. Stanford Holme at Oxford to see if by any chance either of them would be prepared to consider you for a vacancy. More than that for the moment I'm afraid I cannot say to you.

Price refused to take no as an answer and, relying heavily on a parental subsidiary, he moved to London determined to break into his chosen profession. In April the following year he wrote again to the BBC asking for an audition and was informed that "owing to the very large number of artists already on our books it has been necessary to suspend further drama auditions." The nameless clerk went on to suggest that Price reapply in "about six months" time but, on June 4, 1937, his dogged pestering finally paid off and he reported to the BBC for a production of *Crisis in Spain*, a staff training disc never intended for broadcast. For the short engagement, Price was awarded the princely sum of 3 guineas (around $12) for the two days rehearsal and production time.

Though there is no record of it, Val may well have passed Price's name on to John Gielgud, already established as one of the best known and most respected actor-managers in the country. John also had strong connections with Oxford; he made his directorial debut with a successful production of *Romeo and Juliet* for OUDS in 1932, so it is possible that Price evoked this memory when he auditioned to join Gielgud's company. Gielgud had a reputation for helping the waifs and strays of the acting profession and may have felt sorry for the willowy youngster so desperate to work. With practically no professional acting experience, Price joined Gielgud for the 1937-38 season at London's Queen's Theatre and was featured fleetingly in the dual roles of Green and "servant to Exon" in the Shakespeare's *Richard II*. Also in the cast were Michael Redgrave, Alec Guinness and Peggy Ashcroft.

Predictably Price's lifestyle at this time certainly didn't reflect his status as a struggling actor and the recurring pattern of his life was clearly established. He would never have enough money, but the lack of it would never affect his extravagances. His correspondence with the BBC continued during the run with Gielgud and well into 1938 as Price pestered the Corporation unsuccessfully for work. At one point he became so desperate that he considered taking a radio announcer job in Manchester. By the early summer of 1938 he had undertaken Val Gielgud's promised voice tests but the BBC's chief instructor, E.A.F. Harding, was underwhelmed and his handwritten notes record:

> Quite a good medium baritone/essentially modern part actor/ quite good juvenile lead/not very good verse speaker/can act a bit but not perhaps very flexible—has possibilities in good productions/hard worker, agreeable and pleasant/not a character actor.

Many years later Price recalled that fellow actor Nicholas Hannen had said, "Acting's a starving job, my boy. If you're lucky, you may jump over some of the others to fame and fortune; never imagine you are there for long." But if Hannen had intended to council Price against a career as an actor, it fell on deaf ears: Price signed on with a repertory company in Croydon, then a leafy suburb of London, and won some good notices in *I Killed the Count*. A prompt return to the West End was cut short when *A Party for Christmas* at the prestigious Haymarket failed to make it to the festive season and closed in November, leaving Price out of work over Christmas.

The following February he finally made his breakthrough with the BBC and appeared in one of their early television productions, *The Tempest*, followed a month later by *Rope*, earning all of 12 guineas ($50). Price followed this modest success with further appearances in the BBC productions of *Julius Caesar* and *Lady Precious Stream*, and by the summer of 1939 he could with some justification describe himself as a "promising leading man"—certainly promising enough to put down some permanent roots.

While at Croydon, Price had fallen for the striking blonde actress Joan Schofield who, as well as having a love of the stage, also shared a military heritage: Her father was Major-General Arthur Cecil Temperley of Beaconfield. After a whirlwind romance the couple got engaged and then married in July 1939 at St. Paul's Church in Knightsbridge. The family indulged the newlyweds with a honeymoon and, as war clouds gathered over Europe in the summer of 1939, the Prices went on holiday in the shadow of Mont Blanc in the French Alps.

By the time the couple returned to London the prospect of war was stifling the theatre scene and, despite moving to a new address in London's fashionable Sloane Square, Price had no offers of work. He reluctantly accepted a short run outside of the capital at the Oxford Playhouse where his success was overshadowed by world events: On September 3, 1939, Britain declared war on Hitler's Germany. For a time, nothing changed and Price managed to land an important role in *String Quartet*, one of the few new productions scheduled for the West End. Soon enough the realities of war set in and, as London braced itself for the inevitable air raids, the BBC's television drama department was closed down and theatres were boarded up. *String Quartet* was cancelled and Price was again out of work with no immediate prospects. Inevitably he was called on to do his patriotic duty, and in March 1940 he answered the call to arms. Curiously, given his background and the influence wielded by both his father and his father-in-law, Price chose not to serve as an officer. Instead 1552227 Gunner Price DJR reported for duty at the Royal Artillery battery in the provincial town of Sevenoaks, just south of London. Price's role in facing down the Nazi threat was unconventional, to say the least, as Alec Guinness would later relate:

> I ran into Dennis Price, who was a casual friend from the time we had been together in one of Gielgud's productions. "You should join us at Sevenoaks," Dennis said encouragingly. "It's an anti-aircraft battery and there is simply nothing to do. Major Cazalet is a dear, and there are lots of chums, Johnnie and Jack and Hughie and Sebastian among others. (I won't recall, now, who all these Christian names represented.) You can swing as much leave as you want, all you have to say is you have a dinner engagement at the Savoy which you simply can't get out of. I think we should sit out the war very comfortably. Do join us. I'll have a word with Cazzers." Dennis looked very smart in his khaki; a sharp crease to his trousers, shiny boots and a rakish tilt to his cap.

Guinness went on to record with some regret that he was unable to join Price:

Not long after this there were questions in the House of Commons about the Sevenoaks battery; the whole thing was broken up; and Jack and Johnnie and Dennis and Hugh and co. were dispersed to different and less pleasant duties.

In later years studio publicists liked to imply that Price was something of a war hero, but in reality his military career came to an abrupt end in May 1941 when he was released on six months sick leave and then medically discharged. The suggestion has always been that this was stress related rather than a physical injury and, despite his outward *bonhomie,* Price must have suffered at yet another failure to live up to family expectations. This situation was all the harder too bear because his brother, Flying Officer Arthur Thomas Rose-Price, had been killed in a dogfight over the English coast in 1940. Price's older brother, Robert, was in the Welsh Guards and would serve with distinction in North Africa and Italy, eventually attaining the rank of Lieutenant Colonel. Price's own contribution to the war effort was now limited to the BBC radio's World Service, in particular the famous "London Calling" broadcasts. The actor would play military men many times in his career but he never talked about his own service.

Apart from radio, Price was slow to find his way back into regular work. By then the British economy was on a war footing, with most of the film studios taken over by the Ministry of War and used as bases or supply depots. Many theatres had also been requisitioned or closed in the face of the inevitable shortages and those that stayed open had to struggle through the nightly air raids. The noted playwright and songwriter Noel Coward was one of the few who decided to carry on regardless, and in 1943 signed Price to a 33-date morale boosting tour of the English provinces. Price played several small parts in the company's productions of *Blithe Spirit, This Happy Breed* and *Present Laughter* but more importantly he was given the task of understudying Coward. When the tour moved to the Duchess Theatre in London, Price was handed the opportunity of a lifetime, as he later related in a press interview:

> When Noel fell ill one day— not very seriously, so there was no need to say I was sorry and quite honestly I wasn't. It was my chance. I took Noel's part. If Noel hadn't caught that cold, I don't suppose I'd have ever got the chance of doing those parts in the West End.

The whistlestop tour proved an ideal training ground. Price claimed, "I learned more from that tour than I ever hope to learn from anyone." Certainly his growing maturity was attracting the attention of casting directors. Price was seen by Michael Powell, the highly idiosyncratic director, when he appeared in

Dennis Price and wife Joan Schofield relax at home.

Springtime of Others at the London Arts Theatre, Powell and his partner Emeric Pressburger had just completed the lavish Technicolor war film *Colonel Blimp* and, at the time, were considered the most creative and daring filmmakers in England. Their films reflected a unique perspective and sense of humor, and the partnership had produced a series of successful and celebrated films such as *49th Parallel* and *One of Our Aircraft is Missing*. Powell was about to start on a more modest and personal film, which retained a wartime setting but had none of nationalistic fervor of its contemporaries, and he was looking for a fresh young actor to play his leading man

A Canterbury Tale is set in Powell's home county of Kent and reflects the misty-eyed memories the filmmaker retained of his formative years. The film presents three friends on a journey of sorts to Canterbury when they encounter a mystery in a small village. Price plays Sergeant Peter Gibbs who, with Alison (Shelia Sim) and a G.I. (Bob Johnson), sets out to capture a nocturnal prankster who has taken to pouring glue into the hair of local girls. Eric Portman plays the solemn Thomas Colpeper, a local historian, who may or may not have something to hide. The storyline is slight but held together by Powell's sly humor and stunning visual sense, the superb black and white cinematography and a darkly ambivalent performance by Portman, the only familiar name in

the cast. To the modern viewer *A Canterbury Tale* is one of those British films where everybody is either a yokel with an impenetrable accent or talks with a plum in his mouth. Shelia Sim is supposedly a London shop girl but sounds like she stepped straight out of the Royal Academy's speech classes. Price, who is a mere sergeant, sounds like…well, the Oxford educated son of a Brigadier General. Portman aside, the acting is variable, with Price radiating youthful enthusiasm without really making anything of the character, and there is little in the way of on-screen chemistry with Sim. The fan magazine *Picturegoer* didn't agree and christened him one of its "Three men to watch" (the other two were Vincent Price and Dane Clark):

> Dennis is well built, over six feet in height, has brown hair and grey eyes. He combines that with a striking individuality and acting ability.

Irrespective of Price's personal qualities, Powell's visual love poem wasn't a success. The film is simply too idealized and lyrical to attract a mainstream audience in no mood for a gentle romance and lighthearted mystery. But the exposure worked well for Price and he caught the eye of Maurice Ostrer at Gainsborough Pictures, a wholly owned subsidiary of the Rank Organization but operating more or less autonomously from a central London base at Shepherds Bush. (The company also had a smaller studio in London, at Islington, which consists of the two soundstages where the young Alfred Hitchcock learned his trade)

The film mogul J. Arthur Rank had acquired Gainsborough in 1937 with no clear idea of what to do with this company originally founded by Michael Balcon. At the time British films were thought of as either ponderous but worthy, or cheapjack thrillers thrown out to meet quota regulations (an early attempt by the government to protect the industry by regulating the number of British films exhibited—the "quota quickies"). Ostrer offered the public something different: a world of costume melodrama with tousle-haired and brooding men, and smoldering, full-figured heroines. Drawing predominately from female authors, Gainsborough traded on larger than life characters and unabashed sexuality in titles like *The Man in Grey* and *Man of Evil,* which electrified audiences and mortified the critics. Much like the later Hammer Horrors, Gainsborough fashioned a highly stylized product supported by their own repertory company of actors and regular technicians. Indeed many of Gainsborough's better known crew, including Terence Fisher, Les Bowie and Jack Asher—would later turn up at Hammer. James Mason was the studio's biggest star with his cultured voice and contemptuous attitude—on and off the screen; while a toned and handsome Stewart Grainger set pulses racing with an action image modeled closely on Errol Flynn. And there was a clutch of female stars including Jean Kent, Patricia Roc and, most famously, the "wicked" Margaret Lockwood. Dennis Price would soon join Gainsborough's illustrious list.

Price was actually on stage toiling through *Scandal in Barchester* when Ostrer's offer of a long-term contract came through; as always money was tight so it wasn't a difficult decision to make. The first film was an adaptation of Osbert Sitwell's sedate ghost story *A Place of One's Own*, a rare attempt by the British to make a supernatural thriller. James Mason, playing against type, was top-billed as the elderly Smedhurst who buys Bellingham House hoping for a long and restful retirement. It is only after he moves his servants in—Gainsborough characters always had servants—that he discovers the unwanted "presence" of an invalid girl, seemingly murdered there 40 years before. Mason, laboring under some spectacularly unconvincing makeup, gruffly dismisses any suggestion of supernatural phenomena but things change when Annette (Margaret Lockwood), a young friend of the family, arrives. The wan and impressionable teenager proves too susceptible to Bellingham's melancholy and is soon hearing voices and swooning. Enter Price as the skeptical Dr. Selbie who immediately falls in love with the rapidly fading Annette but is at a loss to diagnose the problem. Just as everything seems lost, Annette, in a trance, insists they call the previous family's physician, Dr. Marsham (a dessicated Ernest Thesiger) who arrives in the nick of time and saves the day. The twist in the tail, such as it is, was transmitted to the audience long before the "surprise" ending.

Scripted by Brock Williams, a prolific but journeyman writer, the film marked the directorial debut of Bernard Knowles who had photographed some of the classics of the British cinema including Hitchcock's *The 39 Steps* and *Jamaica Inn.* Knowles and director of photographer Stephan Dade, who would later shoot Hammer's *The Viking Queen*, contrived to make the black and white film look beautiful and turn Bellingham into a genuinely creepy and foreboding place. Unfortunately the narrative plods along at a snail's pace and the actors struggle with superficial characterizations. James Mason is dire, and Lockwood, at 34, was clearly too old and worldly to play a vulnerable and virginal Annette. The fresh-faced Price makes an acceptable if colorless leading man and it is left

Anne Crawford and Dennis Price in *Caravan*

to the veteran Thesiger (best known for *Bride of Frankenstein*) who, at a mere 66 and looking twice that, effortlessly steals the show. The sedate pace seemed to suit the critics but the box-office reception was poor. The female audience, who had panted when James Mason took a riding crop to Lockwood in *The Man in Grey,* couldn't help but be disappointed by the vision of their hero as a little old man and stayed away in droves.

Despite this inauspicious start, Price loved in the idea of being a film star and the financial security his contract brought. Soon after shooting his Gainsborough debut he was confident enough to walk out on John Gielgud's production of *Lady Windermere's Fan* after one week of rehearsals, saying he couldn't tolerate his old benefactor's rehearsal technique. Price, brought in as a last minute substitute for Rex Harrison, had acquired a new-found aversion to prolonged rehearsals, a characteristic that would stay with him throughout his career. Gielgud's reaction isn't known but Price wasn't too concerned; by then Gainsborough had lined up a second starring role.

Caravan stars Stewart Grainger, all toothy grins and rippling muscles, as a 19th century adventurer complete with lacquered hair and razor-sharp sideburns. This was the Gainsborough audiences wanted, with Price playing Sir Francis Castleton, a pantomime villain Basil Rathbone would relish. It is a harmless piece of escapism from Arthur Crabtree, who later would direct the cult classic *Fiend without a Face*, showing no restraint and allowing his cast to play it to the hilt. Price got to camp it up mercilessly, leering after Jean Kent's hapless heroine and plotting his improbably wicked schemes. The fun and enthusiasm was transmitted to the audience, providing Price with his first genuine hit.

In 1946 his burgeoning career received an indirect boost from no less a figure than J. Arthur Rank, the man who *was* the British film industry. Having made a personal fortune in the flour business, Rank, a devout Methodist, first dabbled in cinema to promote Christian ethics, but this led to a rapid induction into the chaotic workings of the 1930s film business. Fascinated by the possibilities and fired by a genuine sense of patriotic duty, Rank started to assemble what became, through a series of mergers and buyouts, the Rank Organization. Described by one rival as "dull and bumbling"—a view that seems to have been shared by anyone who worked for him—Rank was the unlikeliest of moguls, but he had the common sense to leave the artistry to others and apply sound business practices to his growing film empire. In a little over a decade Rank built the only production company outside of the U.S. which could compete with Hollywood on its own terms. Rank provided an artistic haven for such diverse talents as David Lean, Michael Powell and Ronald Neame; at the same time the company owned outright five film studios, including Pinewood, the most modern in Europe, and employed 31,000 people in production, and post-production. On the distribution side, quite apart from its extensive overseas sales arms, the Rank Organization owned 650 cinemas in the UK and could boast an annual turnover in excess of $180 million.

The organization's pious chief had no time for Gainsborough's "bodice rippers"; they offended his moral sensibilities—Lady Rank allegedly walked out of a screening of *The Wicked Lady*—and he felt they did not reach his quality standards. During the war years Maurice Ostrer's success at the box office assured his independence, but in 1946 the seemingly insatiable demand for new films created new pressures. Having identified success in the North American market as his number-one priority, Rank was preparing to match Hollywood with a series of lavish big-budget entertainments. He wasn't exactly putting all his financial eggs in one basket but he was taking a tremendous risk: At a time when the average gross of a successful film in Britain was about $800,000, the musical *London Town* cost a staggering $4 million. Even this was exceeded by *Caesar and Cleopatra*, which cost over $5 million—$1 million more than *Gone with the Wind*! These flagship productions weren't for Gainsborough of course; they would be made elsewhere in the group while Ostrer's stable of actors and filmmakers was expected to provide cheap and quickly made films to keep the cinema circuits full. Ostrer, disgusted at the interference, resigned in protest and was replaced almost immediately by Sidney Box, producer of the sleeper hit *The Seventh Veil*.

To offset his boss's huge investment, Box was instructed to deliver between 15 and 20 new features a year, mixing contemporary thrillers with historical dramas and comedies. In sharp contrast to the "prestige" projects, Box had to content himself with budgets of $400,000 to $600,000. Despite this financial constraint and the obvious difficulties of filming in a country that was still subject to rationing and political interference, Box managed to deliver nine new films in 1947, increasing to 11 in 1948 and, by the time the whole experiment came to an end in 1950, Box had overseen the production of a creditable 44 productions. This was the highpoint of Dennis Price's film career; riding the wave he made 10 movies for Gainsborough between *A Place of One's Own* in 1946 and his last in 1949. (This figure doesn't include several productions for other companies in the Rank stable.) Both actor and studio seemed blissfully unaware of the dangers of overexposure; between the months of March and June 1948 the Rank's Odeon circuit in England hosted no fewer than four new Price movies: *Easy Money*, *Chorus Girl*, *Snowbound* and *Good Time Girl*—not including re-releases and earlier films already in release!

Price was considered the epitome of a British film star. Dirk Bogarde, who later emerged as Britain's biggest box-office star, remembered an early meeting with a Rank casting director:

> He threw a scatter of photographs across the partner's desk. "We're looking for people like that!" he said proudly, indicating Stewart Grainger, James Mason, Dennis Price and a sundry collection of retouched, lip-sticked, hair-creamed gods.

Gainsborough's publicity materials reinforce this image of Price as a matinee idol, describing him as a "tall, dark young man with quiet gray eyes, crinkly hair and a fine speaking voice." The studio publicist also mentions Price's sincerity as an actor:

This quality is typical of Dennis Price the man. To see him on the screen is to know him in real life; he is at all times a genuine person, unaffected by screen stardom, quiet-voiced and with a tremendous reserve of feeling behind his apparent calm. Intelligent without being pretentious, taking his work seriously without taking himself too seriously.

The British newspapers delighted their readers with the snippet that a bulging post bag delivered to the studio each day contained more "fan mail for Mr. Price than was being received in Hollywood by stars like Humphrey Bogart and Cary Cooper!" Price knew his worth. With a contract guaranteeing him an income of $100,000, he was one of the highest paid and most popular actors in the country and his lifestyle reflected his status; no sooner were the checks banked than the money was spent, and he ate at the best restaurants and played the tables in the best clubs.

Inevitably this increase in the studio's productivity meant a decrease in quality and, although Box and his producers, including wife Muriel and his sister Betty, made some interesting films, the decline was obvious: Pre-production was rushed, the scripts were formulaic and the casting was uninspired. Despite his success it is hard to shake the impression that Price was cast mainly because he was available rather than being right for the role. This is particularly obvious in *The Magic Bow*, a bland biography of Paganini with Price offering superfluous support to a hopelessly miscast Stewart Grainger in the lead. *The Last Unicorn* also suffers from miscasting, with Price and Margaret Lockwood creating an unappealing couple rivaling their duet in *A Place of One's Own*. Box seemed unsure whether Price was the next James Mason or Ivor Novello (Price played and sang the Novello role in the remake of *The Dancing Years* and was universally panned).

The departure of a disgruntled Mason for Hollywood in 1947 meant that Price was suddenly promoted to more complex parts and, while the sullen Mason launched a petulant attack on his former employers in particular and British films in general, Price started work on one of his more interesting roles. Conceived as a soap opera, *Holiday Camp* was the brainchild of women's magazine writer Godfrey Winn with additional material from

the playwright Ted Willis (later Lord Willis), Muriel Box, Betty Box and her husband Peter Rogers, the man behind the interminable *Carry On* series.

The premise, a number of tenuously related subplots around a central theme, had already been tested successfully by Gainsborough in their prewar effort *Bank Holiday* starring Margaret Lockwood and, initially at least, *Holiday Camp* was simply an attempt to rework a proven hit. This time the latest national obsession, the holiday camp, provided the location for a collision of unmarried lovers, teenage pregnancies and grieving widows. At the center is London bus driver Joe Hugget and his family including daughter Joan (21-year-old Hazel Court). It would have been pretty routine stuff had Muriel Box not suggested introducing a character based on the real-life sexual deviant Neville Heath whose much publicized trial and subsequent execution was scandalizing the British public. The suave and handsome Heath had been convicted of two murders, with the police convinced he was guilty of up to four more. Heath's modus operandi was to pose as a Royal Air Force officer to win the affection of impressionable young women before subjecting them to bizarre sexual rituals including bondage and mutilation. Hardly the stuff of a domestic drama but the public was fascinated and Box seized the opportunity to exploit some of the publicity.

Price, who came to the film straight from the more conventional thriller *Dear Murderer*, effectively plays a guest role as Squadron-Leader Hardwick, a bogus officer who oozes oily charm and deadly intentions. When the down to earth Joan rejects his advances, Hardwick lures the mousey Elsie (Esma Cannon) to a deserted hillside where she is throttled to death. The censors ensured that cinemagoers were suitably protected and, although the tabloids reveled over every sordid detail of Heath's crimes, his celluloid counterpart is far more restrained. Aiming for realism Box hired former documentary filmmaker Ken Annakin to direct, using actual locations in the famous Butlin's holiday camp—off-season of course, which meant a chilly December had to stand in for the English summer. To ensure that none of the cast succumbed to pneumonia, the swimming pool sequences had to be recreated in the studio using one of the largest sets built for a British film.

Adding to the documentary feel, *Holiday Camp* features a cameo by Gainsborough contractor Patricia Roc, who is seen judging a beauty contest as herself. Rank charm school starlet Diana Dors also has a walk-on. Disappointingly Annakin decided not to shoot the murder scene on location; instead, an obviously artificial hillside was created in the studio, undermining an otherwise effective sequence. Nevertheless Price's subplot remains the best thing in the film, with the actor effortlessly switching from duplicitous charm to malevolence. This is Price at his best, all the more surprising given the near constant work commitments he had at the time. Having come from the set of one film, the actor shot his scenes and then immediately went straight into filming his next. Hazel Court remembered that he showed no sign of any strain:

Price in a publicity shot for *Holiday Camp*

Dennis was delightful, an absolute joy to work with, he was so charming but a big star and I was a bit in awe of him. Later we worked together on the stage and I really got to know him well and realized that he didn't take himself or this whole star thing too seriously then. He had such a wicked sense of humor; he was always playing tricks on the cast he said Laurence Olivier taught him!

Expectations for *Holiday Camp* weren't high but the film stormed its way into the Top 10 Box-Office Earners list in Britain, recovering its costs in the first three months of release and eventually spinning off three sequels. But while Annakin was still in the cutting room, Box was under considerable pressure to produce a surefire hit. Gainsborough may have been hitting its targets for volume but Box was slipping in terms of box-office success. Out of desperation rather than design, Gainsborough announced it would start shooting *Jassy* under the direction of Bernard Knowles. It was a project that started under the previous regime, a return to full-bloodied Gainsborough Gothic crammed with gratuitous violence, plunging necklines, passionate love affairs and associated murder and mayhem. In other words, precisely the sort of overwrought melodrama Box—and Rank—despised.

When he accepted the job, Box knew he was being handed a poisoned chalice—the cupboard at Gainsborough was practically bare at least as far as suitable projects were concerned, and *Jassy* represented one of the very few projects ready to start shooting. Margaret Lockwood, having recently escaped the stigma of Gainsborough Gothics by signing a contract with Rank, was, much to her annoyance, loaned back to Box to play the title role, a tempestuous gypsy scheming her way through English society. Box hated the film almost as much as his star, but if he had to do it, he resolved to do it well, and *Jassy* was one of only two films the company ever shot in Technicolor.

The publicity department did its best to suggest a passionate collision between the stars and Price and Lockwood who, playing opposite each other for the fourth time, were invariably depicted in full embrace. Price had no more than an extended cameo as Christopher Hatton, a dissolute aristocrat more interested in gambling and debauchery than the running of his estate, who somehow finds time to come between Jassy and her true love. Hatton's much deserved demise, a suicide after incurring ruinous gambling debts, is then blamed on the calculating

Lockwood who is arrested for murder. Proving his utility value to Box, Price was a last-minute replacement for Peter Graves, and donned the age makeup to play father to Dermot Walsh for the second time. (32-year-old Price had fulfilled the same function the previous year in *Hungry Hill*). Price made a better job in character makeup than Mason and seemed attuned to the over-the-top spirit of the whole adventure, something that could not be said of Lockwood, and the film labors badly whenever Price is not on screen. Box approached *Jassy's* release and exploitation as a necessary chore but the careful aping of the previously successful formula paid dividends. While the critics were unanimously unimpressed, the public voted *Jassy* fourth place in the "Daily Mail National Film Awards" with Price, who also had *The White Unicorn* on the list, featuring in the Top 10 Most Popular Stars. However, box-office receipts were down and Box seized the opportunity to close the book on the Gothic cycle.

Price and Margaret Lockwood in *Hungry Hill*

By now a colorful death scene was considered a feature of a Dennis Price movie: *Dear Murderer* and *Good Time Girl* have him ruthlessly done in; he dies of a fever in *Hungry Hill* and *The Bad Lord Byron*; is crushed to death in *Master of Bankdam*; and, best of all, is mauled by a hog in *Caravan*. Two years and several more colorful deaths later, Price complained to *Film Parade*:

> The one thing I hate more than anything else is being described as "that actor who always gets killed or dies before the end of his films." I am not seriously objecting, but the trouble is that I've come to a sticky end in nine films and I don't like being constantly reminded of it.

The reviews for these films were generally mixed but Price always seemed to catch the eye, a situation he treated with some modesty, as he told the *Daily Express*:

> Don't thank me, thank the director. It was just a job for me to keep a roof over our heads for the wife and me. I didn't do a thing except act and talk as the director told me.

To meet Rank's targets, Box could have anything up to five films in development or production at the same time; for someone like Price, who was always in need of money and not too concerned about the size of his part, it was an environment where he could work almost continuously. He continued to jump from film to film, and *Snowbound* and *Helter Skelter* followed in quick succession. In an interview with *Contemporary Cinema* he summed up his philosophy by quoting a personal idol:

> Leslie Howard said, "Never throw a script out of the window. If you do you may be sure that someone will pick it up and never be rude to anyone on the floor unless you are certain you are right. And then don't say it!"

As a rule British films fared poorly in North America, with only one or two notable exceptions (*The Private Life of Henry VIII*, for example). As far as U.S. distributors were concerned, British stars were never accepted as marketable until they made the transition to Hollywood. Price's films, like all Gainsborough movies, were geared for domestic consumption and had limited prospects outside the UK. *Easy Money*, another of Box's multi-story compilations, features a number of individuals and their reaction to the sudden wealth offered by winning the football pools—a sort of national lottery based around soccer results. Despite being mildly entertaining, with Price (billed second) doing well opposite Greta Gynt in the third of the four episodes, the parochial subject matter and the relatively low budget destined the film for a limited audience even in its native country. Price, although considered a major star in England, remained practically unknown in the States.

While carefully balancing the needs of the front office, Box tried from time to time to push the company into something more worthy. *The Lost People* was unique in dealing with a very real social problem from a European rather than British perspective. Playwright and journalist Bridget Roland had been in Germany soon after the collapse of the Nazi regime and had seen first hand the horrors of Belsen and Buchenwald. She had also witnessed the suffering and depravation faced by the refugees streaming out of the slave factories or fleeing the march of the Soviet armies. Roland attempted to tell something of their story in the successful but harrowing play *Cockpit* which was purchased by Sidney Box and rewritten by Muriel Box as *The Lost People*. The story centers on an abandoned theatre where the human debris of war is huddled under the watchful eyes of a small unit of British soldiers, led with youthful enthusiasm by Ridley (Price). "You are very young, Captain, to play godfather to the whole of Europe," says Gerard Heinz's world-weary professor and, as the tensions begin to mount, Ridley is powerless to prevent the refugees turning on their nominal benefactors—as well as each other. Faced with paranoia and resentment bred by starvation and disease, the soldiers have little more to offer than words of comfort.

Price, back in uniform, gives a solid performance in a role intended to be symbolic of the Allied position, full of good intentions but largely impotent. He doesn't quite come to grips with Ridley's inner turmoil but certainly holds his own in a cast that includes fine performances from Richard Attenborough, Mai Zetterling and Herbert Lom. An unusually intelligent effort by Gainsborough's standards, *The Lost People* was well directed by Bernard Knowles and photographed by Jack Asher and hints at the direction Box would have taken the studio had he been given a free hand. It wasn't to be, however; respected by critics perhaps more for its subject matter than the style, the film was not popular where it counted—at least for the Rank accountants—in ticket receipts. While Box continued to battle against a regime that counted dollars above quality, his star came out firmly on the side of box-office. Price, interviewed in *The Leader* in January 1948, said:

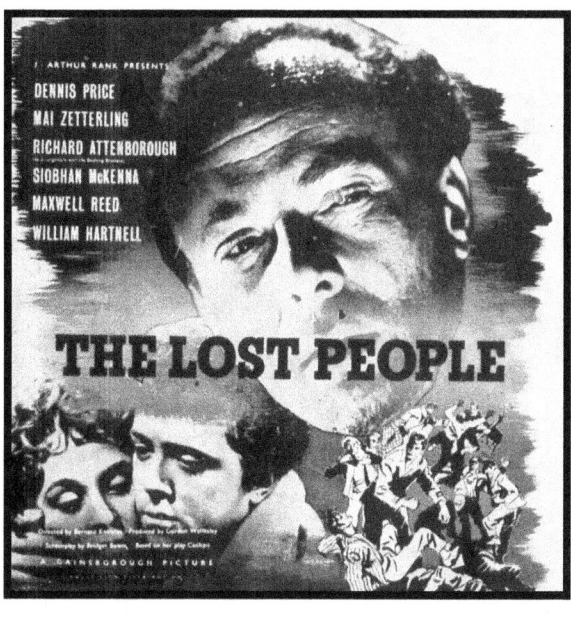

> Of course a film mustn't be bad or it will flop. But what do you mean by bad—*Caravan*? I beg your pardon-it made £400,000. Who is to be the judge of quality? In the last resort it's what comes into the till that counts.

The poor performance of films like *The Lost People*, hit Box's self confidence as well as his credibility with Rank; as far as the latter was concerned Gainsborough should continue to churn out sequels to *Holiday Camp* and little else. In an effort to prove he could increase the box office *and* improve the quality, Box committed to make two films that would be crucial to the future of the company, *The Bad Lord Bryon* and *Christopher Columbus*. Price took the title role in the former, one of the most expensive films made under Box's reign and by far the most important role of the actor's career. At the same time Price signed for Gainsborough's sister company Ealing, opposite Alec Guinness, playing in a film that was to prove a landmark in British cinema, *Kind Hearts and*

Coronets. These two films, released within weeks of each other in 1949, marked the pinnacle of his stardom and in different ways could be said to define Price's professional life.

Price hadn't been the first choice to play the role of Byron; the prodigal James Mason was ready to make his peace with the British film industry if an accommodation could be reached with the taxman. Mason had written to Box expressing interest in a new Gainsborough contract, guaranteeing him a film a year in England and freedom to work in California. Box, who got on famously with Mason during *The Seventh Veil*, was confident enough to pencil his name next to the title roles of Byron and Columbus. When Mason finally dropped out, a disappointed Box was ready to listen to suggestions that Price could step up to play what the studio's publicity described as "a man who shocked and fascinated the world." Price's agent had canvassed heavily on the actor's behalf and it was a role that Price badly wanted to play— despite the impression he gave to the *Daily Mirror* that it somehow landed in his lap:

> I shouldn't be playing the part at all. It's a role for Laurence Olivier or Eric Portman; they could make a wonderful job at it. But you know what things are like in the film business these days. Costs are being cut and all that. And you see old man, I'm cheap.

Price's intense desire to play Byron has been interpreted widely as a close identification with the character, the famously "mad, bad and dangerous to know" poet and libertine. It was true that behind the facade of a happy marriage, Price's own sexuality was in turmoil but even so he could hardly be compared to the tormented Byron whose hedonism alienated him from society. The much more prosaic answer is Price wanted to stretch himself and prove his worth against the actors like Olivier and Portman. Byron was a role far removed from any of his previous film work and would provide a platform to establish himself as an actor rather than a mere film star. Price threw himself into research, claiming he read five separate biographies of the poet, as well as visiting actual locations in both Italy and England. As production drew nearer, Price took a jaunt to Byron's ancestral home in Mansfield, posed in full costume for a series of publicity stills and warbling to the press that he had felt the presence of a "dim cloaked figure." Later, filming in Venice, he claimed he heard a voice singing in English, which could, he bizarrely deduced, only have come from Byron himself.

While Price was occupied with all this "preparation," Scottish director David MacDonald, who had directed *Snowbound* and would also take the reins for the Columbus film, was working on the script. As a measure of his commitment to the project Box allocated a budget of $800,000, modest by Rank's standards but a substantial slice of the studio's dwindling production fund. (*Christopher Columbus* would eventually come in massively over budget at $1 million). Gainsborough pulled out all the stops to ensure that their film was as accurate as possible. Muriel Box noted in her diary that "we tried to make it authentically correct in every detail...*Byron* was historical in a literal way and was extremely well documented." But it was the attention to historical fact that created problems for the censorship bodies in both Britain and the U.S. Rank insisted that all of the company's scripts be submitted to the Breen office in the U.S. for prior approval and a number of changes were demanded including the toning down of Bryon's incestuous relationship with his half-sister (Linden Travers). The British censor and the Rank accountants then had their say and, by the time a shooting script was ready, the project had five credited writers, including future James Bond director Terence Young.

To add to the confusion, Price and producer Aubrey Baring, touring Italy on a research mission, began to send their own suggestions back to MacDonald and the posse of scriptwriters in London. MacDonald was handed a muddled script that tried to accommodate all the changes and vested interests and still retain some sense of the poet's life. The film then suffered again in post-production when the British censor, seeing the actual footage, weighed in with further objections and scenes already in the can had to be scrapped and reshot. The final film bore all the scars of those rewrites and compromises; the narrative is fuzzy and unfocused, characterization is weak and the dialogue leaden. A stronger director would have torn pages out of the shooting script and tightened the narrative but MacDonald filmed what he was given, the end result being a turgid mess.

The film opens with Byron on his deathbed hallucinating that his legacy is on trial: Would history judge him as a great poet and freethinker or a misogynist and a wastrel? Witnesses from throughout Byron's life are summoned to replay via flashback their encounters with him; notable amongst the throng is Joan Greenwood as the besotted Lady Caroline Lamb. Greenwood's smoldering sexuality makes Lamb the film's only memorable character and her attempted suicide

Dennis Price and Joan Greenwood in the obscure film *The Bad Lord Byron*

provides the one really good scene. The fact that such reliable performers as Ernest Thesiger, Wilfred Hyde-White and Mai Zettering can make little of their material sets out the challenge Price faced in the title role and sadly the actor wasn't really up to it. Clearly miscast, Price fails even to hint at Bryon's inherent cruelty and after the censors had effectively emasculated him, Byron is left not so much mad and bad as petulant and slightly naughty. The actor is not helped by the overly theatrical dialogue, MacDonald's flaccid direction and limp narrative, which reduces Byron's unrestrained libido to youthful high spirits. Even the services of a very competent editor, James Needs, who cut many of Hammer's better films, couldn't impose any structure or pace. Box was under no illusions, and his wife Muriel noted in her diary, "Sidney saw the rough-cut of Byron yesterday and said it was shocking." But Gainsborough was fully committed and Box sanctioned a massive publicity campaign hoping that he could talk the film into being the hit he needed. Price, doing his bit, approached the BBC suggesting a program of readings from Byron's best poetry to coincide with the film's release. The BBC politely declined but Box's policy of raising expectations proved disastrous.

When *The Bad Lord Byron* opened, critics savaged the film, with Price receiving the worst of the backlash. The public then voted with their feet, leaving him distraught and humiliated by the failure. Speaking to *The Guardian* newspaper in 1953 he conceded, "I know I was terrible. Then everything about it was." Having invested so much enthusiasm and energy into his preparation and performance only to have it rejected left Price shattered. With *The Bad Lord Byron* Price's brief flirtation with character acting came to an end, from now all of his performances would be variations on his own personality. It also brought to an end, at least in his eyes, his career as a leading man; much of his later humility about his Gainsborough days would stem from this one failure.

At the same time that Dennis Price was receiving his worst professional disappointment, he was also appearing in what could arguably be regarded as his best film, Robert Hamer's *Kind Hearts and Coronets* which opened in

Britain in June 1949 (the U.S. release was held up for exactly one year). Like *The Bad Lord Byron*, Hamer's film is told predominately in flashback, with its leading character, the effete Edwardian haberdasher Louis Mazzini, relating his memoirs while awaiting  execution for a murder he didn't commit. As the story unfolds, eight murders he did perpetrate come to light! Where *Byron* is leaden and shapeless, *Kind Hearts and Coronets* is witty and elegant; and where critics reviled *Byron*, Hamer's film was celebrated as the pinnacle of what became known as Ealing comedy. In fact *Kind Hearts and Coronets*, adapted from a Victorian novel by Roy Horniman, doesn't actually resemble the Ealing comedies; it does play with manners and class, as do the best of Ealing, but it does so with uncharacteristically cynical wit.

Mazzini (Price) refuses to accept his position as the black sheep of the decaying D'Ascoyne family, a legacy from his mother's marriage to a penniless Italian opera singer. Robbed of what he feels is his rightful inheritance, he embarks on an elaborate plan to murder his way to the title. Along the way Hamer affords his anti-hero two romantic attachments: the headstrong Sibella (played once again with languorous sexuality by Joan Greenwood) and Edith (Valerie Hobson), the beautiful and stately widow of one of his victims. This love triangle provides much of the humor in the film, as Mazzini prevaricates over which one to marry: "While I never admired Edith as much as when I was with Sibella," Mazzini sighs, "I never longed for Sibella as much as when I was with Edith." In complete contrast to Byron, Price is perfectly cast as the witty murderer, his timing and delivery can't be faulted, and the *bon mots* trip off his tongue with ease: "It is so difficult to make a neat job of killing people with whom one is not on friendly terms." After downing Lady Agatha's balloon, Mazzini quips, "I shot an arrow in the air. She fell to earth in Berkleley Square." Price is both a joy to watch and hear as Mazzini's narration mixes cool detachment with cynicism: "I had not forgotten or forgiven the boredom

of the sermon of young Henry's funeral and I decided to promote the Reverend Lord Henry D'Ascoyne to next place on the list."

In the original British version, the conclusion is deliberately ambiguous. Mazzini's highly incriminating autobiography seems to fall into the hands of the law just as he has won his freedom and the girl (he gets presented with the choice!). Hamer was spared the sort of script interference that had destroyed the Byron picture but this final scene fell afoul of the Breen office, with the ruling that Mazzini's fate ran contrary to the Production Code edict that crime should not be seen to pay. As a consequence American audiences were treated to an additional scene confirming that the incriminating manuscript ended up with the proper authorities.

Despite dominating every scene, *Kind Hearts and Coronets* was never considered a "Dennis Price film." That honor is reserved for Price's former stage colleague, Alec Guinness, a major character star who would go on to appear in many of the recognized Ealing "classics." His showy turn as the D'Ascoynes—all eight of them—established Guinness' reputation as a "man of a thousand faces" and set the benchmark for the generation that followed; Peter Sellers in particular was obsessed with the idea of emulating the feat. With the benefit of hindsight it is obvious that Guinness is offering no more than a series of wigs and funny voices rather than characters, and the actor himself called them "pretty cardboard." Price on the other hand is superb as Louis, effortlessly elegant and cold blooded as he anchors the film and creates much of the comedy. While most contemporary critics raved about Guinness, Price did attract some attention. The *Monthly Film Bulletin* announced, "Dennis Price, humorous, polished and sinister, gives a brilliant portrayal." *Kind Hearts and Coronets* was, the magazine concluded, "an exceedingly funny film." Michael Balcon, then the head of Ealing, noted in his autobiography that Price's "elegant, stylized, beautifully acted portrait of a multiple murderer is a piece of high comedy acting which has never perhaps had its proper due."

Alec Guinness was in no doubt where the plaudits should lie. Some years later, when it was suggested he completely overshadowed Price, he snapped, "Its mythology, I revered Dennis." The film's title comes from a line of Tennyson's poetry: "Kind hearts are more than coronets / And simple faith than Norman blood." Hamer's literate script also contains allusions to Shakespeare and Chaucer.

While enjoying success in Britain—though it couldn't be considered a major hit—the release in the U.S. was spotty and unrewarding. Despite this, the film's reputation has grown over the years: In 1999 the British Film Institute poll put *Kind Hearts and Coronets* seventh on the Best British Film list, ahead of such standards as *Bridge on the River Kwai*, *Don't Look Now* and Olivier's *Henry V*. At one point Mike Nichols announced a remake with Robin Williams in the Alec Guinness role(s) and Will Smith as Mazzini—mercifully it never happened.

If ever there was a moment for Price to consider joining the exodus of British actors to Hollywood then this was it. But at the UK premiere of *The Bad Lord Byron*, before both the U.S. release and the critical backlash, Price was asked by reporters if he would consider a career in American films:

> Any British actor who leaves Rank now is foolish. Give me Shepherd's Bush any day. Hollywood doesn't attract me. And the columnists…I'm all for publicity but not that kind. I want my private life to myself.

In an article ghostwritten for Price and appearing in *Film Parade*, he projected this same image of contentment with his lot, describing himself as "an average sort of fellow, tolerant, with a sense of humor and understanding. I try not to be prejudiced and to appreciate the other person's point of view." Happily posing with daughters, Susan and Tessa, he offered his recipe for a successful picture:

> Begin with a good story; then a director who is sympathetic and knows his job, and an enthusiastic and experienced cast. All of these are important, but are of no avail unless there is

teamwork in full measure from all of those involved in the production, from the humble clapper boy to the all-important producer. Realizing all that, can you imagine anything more irritating than the actor who comes on set without knowing his lines? Not only is it intensely annoying for the people with whom he is appearing, but holding up production is a very costly business involving a waste of money, which would be far better employed in the making of more and better pictures.

Unfortunately the choice of employer and the relative luxury Price had enjoyed over the previous five years was about to come crashing to an end. In 1949 the British film industry collapsed. Rank's bold expansion policy, the complete failure to break into the U.S. market and a series of ill-conceived experiments, such as the infamous Charm School, chipped away at the company's prestige and its bank balance. Although not obvious at the time, the fatal blow had actually been delivered two years earlier when the British government was desperately trying to control its balance payments deficit. The massive debts inflicted by the war left gold reserves at an all time low and rationing was reintroduced on food, petrol and luxury items, as well as a ban on foreign travel except for business reasons. The socialist government then turned their attention to the film industry where Britain represented around 25 percent of the world market, with the vast slice of these earnings going straight to bank accounts in California. The administration, ignoring the protests of Lord Rank, announced the Dalton Duty, an *ad valorem* tax of 75 percent on the value of all imported films. Hollywood distributors immediately retaliated with a boycott of British cinemas, a move the Department of Trade argued could only benefit the indigenous industry. There was only one wrinkle in the plan: finding enough new films to keep cinemas open. J. Arthur Rank, who had campaigned vigorously against the legislation, accepted the assurances of the government that there would be protection if the situation changed and reluctantly agreed to fill the gap with an ambitious program of some 43 new features over the coming 12 months—an investment in excess of $38 million! The trade war proved a storm in a teacup; within months the British government brokered a compromise agreement and cinemas were again opened to competition. In reality the backlog of new films at the beginning of the dispute was so great that most cinemagoers were oblivious to any change. By then Rank was fully engaged in his production program, but when the mogul went cap in hand to the future Prime Minister and then President of the Board of Trade, Harold Wilson, he was told the government had agreed with the Americans not to introduce protectionist legislation. Wilson blithely announced that British films would be expected to compete in equal terms with their Hollywood counterparts.

It was a ruinous exercise for the Rank Organization: The British public liked British films from time to time, but not an exclusive diet of them, and even the best of Rank's films couldn't stand alongside the much more polished Hollywood product. Movie after movie was simply dumped after only a token release. This couldn't have come at a worse time: The huge losses on the "prestige" projects added to Gainsborough's flops meant a loss for 1949 of $13.6 million. In an announcement to investors Lord Rank conceded the overdraft stood at over $66 million and, with immediate effect, he would be withdrawing from the active running of the business. The company that bore his name was handed over to the accountants. Gainsborough was closed down and Sidney Box released from his contract; all the actors, including Price, were sacked. The failure of the Rank Organization plunged the whole of the British film industry into recession.

Rank's most requested photo

At the same time Price's marriage was falling apart. When they married, Joan put her duties as a mother first; she hadn't given up acting but restricted her occasional appearances to London runs, including *Great Day* and *The Country Wife*. While fan magazines showed Price as a happy and home-loving man, the studio's publicity machine liked to mix up his screen roles with his personality. Somewhere along the line this naturally charming *bon viveur* became a gentleman rogue, the type just as like to covet a lady's jewelry as her affections—the archetypal " man women love to hate." In truth the actor hated the carefully crafted persona and the attention his status brought; he dreaded the endless personal appearances at cinemas—publicists would arrange as many as three a night—or opening village fetes and garden parties where one was always required to play the "movie star." Maintaining this façade took its toil: Price was always a spendthrift but his gambling was now a problem and he was drinking heavily. There was also a far darker side to the actor's personality.

In 1984 the formidable actress Hermione Baddeley published her life story, and for the first time Price's sexual proclivities were openly stated. The actress, who had been romantically linked with Price some years earlier by some over-zealous newspaper columnist, turned up at a social event with bruises on her face—the result of a tempestuous affair with Laurence Harvey. In a casual aside she noted, "Dennis Price...had sharp eyes for he whispered: "Some of my boyfriends knock me about too." Then he winked. "I quite enjoy it." John Frazer, who costarred with Price on stage and screen, repeated the accusation in his 2004 autobiography, claiming, "separated from his wife when he discovered late in the day that he preferred a beating-up to intercourse and that men were better at it." On October 24, 1950, a magistrate heard Joan's petition for divorce on the grounds of adultery. It was uncontested and she was awarded costs and custody of the children.

With the end of Gainsborough, Price's film career stalled and he struggled to get work even in the few films that were being made. Between *Kind Hearts and Coronets* and a cameo in the Boulting brothers' all-star jamboree *The Magic Box* three years later, he completed only one film, the routine thriller *Murder without Crime* indifferently directed by J. Lee Thompson. Money was tight so Price sold his car and moved into a much smaller apartment in Egerton Gardens, a Chelsea address close to the Victoria and Albert Museum. As financial problems piled up he seemed dogged with bad luck. During the fall of 1953 he got a good part in the murder play *Blind Man's Buff* and hoped it would see him through until Christmas, but the show flopped and closed after a few weeks. Price signed for another West End play scheduled to open in December and, to fill in time, took the only work available, a television drama called *Eight Witnesses* to be shot

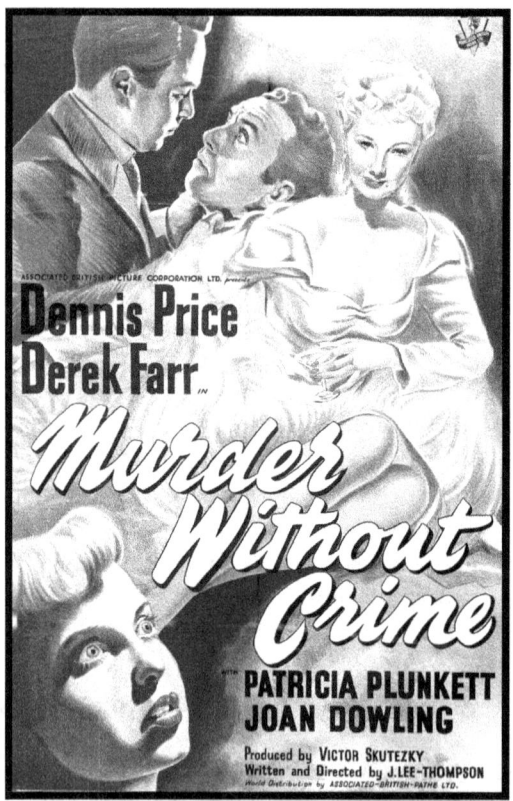

in Germany for television. In Munich he contracted pneumonia and by the time he recovered, he had lost out on the play. When the Inland Revenue presented a bill for back taxes, Price was too proud to seek refuge in bankruptcy and instead reached an agreement to pay all monies owed over the coming years; it was the start of what was to be an acrimonious relationship with the tax authorities. Only two years earlier the actor was could be seen at London's most fashionable nightspots and restaurants; he would be quaffing champagne at The Caprice or buying dinner for friends at Les Ambassadeurs. Now he could be found eating alone in the lounge bar of his local pub, The Rose and Crown. The theatre still offered an outlet and he appeared in a number of productions, including a 19-city tour of the U.S. with John van Druten's whimsical play *Bell, Book and Candle* starring Rosalind Russell. He then joined *Husband's Don't Count,* a lifeless farce, which opened in the provinces and crawled fleetingly into the West End. It was during the latter that Price, interviewed by the *Evening Standard*, offered some insight into his current position:

> Perhaps this job may prove the road back to the studios, too, if producers and the public recognize my name. There is one tentative offer already—not for a big movie—but I may accept it even though it would mean working all day as well as night. After all this time I feel cinemagoers should have a gentle reminder of my existence.

In the same interview he belatedly acknowledged the damage done by making so many films in such a short space of time: "It was far too much, I realize that now, too much for me and far too much for the public." When the offers finally did come they were for B movies made by independent companies with production values to match their lowly ambitions: *Murder at 3:00 AM* directed by Francis Searle, *Time is My Enemy* directed by Don Chaffney and *The Frightened Bride* costarring Andre Morell. Still in the mind of the producers, he retained his marquee value; when he appeared for London Films, a subsidiary of Rank, in the inoffensive comedy *Lady Godiva Rides* he was awarded top billing for what amounts to a cameo. During this time

Price made only one significant film, *The House on the Square,* a time travel-love story financed by 20th Century Fox starring Tyrone Power and directed by Roy Ward Baker. Then early in 1954 Price started working on *For Better, For Worse,* an inane marital comedy starring Dirk Bogarde, which came very close to being the last film he ever made.

Homosexuality was at that time still illegal in both Britain and the U.S. Despite a general acceptance, particularly by the British intelligentsia, and more so in the arts than any other walk of life, the early 1950s brought a return to the intolerance more suited to the days of Oscar Wilde and his celebrated lawsuit of 1895. The reaction sparked the defection of the openly gay traitor Guy Burgess in 1951 and the outcry that followed. The growing unease became a backlash after the trial of assistant film director Kenneth Hume and Lord Montague of Beaulieu for sexual assault on a boy scout. The newspapers and the police conspired to give maximum publicity to the ritual culling of what many senior officers, magistrates and civil servants regarded as the nation's unworthy. Noel Coward's biographer Sheridan Morley noted:

The House on the Square (1951) was also released as *I'll Never Forget You.*

> A lot of people were suddenly aware of a witch hunt as potent as the one being contemporaneously waged on supposed Hollywood communists by the McCarthy tribunals in the U.S.A.

Some of the biggest stars were affected. Anton Walbrook never reconciled his personal and public lives, and his career ground to a halt; he would complete only three films between 1955 and his death in 1968. Prominent figures in film and theatre suddenly relocated abroad, most noticeably Noel Coward. Those who stayed, like the newly knighted John Gielgud, risked not only arrest but trial by media and public humiliation. On October 21, 1953, Gielgud was arrested and charged with "homosexual importuning" in Chelsea, fined $30 and made to apologize to the Court. The headlines in the *Evening Standard* screamed, "Sir John Gielgud fined: See Your Doctor the Moment You Leave Here." Alec Guinness had been arrested in 1946 for the same act and escaped press attention by giving a false name. Guinness, who was married, never really recovered from the shame and developed an obsession about his privacy.

There were three options available for gay men in Britain: suppress the natural instinct to find a partner and live a lonely and unfulfilled life; discreetly indulge behind the façade of a marriage to a woman (what the scandal sheets dubbed a "beard"); or live openly with a same sex partner and face the fear of exposure. In 1954 Price was involved with a Canadian actor but the relationship ended badly, leaving him alone in his apartment, depressed by the state of his career, and with money problems mounting. On the April 19, 1954, Easter Monday, Price tried to take his own life.

Events prior to the incident had been nothing but routine; he had spent the week working with Bogarde and then on Saturday took his daughters to the cinema. The Saturday evening was spent having a quiet drink at The Hour Glass where the landlord said he was in a serious conversation with a "chap called Bobby." There was no filming on Monday morning so, last thing on Sunday evening, Price told his housekeeper Mrs. Lamb to "forget about me until lunchtime; I need a really good rest." The following morning at 8:00 when Mrs. Lamb went to make herself a cup of tea she found the kitchen door jammed and the house filled with the smell of gas. Forcing the door open, she was able to drag the unconscious actor to the window and then summon help from a neighbor. A police officer arrived on the scene quickly and was able to revive Price with artificial respiration; he then was rushed to the intensive care unit at St George's Hospital, Hyde Park.

The press of course loves a "fallen star" story and the next day the front pages were full of his brush with death and the dramatic efforts to save him. By then Price's condition was described as stable and he was moved to more comfortable surroundings at Morley Hospital in Wimbledon. Joan, who had been at his bedside throughout, told the *Daily Sketch*:

Convict Actor On Morals Charge

LONDON (₳)—West London Magistrate's Court Wednesday convicted Sir John Gielgud, famed Shakespearean actor, on a charge of persistently importuning male persons for an immoral purpose. He was fined 10 pounds ($28I) and told to see his doctor at once.

The balding 49-year-old Gielgud, peering from horn-rimmed spectacles, pleaded guilty and said: "I cannot imagine why I was so stupid. I was tired and had a few drinks. I was not responsible for my actions."

Magistrate E. R. Guest said:

"See your doctor the moment you leave here and tell him. If he has any advice to offer take it because this conduct is dangerous to other men, particularly young men, and is a scourge in this neighborhood . . ."

Gielgud is a bachelor. There were no previous convictions recorded against him.

Gielgud, stage star for 20 years, was knighted by Queen Elizabeth II in the coronation honors list last June.

Last year he went to Hollywood for the first time to play Cassius in the film "Julius Caesar."

> Our marriage was dissolved 3 1/2 years ago after many years of happiness. I shall make it my business to look after him till he is well. My only concern is that he will get fit and strong as quickly as possible. To do that it is important he feels he is not neglected. We are very good friends and always have been.

Under the circumstances the journalists were remarkably kind to Price, there was only the slightest hint of his sexuality in the reference to "Bobby" but otherwise the focus was very much on his fall from grace and his brushes with the taxman. He was depicted as a charming but sensitive man who spent as much time as he could with his children and lived a quiet, unassuming life. On the whole one has to admit the coverage did his image a great deal of good. One paper reported that his first words on being revived were "What glory, Price?" which is either total fiction or suggests he had prepared a suitably witty rejoinder. This, and the subsequent upswing in Price's career, created the myth that the whole thing was a staged publicity stunt, which seems unlikely—had Mrs. Lamb followed instructions, he would have been long dead before she arrived.

Whatever the truth the attention Price received from family and friends, as well as press and public, gave him the impetus he needed to get back on track. He took a short break, 10 days in the country with Joan and the girls, and then returned to finish *For Better, For Worse*. By then the future looked brighter, and he had been inundated with goodwill letters from fans; as he told the *Daily Mirror*, "My plan is to try and get good costume films or solid acting roles. I am going to stop playing those precious romantic juvenile leads." In fact Price had already signed for a costume film, Terence Young's trashy *That Lady*, starring Olivia de Havilland as the one-eyed Princess of Eboli. It wasn't a success.

Price would talk often about this part of his life in many interviews over the years without really giving anything away. His homosexuality was never openly discussed and certainly he never publicly acknowledged it—it remained illegal for most of his life. That such a sensitive man could put the scandal of an attempted suicide behind him speaks volumes for his strength of character. That he would go on to play no fewer than six openly gay roles over the remainder of his career speaks volumes about his bravery.

In 1955 Price made a return to quality films when he was cast as Major Frank on *Oh Rosalinda!*, Michael Powell and Emeric Pressburger's revamped version of Johann Strauss' operetta *Die Fledermus*. The role had been written for Noel Coward, who declined, and then offered to David Niven who took one look at the script and decided he was "busy." Price couldn't afford to be so fussy; broke and, despite his public bravado, a long way from recovery, he took the minor role of a British army major in this Cold War comedy of errors. Powell, who had worked with Price at the height of his fame, described the actor as "sick and broken and always elegant and well mannered" and cast him more out of pity than anything else. It was hardly a significant role for Price and he was billed below Michael Redgrave and Anton Walbrook, but Powell and Pressburger were still considered important filmmakers. Sadly, despite success with similar subjects in the past, Powell's touch failed him and the film turned out to be a soulless affair disliked by practically everyone.

The film did publicize the fact that Price was again available for work and he moved quickly into a comedy called *A Touch of the Sun*, acting as a straight man for the slapstick antics of burlesque comic Frankie Howerd. It was a half-witted effort which deserved its rapid descent into obscurity but it marked a turning point for Price. Returning to full health he was being cast in comedies rather than dramas and for the next decade or so, comedy was to dominate his work on stage, television and film.

By the mid-50s, the British economy had picked up and the film industry was recovering something of its confidence. A leaner and fitter Rank Organization was better able to deal with the twin threats of television and the undiminished dominance of U.S. films. The accountant John Davis was in charge and out went the lavish projects, the stable of contract artists and the mega-budgets, as he established himself as either the savior or the destroyer of the British film industry (depending on which side of the fence you sat). Davis introduced the principal that films must recover their costs in the domestic market, and the new Rank concentrated on popular comedies and contemporary thrillers.

Price renewed acquaintances with his former employer for another empty-headed musical, *Charley Moon*, made by British Lion, Alexander Korda's old company and now a subsidiary of Rank. It was designed solely as a vehicle for popular entertainer Max Bygraves with Price mugging through a series of

Price in *Charley Moon* with Max Bygraves and Shirley Eaton

contrived indignities including a pantomimic goose and later in drag as an "ugly sister". The film, which also stars Shirley Eaton, did allow Price the relative luxury of being in a popular success. He then appeared in a well-received tour of *Blithe Spirit* with Kay Kendall, after which he went straight into a new production, *The Ball*. He was still appearing in *The Ball* on the second anniversary of his suicide attempt and took the opportunity to reflect on the event. In an interview with the *Daily Express* he admitted:

> My career as an actor was at a low ebb. I had made a row of bad films in quick succession. There was money in the bank but my self-esteem was bankrupt. My private life too was in a mess.

Talking about his journey back from the brink, he said:

> It wasn't easy. People I'd known and worked with for years hardly knew how to approach a man who had almost died. There were awkward pauses; the wrong things said. I felt like a ghost who was haunting the wrong house. I decided the only thing to do was to behave as though nothing had happened. Not an easy assignment. I ate at my usual restaurants. I went to the usual clubs. I tried desperately to create the appearance that I was living a thoroughly normal life. And my performance— the hardest I have ever had to give—was a success.

Price's efforts paid off with the Boulting brothers' *Private's Progress*, a send up of British class values in a wartime setting. The Boulting twins, Roy and John, had been at the cutting edge of British cinema for two decades, making the Oscar-winning documentary *Desert Victory* and the gritty gangster thriller *Brighton Rock*. In the mid-50s they graduated to lighter material with a stream of social satires, usually starring Ian Carmichael, invariably as a chinless aristocrat. In *Private's Progress* Carmichael plays to type as the dim but nice Stanley Windrush who, despite his breeding and background, fails to make the grade as an officer and end up slumming with the other ranks. Of course, the working classes, represented by Ian Bannen, Kenneth Griffith and Richard Attenborough, are all work-shy opportunists out to screw the system for a quick buck. The officers, on the other hand, are buffoons or self-serving schemers, Terry-Thomas and Dennis Price, respectively. At the core of the film is the clash between the two classes but it is held together with a loose narrative about "liberating" some art treasures from the retreating Nazis. Along for the ride are reliable performers George Coulouris, Christopher Lee and Thorley Walters.

Private's Progress features George Coulouris on the right.

Private's Progress is a witty and intelligent riposte to the endless Boy's Own war films which filled cinemas during the postwar years, with Price in fine form as the conniving Bertram Tracepurcel (Uncle Bertie) effortlessly twisting the nation's war effort to his own advantage. It is the sort of film that official channels had dreaded would be made. After seeing an early copy of the script, the War Ministry had refused all requests for assistance, leading the Boultings to open the film with the sarcastic credit, "The producers gratefully acknowledge the cooperation of absolutely nobody." The film's two rogues, Richard Attenborough and Price, share top billing in what the *New York Herald* called "the funniest film of the year." London's *Evening News* was also impressed: "Dennis Price in one of his *Kind Hearts and Coronets* moods of suave villainy…I have seldom seen funnier performances. Attenborough and Price are brilliantly bogus." *Private's Progress* went on to fare amongst the top earners in the UK, inspiring a run of increasingly broad military comedies, many of which would feature Price—ironic, given his own brief army experience.

Price more or less carried the Tracepurcel character into the entertaining comedy *Your Past is Showing* where he is seen at his most clinical and calculating as Nigel Dennis, publisher of the scandal sheet "The Naked Truth," who discovers there is more profit to be made in blackmailing his victims than exposing them. This being a comedy, the blackmail is all pretty innocent and

socially acceptable: Authoress Peggy Mount strayed from the "path of righteousness" in the Far East, while insurance tycoon Terry-Thomas dallied once too often with a pretty girl. In the opening scenes, Price's little visits to his "clients" drive several to suicide. "Pay up in a fortnight," he demands, "or I'll publish." After several botched attempts to solve their problems by murderous means, the remaining victims—by the end of the film they number more than 300—band together to put an end to it for once and all. The script doesn't give the leading players anything radical to do, so all of them play to their well-worn stereotypes: Peggy Mount is a belligerent battleaxe, Terry-Thomas a lecherous but ineffective rogue and Price, ice cold and smooth as silk, the duplicitous baddie. Shirley Eaton plays a model with a dubious past, while Peter Sellers as an odious television personality is allowed to mug furiously through a parade of pointless disguises. Nevertheless the film is very funny; titled *The Naked Truth* it played very well in Britain, helping to reinforce Price's new screen image as a smooth baddie. Terry-Thomas, who would go on to make five more films with Price, recalled in his autobiography his costar was:

> Most likeable. He arrived every morning with a basket of beer slung over his shoulder. As the day went by he methodically got rid of it. All of it! Well, he was a very practical chap and he didn't want to carry any of it home.

Price was also in demand on the stage where his brand of light comedy was very much *en vogue*. He appeared at the Fortune Theatre in London in Hugh Burden's popular comedy *To My Love* and then in 1957 toured South Africa with *Separate Tables* playing Major Pollock, followed by a national tour of *Table by the Window*. In January 1958 he opened in the farce *Be My Guest* starring alongside June Baxter. The small screen also turned into a lucrative sideline for Price and he was a regular in entertainment shows like *Chelsea at Nine* playing in various skits, as well as appearing in panel games and chat shows. In March 1959 he returned to BBC radio for the comedy *The Navy Lark,* which proved massively popular at a time when television was winning the ratings battle. Unfortunately Price quit after the first season to appear on Broadway and the show, recast with Stephen Murray, went on to run for a record-breaking 17 1/2 years! Price's New York debut as Hector Hushabye in *Heartbreak Hotel* wasn't well received and the show closed early.

With all his radio and stage commitments, Price made only one film between 1957 and 1959, a torrid tale of murder and blackmail called *She Played with Fire* starring Jack Hawkins. When he was available again it was predictably in a comic role and one that should have meant a splendid return to quality cinema. *How to Win without Actually Cheating,* neatly summed up by its British title *School for Scoundrels*, again teams Price with *Kind Hearts and Coronets* director Robert Hamer, and features some of the best comedy talent in England, including Ian Carmichael, Terry-Thomas, Janette Scott, and John Le Mesurier. Based on Stephen Potter's frightfully British "Gamesmanship" series of books, the film stars Carmichael as the perpetually befuddled Henry Palfrey, who seems destined to always lose out to "that absolute rotter Delauney" (a leering Terry-Thomas) until he discovers the work of Professor Potter (the magnificent Alistair Sim), founder of the

"Lifeman College" devoted to teaching the hidden art of always coming out on top. Price was given an eye-catching cameo playing Dunstan Dorcester, a dodgy car dealer in a role originally intended for Peter Ustinov (who in fact had written the first draft of the script). Sadly the decline in Hamer's skills during the intervening decade was all too obvious. A recovering alcoholic, Hamer fell off the wagon during the filming and his behavior became so erratic that producer Hal Chester had no choice but to replace him with Cyril Frankel, director of *Never Take Sweets from a Stranger*. In fairness to Hamer he was working with two acknowledged reprobates, Price and Terry-Thomas, both of whom would happily join him at lunchtime for a tipple, but his forced removal from the project more or less finished him in the industry. Hamer never directed another film and cirrhosis of the liver killed him in 1963. *How to Win without Actually Cheating* shows all the signs of this disrupted shooting and only has brief flashes of the wit and elegance of Hamer's earlier work. These unique British books had once been considered by Carl Foreman as a vehicle for Cary Grant. However, with Carmichael in the lead, there was little to appeal to international audiences. Terry-Thomas, in one of his trademark bounder roles, saved the film from obscurity, But despite solid supporting performances it fizzled to a quiet death at the box office.

Price's next film was everything that Hamer was aiming for and missed. *I'm Alright Jack* is the Boultings' sequel to *Private's Progress,* transplanting the blundering Windrush from the army to the factory, with military pomposity replaced by rabid trade unionism. Having accepted a job in Uncle Bertie's armaments factory, Windrush finds himself an unwitting pawn in a plan to swindle an Arab trade delegation into over paying for the latest missile shipment. Price, oozing self-satisfied smugness, schemes over a glass of brandy and cigars with fellow magnate Richard Attenborough, while Terry-Thomas fumes as the dimwit Major Hitchcock. Margaret Rutherford and a winsome Liz Frazer, who won a British Academy Award nomination for Best Newcomer, augment regulars Ian Carmichael, Miles Malleson and John Le Mesurier. Stealing the show is Peter Sellers with a bravura performance as the Soviet-obsessed trade unionist Fred Kite, beady eyed and simmering with rage and class indignation. The role made a star of Sellers and won him the British Academy Award for Best Actor; the Boultings' also picked up the Award for Best Film. The success with critics and the public ensured that Price was well and truly typecast and with only one or two notable exceptions his film roles over the next few years were variations of Bertram Tracepurcel.

Sadly all the comedies Price made following *I'm Alright Jack* show an ambition and imagination to match their low budget. *Double Bunk* features Ian Carmichael and Janette Scott as a likeable couple on a boating holiday coming up against the fiercely snobbish and competitive Price, seething in pantomimic caddishness. Liz Frazer and Sid James are also featured and, while the film's climatic and chaotic boat race is fun to watch, one is left wishing for something a little more ambitious.

Hammer, taking a break from its usual horror fare, then cast Price as Captain Von Krisling, a German version of Bertie Tracepurcel, whose tiny German command finds itself at loggerheads with Thorley Walters' contingent of Brits stranded somewhere in the Adriatic Sea. *Don't Panic Chaps* was adapted from a radio play by Ronald Holroyd and directed by journeyman George Pollack, better known for his sedate "whodunits," but it fails to rise above the routine with Price playing a singularly unconvincing Junker aristocrat. Hammer's James Carreras tried to talk up their efforts by announcing it as "our funniest film yet!" but Columbia, the U.S. distributor, must have been disappointed by just how insular the humor was.

Hammer put Price into a navy uniform for *Watch It Sailor,* based on the characters created for the stage by Falkland Carey and Phillip King and directed by Wolf Rilla, better known for *Village of the Damned.* It afforded Price top billing again and this time he was on the side of the Allies as Lt. Commander Hardcastle in a poor imitation of *The Navy Lark.* Despite featuring Liz Frazer and Vera Day, the film is a crashing bore and curtailed Hammer's efforts in the comedy market until the 1970s. *Watch It Sailor* also features Frankie Howerd in a brief cameo (returning a favor for Price who had acted his straight man in the television show *Ladies and Gentle-men*). Howerd became another victim of the scurrilous gutter press when a Sunday newspaper ran with the headline "Frankie Howerd Stole My Husband!" The comedian's fragile self-confidence was destroyed and it took him over a decade to recover anything of his career.

Price was then typecast in *The Millionairess* which opens with a group of suited businessmen mourning the death of their former benefactor and saluting his heir with "the millionaire is dead, long live the

millionairess." Statuesque Italian beauty Sophia Loren plays the title role, the richest woman in the world searching for true love in London's docklands and finding an incorruptible Indian doctor (Peter Sellers, once again in silly voice mode). Price is smoothly charming as a lecherous psychiatrist whose designs on the impressionable Loren earn him a ducking in the Thames. It isn't much of a role but then it isn't much of a film. The comedy is labored and the direction by the usually reliable Anthony Asquith uninspired. Only the veteran scene-stealer Alistair Sim rose above his material to remain watch-able throughout. By now, even in serious films, Price was being used as the light relief. *Breakout*, a dreary POW escape yarn starring diminutive action hero Richard Todd, cast him as the outrageously campy Captain Callander, more interested in mounting an ersatz version of Hamlet than escaping.

Price did manage to lend his name to one very good film during this period, thanks to the intervention of Alec Guinness. Ronald Neame's superb black comedy *Tunes of Glory* stars Guinness and John Mills as feuding officers battling for control of a tradition-bound Highland regiment just after the war. It was Guinness who persuaded a reluctant Neame to hire Price for the calculating Major Charles "Charlie" Scott M.C., the battalion's executive officer who desperately tries to play both sides against each other while coming out on top. A big hit in Britain, the film is efficiently directed by Ronald Neame and superbly acted by the principals, with Price looking very fetching in a kilt and every inch the Highland officer. The film also earned him his best notices for

some time: The *Daily Express* singled out the "wonderful performance as a caddishly smooth major from Dennis Price."

Less impressive was *Oscar Wilde* in which Price plays Robert Ross, the playwright's close friend and confidante, in a lackluster biopic. It features a starry cast including Ralph Richardson, John Neville and former Gainsborough starlet Phyllis Clavert, but a limp script and Robert Morley, too old for his part, makes a dire Wilde. Price is very good and it's a shame the days when he could have been considered for the title role were gone—with his wit and intelligence he would have made a far more charismatic Wilde. Price also popped up opposite Peter Finch in the political drama *No Love for Johnnie* about a British politician whose career is endangered by his libido. Directed by Ralph Thomas, who was on surer ground with his comedies, it features performances by Mary Peach, Donald Pleasance and Stanley Holloway, but it is no better than average. If the film had something to say about politics or politicians it loses the message along the way.

Basil Dearden's film *Victim,* very clear on its social comment, is much sterner stuff. In 1957 the government-sponsored "Wolfenden Report" had recommended sweeping changes to Britain's archaic homosexuality laws, but successive Prime Ministers shied away from the potential hot potato and the debate rumbled on with no sign of a resolution. In the meantime, the situation, to use Dearden's words, created a "blackmailer's charter" with otherwise law abiding citizens held to ransom over their sexual proclivities. Dearden was all

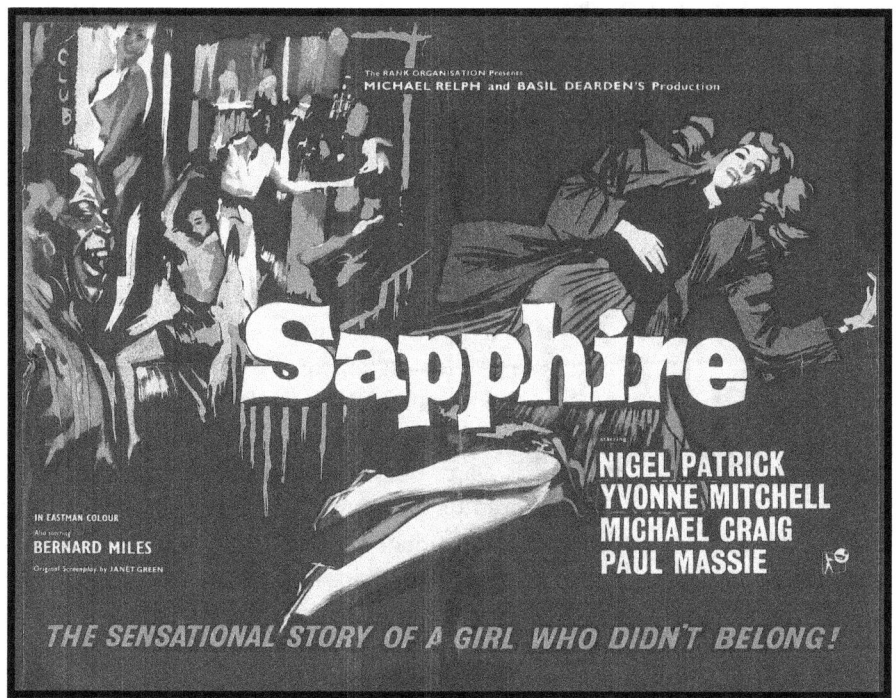

too aware of the commercial impact of controversy, having earlier tackled racial prejudice in the successful thriller *Sapphire*. He seized on the contradictions and managed to get the story of homosexual lawyer Melville Farr off the drawing board—despite the fact that no major studio or star would touch it. Raising the money independently, Dearden was turned down by every leading actor he approached, including Peter Finch, Jack Hawkins and Price's old Gainsborough stable mates, James Mason and Stewart Grainger. Finally the director approached the one star he thought would never touch it: Dirk Bogarde. The actor, once the darling of the Rank Organization, was coming to the end of his contract and tiring of the insipid work offered by the studio. Ignoring the warnings from his agent that it could kill his career, Bogarde agreed to play Farr.

Dearden's film makes the bold assertion that 90 percent of all British libel cases were related to homosexuality, and Farr is depicted as a high-flying lawyer who falls afoul of a blackmailing ring. Attempts to elicit help from the gay community prove futile and Farr is left to tackle the villains more or less on his own, and then face the consequences. Bogarde's casting raised eyebrows in the industry where his homosexuality was an open secret—despite strenuous efforts by the Rank publicists to divert public attention. For Price, the film must also have brought back unfortunate memories but he agreed to play Calloway, a successful stage actor who is being blackmailed by the odious Sandy (Derren Nesbitt). The clearly rattled Calloway refuses to help Farr in his campaign, preferring instead to pay up and shut up. It is a compelling performance from

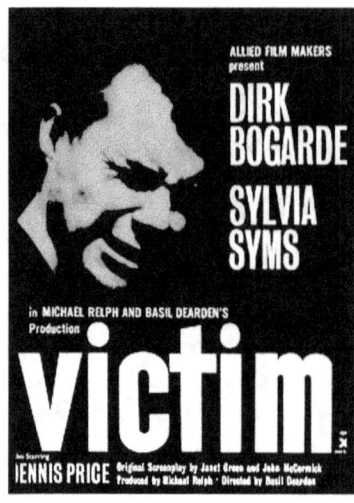

Price who, despite third billing, is only given three scenes to convey Calloway's absolute terror of exposure. In one particularly telling line he says, "I never mix with anyone but my own kind. Why can't I do what I find natural without the risk of prison?"

To his credit Dearden doesn't portray the victims as mincing queens but ordinary, rather mundane little men (a hairdresser, a book seller) and the film plays more like a thriller rather than a political statement. Sex is never depicted nor even mentioned. Beautifully photographed and sensitively acted by the entire cast, particularly Bogarde, the film was in 1961 a remarkably bold statement and much of the credit has over the years focused on its star. Bogarde had been living more or less openly with a male partner for a number of years, and drawing attention to himself was certainly a brave act. At the time Bogarde told the press he was "a heterosexual playing a homosexual" and even as late as 1991, when this sort of thing was of little consequence, Bogarde admitted in a television documentary that, "all of the actors in *Victim* were straight except for Dennis Price." Through five volumes of autobiography, Bogarde never openly admitted his sexual proclivities. While it is true that Price never discussed his sexuality, it is equally true that friends and colleagues may have seen the autobiographical elements in the role of Calloway, a taciturn but successful stage actor. The parallels with real life may be even more striking: In 2002 Robert Ross' biography of Terry-Thomas identifies Price as a lifelong victim of blackmail!

The British censor John Trevelyan had earlier cautioned Dearden against making the film, claiming, "no film dealing with homosexuality had ever made money in Britain." Later, faced with what was clearly a superior thriller, Trevelyan awarded *Victim* a "X" certificate, which in Britain meant it could not be screened to children under the age of 16. Apparently the censor was particularly concerned about the subject matter and strong language, especially the word "homosexual," which was heard for the first time in a British film. In the U.S., *Victim* was denied a MPAA seal under Section III (6): "Sexual perversion or any inference of it is forbidden." *Time*'s reviewer echoed that theme:

> A coyly sensational exploitation of homosexuality as a theme—and, what's more offensive, an implicit approval of homosexuality as a practice...Nowhere does the film suggest that homosexuality is a serious (but often curable) neurosis that attacks the biological basis of life itself.

In England, *Films and Filming* recognized, "for all its faults, this is a landmark in British cinema," and the British Academy, always keen to recognize worthy films, awarded *Victim* two nominations, including Best Screenplay, but shied away from an actual award. All the controversy was good publicity and the film was a box-office hit.

After *Victim,* Price went into an unbroken run of comedies, few of which had any lasting value. *The Rebel* is a vehicle for radio comedian Tony Hancock, and retained some cult status after his suicide, but is pretty dull. *The Pot Carriers* for Peter Graham Scott isn't much better but gave Price the distinction of playing the likeable con man with the curious appellation "Smooth-Tongue" Bertie. Price also appears in *The Cool Mikado*, an odd little film for the precocious Michael Winner, who still had *Death Wish* and *The Sentinel* ahead of him. Price had already picked up pocket money for Winner's short film *Shoot to Kill* in 1960 and appears in his inane musical *Play it Cool,* starring pop acts Billy Furie and Helena Shapiro. *The Cool Mikado* is of marginally more interest, at least to connoisseurs of bad movies. Winner had intended to make an updated version of the Gilbert and Sullivan light opera on a microscopic budget. His worthy intentions, such as they were, were undone by the inept staging and some truly dreadful performances from a host of forgettable stand-up comedians.

Winner could not afford stars so he went for "names" desperate for work and money: Dermot Walsh, Price's erstwhile "son" in *Hungry Hill* and *Jassy,* was nearing the end of his career and popped by for a few days work, as did Frankie Howerd who was otherwise unemployable. Winner was honest enough to tell *The Times*, "I admit it was a big failure…it was ahead of its time, that was the real trouble. OK, so some say its time will never come." It least Price was afforded one good line; when asked if he was attached to the British government he says, "Not particularly!"

Better, but not by much, is *The Amorous Prawn* based on the West End stage hit of the same name. Joan Greenwood stars as an impoverished army wife who uses her husband's absence as an excuse to rent out the regimental home to American tourists. Ian Carmichael is amongst the soldiers dressed as servants waiting on the guests, while Price plays a visiting politician caught in a compromising position with barmaid Liz Frazer. Price milked his scenes for their entire comic lechery but he was fighting an uphill battle against a mediocre script and dull direction. It wasn't successful initially and still flopped after a rushed re-titling to *The Playgirl and the Minister*, a blatant attempt to cash in on the very topical Profumo affair—later the subject of its own film, *Scandal*. (Hammer had earlier announced its own version of the play with Greenwood and Carmichael, and Robert Beatty in the role of the MP, but the option expired when interest in comedies waned.)

None of these films are particularly good or memorable but at least *The Pure Hell of St. Trinians* can claim something approaching cult status. The *St. Trinians* series is a uniquely British phenomenon that owes its existence solely to the comic value of 20-something starlets dressed as schoolgirls. This was the third in a series that ran to five films and picks up after an arson attack on the school and the girls are handed over to the care of a dubious child psychiatrist (Cecil Parker, taking the role over from Terry-Thomas). Parker embarks on the gloriously politically incorrect plan of kidnapping the sixth-form girls and selling them into forced marriages with the sons of Arab sheiks. A close analysis of the basic ingredients probably reveals more about fans of the series than they would be comfortable admitting, so it may be best just to write off all the St Trinians movies as harmless fun and leave it at that. Price's brief cameo adds little value to a cast that includes Sid James and Michael Ripper, with Edina Ronay and Erica Rodgers amongst those squeezed into school uniforms. It also stars Liz Frazer, in one of her six films opposite Price, and she remembers him very fondly:

> He was absolutely charming and it was my pleasure to work with him. He was very gay, not camp I mean, but very fastidious, proper. But a very sweet man, charming and always very easy to work with. There was no big star attitude about him at all.

Price was played off against another regular collaborator, Terry-Thomas, in George Pollack's comic murder mystery *Kill or Cure*. Terry-Thomas plays an inept private detective investigating a murder at Price's private health club, supported by Eric Sykes as his dimwitted sidekick and Lionel Jeffries chewing scenery as a neurotic policeman. Price is charmingly sinister, and the film has moments of humor sprinkled throughout. It was soon after *Kill or Cure* that Terry-Thomas abandoned the U.K. in search of more meaningful roles in Hollywood and, while he would be hopelessly typecast as the typically British bounder, at least he had the recognition (and salary) that goes with international success.

Pollack was on surer ground two years later with his next film featuring Price, the Agatha Christie movie *Murder Most Foul* with Margaret Rutherford in her trademark role of Miss Marple, although the film is actually an adaptation of *Mrs McGintys Dead*—a Hercule Poirot novel! Like all of Pollock's films it has a cozy feel, evoking a world of garden-party poisoning and Home Counties mayhem that existed nowhere except in the minds of writers like Christie. As an altogether too devious theatrical agent, Price is amongst the suspects.

Price was given more to do in another low budget comedy, one which has acquired a remarkable reputation over the years, even inspiring a bestselling paperback novel. *No Place like Homicide* (or *What a Carve Up!* in England) was conceived as a vehicle for the comedy talents of Sid James and Kenneth Connor, refugees from the *Carry On* series. Loosely based on the "old dark house" whodunits, the film features Connor traveling to a remote country house to claim an inheritance from an aristocratic family he has never met. Appropriate to the genre, all the claimants begin to die off one by one in increasingly bizarre fashions. Appearances by Shirley Eaton, Donald Pleasance, Michael Gough and Esme Cannon, Price's victim from *Holiday Camp*, liven things up a bit but, apart from some inspired moments, the humor is very much in the style of the "*Abbott and Costello Meet...*" movies. Price plays ice-cold Guy Broughton whose scripted fondness for alcohol must have caused the odd knowing glance amongst the cast and crew, but it is yet another variation of Bertie Tracepurcel. Still the film proved very popular with viewers who flocked to the *Carry On* movies, and it has retained a fan base to this day.

In the early 1960s, television continued to offer Price a productive outlet for his talent and he played in several quality plays, including Rudolph Cartier's remarkable *Lady of the Camellias,* for the BBC. Price was also appearing on the stage, albeit in lightweight comedies rather than recognized classics; in May 1963 he traveled to Dublin for a popular run of *Not in the Book* but the time for this type of material was coming to an end. The arrival in the West End of "angry young men" actors like Albert Finney and Alan Bates, as well as the hard-hitting works of John Osborne and the subversive comedies of Joe Orton, alienated a generation of actors from an audience now demanding more realism and social drama. Price's acting style seemed quaintly old fashioned and he would increasingly appear as novelty value more than anything else. His last stage role of any consequence was in *Any Wednesday*, another lightweight comedy, where he topped a bill that included John Fraser and Moira Lister. Price may well have continued to appear on stage had it not been for his drinking which had first reared its head in the 50s and by the mid-60s had taken a firm hold. In his divertingly catty autobiography, Fraser reported that Price's behavior was creating problems for theatre actors who, unlike their film counterparts, did not have the luxury of a re-take:

> He never drank tea or coffee even first thing in the morning. A crate of Guinness a day was his consumption, starting at breakfast. He was always drunk of course, but never fell over and could with occasional lapses and in a general sort of way stick to a script.

Fraser also revealed Price's personality changes that accompanied his drinking: Following an incident with his partner at the time, which left him with a hand in plaster, he insisted that a matinee performance must go on:

> Dennis' "charming cad" personality changed abruptly. He became hard, cruel and vicious. It made my flesh creep. The piece was a comedy, but the laughter died on the audience's lips.

When challenged, Price apologized profusely and in the twinkling of an eye was restored to his debonair, charming self. Moving away from stage work, Price's association with the BBC would have one last final flourish but he soon became totally reliant on films as his source of income. By then he was well and truly pigeonholed as a B movie actor and increasingly his film work was limited to low-budget programmers. He recognized his fate and accepted it with quiet resignation. "I have no illusions about myself. I am a second-rate feature actor," he told the *Daily Express*, adding, "I am not a star and never was, even in the old Rank days. I lack the essential spark, you see." As the

years passed he became almost a standard fixture in low-budget horror and exploitation movies.

Terence Fisher, another refugee from the demise of Gainsborough, had built a new career directing the best and most successful of Hammer's horror movies, including the groundbreaking *The Curse of Frankenstein* and *Horror of Dracula*. The relative failure of his most recent efforts *The Curse of the Werewolf* and *The Phantom of the Opera* had left him out in the cold at Hammer but no one doubted his ability to bring a film in on time and budget. It was this quality that made him an attractive option for low-budget filmmakers eager to add a touch of style to their product. Enter American producer Robert Lippert, actually a close collaborator of both Hammer and Fisher going back to the programmers of the early 50s. With exploitation giants AIP milking the teenage market in the U.S. with a diet of chills and laughs, Lippert reasoned that a spoof horror movie could be turned out quickly and cheaply, using both the talent and sets left over from the genuine article. The result was a concoction called *The Horror of It All*, in truth little more than a vehicle for one-time teen idol Pat Boone.

The script by Ray Russell, who had been involved in the much more creditable *The Premature Burial*, was a re-working of *The Old Dark House*, already remade as an unsuccessful "comedy" by Hammer the previous year. Boone stars as an American salesman visiting the old country with his fiancée (Erica Roberts) who is keen to impress her decidedly eccentric English family, the Marleys. The in-laws-to-be consist of the usual stock characters: the vamp Natalia (a splendidly Addams-esque Andree Melly), a mad inventor uncle, a bedridden Grandfather and so on. And of course their crumbling and isolated mansion comes complete with "some thing" living in the cellar. Roberts, an attractive if bland leading lady, is certainly much more tolerable than Boone whose mugging becomes increasingly irritating as the film grinds on. Price grasped the need to play it light and brings some humor to the role of Cornwallis, a dapper ex-actor and the prime suspect as the Marley's begin to disappear one by one. By then the feeble script and flat direction make it hard to care about who is behind the murders and why. Fisher's initiation to teenage exploitation comes with little enthusiasm and he clearly sensed the worst when, just prior to the film's UK opening, he told the press, "It's a musical comedy, or rather a musical parody of horror films…For me it was a sort of experiment and I am not sure whether or not I did a good job with it." Unfunny and tiresome, *The Horror of It All* is summed up by the cringing tagline, "When boy meets ghoul…its laughs at first sight!!!" *Variety* was unimpressed with its "weak mixture of unfunny gags and standard horror situations that get laughs when they aren't supposed to."

Price, who had spent most of his Gainsborough years hopping from one project to another, was an old hand at working on back-to-back movies and used to the pressures it brought. He was also good at repressing his personal demons, having spent a lifetime living behind a façade. As Renée Glynne, the continuity girl on *The Horror of It All,* remembered, he gave every indication of being relaxed:

> He was lovely, and very gay in the accepted sense of the word. The others like Redgrave had their double lives, Denholm Elliot, a wonderful actor, was so jumpy it was like he was spring-loaded. Dennis was perfectly laid-back and actually rather fun in a dry sort of way; and he was always on time and always knew his lines.

Price also seemed much more comfortable with his screen image as a "light heavy," being equally adept at comic and villainous roles, than he ever was with the matinee idol tag. Ten years earlier, he had discussed typecasting with *The Guardian* newspaper, concluding:

> I am quite happy to be a villain. I could play in light comedies until I dropped but weak characters are the strongest to play. I wish George Sanders would drop dead, then I would get all his parts!

The reference to George Sanders is an interesting one; superficially the two men were a lot alike and, in their later years, their careers shared the same downward trajectory, with Sanders ending his days in much the same type of films as Price. However, as screen personalities, the two men were cast in very different roles: Sanders brand of villainy is attractive to women; indeed his appeal was largely with female filmgoers. Price on the other hand played the sort of villains that women prefer to avoid.

Price stayed with Fisher for another Lippert project, *The Earth Dies Screaming,* a B science-fiction movie vaguely reminiscent of the Hollywood alien invasion flicks of the 1950s. The script by Harry Spalding, who had penned *The Day Mars Invaded,* features such reliable sci-fi standbys as a disparate group of survivors, abandoned streets, menacing robots and reanimated corpses.

To lend the film some international appeal, former cowboy star Willard Parker and his wife Virginia Field were imported to play the leads Jeff and Peggy, but neither felt the film merited anything more than a perfunctory performance. Parker seemed at least 10 years too old for the role of a top test pilot and Field, with the hair and eyebrows of Joan Crawford, seems totally uncomfortable with her underwritten part. Price plays Taggart, a self-serving opportunist, who challenges Jeff for leadership of the survivors from what appears to be the beginning of

an alien invasion. "Whoever did it has won the war," says Taggart balefully. "All they have to do is move in and take over." The strong supporting cast includes Fisher favorite Thorley Walters as a bumbling drunk, Vanda Godsell as his wife Violet, who is sadly killed off too early, and a young Anna Palk, creating sympathy as a pregnant girl. David Spenser as the petulant teenager Mel, another of Lippert's concessions to the youth, is quite awful. The painfully low budget and three-week shooting schedule worked against the best endeavors of cast and crew but by accentuating the characters and subplot Fisher manages to hold attention for the better part of 62 minutes.

The early sequences are by far the most effective, despite the handicaps of poorly edited stock footage and wobbly plastic robots. The centerpiece is set in an abandoned inn and shot on a standing set at Shepperton, works very well, emphasizing the growing menace from outside and the frictions inside. Taggart spits lines like, "That's all we need, a cheeky kid and a pregnant girl!" as Jeff gradually emerges as the dominant male. Taggart has a much more realistic grasp of the situation than Jeff, and when the latter starts to spout lyrically about the future, Taggart brings the group back to earth with a sneering, "There aren't any rules, there isn't any order; we can make any world we like." The relationship between Taggart and Peggy is particularly interesting. Price first appears brandishing a gun, which he dismisses as necessary for the protection of Peggy, but it remains glued to his hand, and is in practically every scene thereafter.

Intriguingly but for no logical reason, Taggart has convinced Peggy to pose as his wife. "You and I made a bargain," he tells her later without further elaboration. He clearly regards Peggy as a possession, casually ordering her around, and when he makes his break from the group he abducts her at gunpoint. The lack of sexual chemistry between them is blindingly obvious; apparently, he is doing it simply to stop Jeff from having her. Taggart remains the only character who is more than a cipher; everyone else could have cards around their necks with the characterizations summed up as "hero," "girlfriend" and so on.

Taggart by contrast is an enigma: He is clearly intelligent and well bred, dressed immaculately throughout, even when asleep, yet he is as adept at the use of firearms as he is picking locks. He is also the only one not to reveal where he was when the gas attack started; when everyone else speculates on the reasons for their survival at length, Taggart ignores the question. Sadly having set up the intriguing situation, Fisher and Spalding do nothing with it. To his considerable credit, Price, helped to a large extent by a sympathetic director, turned Taggart into a particularly interesting character. He delivers a major performance in a minor movie, and is extremely effective at playing the duplicitous Taggart as a conniving, greedy villain whose character flaws lead to his own destruction and subsequent resurrection. The scene where Price leaps at the flames to save the now worthless paper money is particularly revealing, the realization passing over his face that he has gone beyond the pale is as subtle as it is final. In the confrontation between Taggart and Willard Parker, Price manages to evoke both revulsion and sympathy.

Fisher, who was never totally comfortable with science-fiction subjects, does well with the first appearance of the now undead Violet and he even creates suspense when the painfully slow-moving zombies trap Peggy. The film only falls apart in the last third when the heroes mount an impromptu attack on a radio antenna. Suddenly Fisher is directing an action movie. The carefully established atmosphere is lost amongst the poorly staged gung-ho stunts, and even the well sign-posted but chilling reappearance of Taggart fails to get the film back on track. Most critics who bothered to see the film sided with the *Kine Weekly's* dismissive "juvenile nonsense," and after a brief release it disappeared with out trace. Suggestions that *The Earth Dies Screaming* was to influence Romero's *Night of the Living Dead* can be dismissed despite a few superficial similarities.

The V.I.P.s could not have been a greater contrast to the two Lippert films; not only was MGM's lumbering soap opera a return to A movies for Price but, at over $4 million, it is the most expensive film on his crowded filmography. The original script called *International Affair* was written by playwright Terence Rattigan (in an attempt to relieve the tedium at a fog-bound London airport) and was supposedly based on an attempt by Vivian Leigh to elope with her lover Peter Finch. The couple allegedly got stranded at Heathrow waiting for the fog to clear, which allowed Laurence Olivier the chance to retrieve his errant wife. When MGM cast Richard Burton as a lovesick but neglectful husband and Liz Taylor as his faithless wife, the film took on a life of its own. Amongst the stars vying for screen time are Orson Welles, Louis Jourdan and Rod Taylor, while Margaret Rutherford, Maggie Smith and Michael Horden provide staunch support. The director was former Gainsborough contractor Anthony Asquith, who had made *The Millionairess,* and cast Price as Commander Millbank, personal assistant and general dog's body to Burton with whom he shares most of his scenes. Essentially it a peripheral role he plays with quiet aplomb in a huge film. That MGM managed to double their investment on the initial worldwide gross was due largely to the media circus that continued to stalk Burton and Taylor, rather than any inherent quality of the film. With such an underdeveloped character, Price was largely ignored by the ballyhoo and the film did little to halt the general decline in his career.

In 1963 London-born Richard Gordon made *Devil Doll*, a minor but effective tale of a psychotic ventriloquist and his malignant dummy, not dissimilar to Von Stroheim's *The Great Gabbo*. *Devil Doll* top-bills Bryant Haliday, an actor who worked for Gordon again in *The Projected Man* and *Tower of Evil*, and was shot in black and white for less than $50,000 — modest even then. The director was Canadian maverick Lindsay Shontoff who would spend the next 30 years making either the most entertaining or the most risible British exploitation

Curse of the Voodoo

pictures, depending on your perspective. Although it wasn't popular with critics *Devil Doll* was successful enough to merit a follow-up and Gordon reunited his director and star for *Curse of the Voodoo*, adapted from the original script *The Lion Man* by Brian Clemens under the name of Tom O'Grady.

With a narrative that spans two continents, *Curse of the Voodoo,* on paper at least, was a more ambitious film, and certainly Clemens script makes more than a passing nod to the Val Lewton RKO movies of the Forties. The film opens in darkest Africa where Haliday's big game hunter, Mike Stacey, and his companion Major Thomas (Price) are stalking a wounded lion through the bush. The hunters fall afoul of the isolated Simbazi tribe, who hold the beast sacred, but Stacey dismisses the idea that the witchdoctor has cursed him. On returning to London Stacey is tormented by apparitions ranging from being chased by a lion to encountering a Simbazi tribesman on a London bus! The only way he can be freed from the curse is to return to Africa and kill the witchdoctor—a task he completes by running him over with his jeep. Unlike *Devil Doll,* where Shonteff creates moments of unease and genuine frisson, *Curse of the Voodoo* has a rushed and amateurish feel, and only in the closing sequences, as Stacey runs out of ammunition, is there any sense of tension. Even with a limited running time Shonteff fails to overcome the clichéd script and a microscopic budget, which required a rainy Regent's Park in central London to stand in unconvincingly for the African plain. One can't fault Gerald Gibb's effective cinematography but even he can't fully compensate for the obvious inserts of

African footage and the generally slow and uninspiring direction of Shonteff. Haliday, who is more of a screen presence than an actor, is genuinely unsettling in *Devil Doll* but wooden here, and Price, despite second billing, has his screen time limited to African sequences at the start and end of the film. *Variety* described Haliday and Price's performances as "robotic," concluding, "as suspense, flat acting and trite story add up to soggy thrills and as a shoestring production it's pretty threadbare." Looking back four decades years later, Producer Gordon admitted, "It's not the film I would like to be remembered for," but he remained convinced about his cast:

> I thought that Bryant Haliday was well enough known in England and that Dennis was a good name—particularly for a low budget movie and he would help sell it to the circuits. He did a very good job, he was in good shape at that time, physically I mean, and I thought he gave a very good performance.

Given the general standard of his movies it was hardly surprising that Price then reported for B movie king Harry Alan Towers for his version of Agatha Christie's creaking stage play *Ten Little Indians* directed by George Pollock. Towers was a one man film industry and over the years produced dozens of movies ranging from *Fu Manchu* to *The House of Usher* and practically everything in between. Dealing almost invariably with exploitation subjects in the public domain, the typical Towers movie mixed the same ingredients: sex, violence and a smattering of familiar, if fading, names in cameo parts. His films also relied heavily on overseas financing and complex pre-sales deals across numerous countries, which led to a distinctive eccentricity in locations and cast. Towers seldom let a good idea slip, and this version was to be the first of three attempts at the tale, with diminishing results over the years.

Ten Little Indians

Sticking to the traditional route of bringing a motley crew of people together in a remote location, Towers opted to exploit tax breaks and shoot in a

Dublin mansion dressed to double, rather unconvincingly, for a castle atop a snow-covered Alpine peak. Predictably the cable car is out of action and the 10 guests are marooned on their mountain perch to hear the reading of a will, a narrative device which was already old hat when it turned up in *What a Carve Up!* Promising what the press book calls "an international cast of leading players," including has-been pop singer Fabian playing a has-been pop singer called Mike Raven, Stanley Holloway as a famous detective, Daliah Lavi as a well-known actress, and Price as Dr. Armstrong who, in common with everyone else, has a guilty secret to hide. Television's Wyatt Earp, Hugh O'Brien, has top billing while Shirley Eaton provides the glamour and Leo Glenn adds menace as the shifty General. The veterans in the cast all try their best but the film crawls interminably towards its predictable conclusion, with O'Brien and Eaton seemingly the only survivors. Justifiably ignored now, the film has one minor claim to fame: the William Castle-like gimmick of stopping the action with a ticking clock and giving the viewers 60 seconds to guess the identity of the murderer. A voiceover encourages viewers to discuss who did it with the person in the next seat while being subjected to a painful re-run of the crimes. Anyone with a passing acquaintance with Christie adaptations will not be surprised to learn that the killer is in fact the Judge, appropriately named U.N. Owen, played with affable eccentricity by Wilfred Hyde-White, who removed himself from suspicion by faking his own demise. The whole thing is rather too lightweight and cheaply produced to make any impact, thus deserving its lukewarm reception. George Pollock retired from the business soon after the film opened.

Price and Ian Carmichael in *World of Wooster*

Price then enjoyed an unexpected career revival playing the obsequious gentleman's gentleman, Jeeves, in the BBC's hugely popular comedy series *World of Wooster*. Adapted from the mannered but witty writings of P.G. Wodehouse, the series starred Ian Carmichael as the upper class twit Wooster—an older version of Stanley Windrush—and was intended to run for six episodes. Eventually it stretched to three years giving Price the security of employment he hadn't enjoyed since his Rank days, a situation he didn't take for granted:

> This role of Jeeves is the best opportunity I had for a number of years. I know damn well they tried to get other people

before they turned to me but when I was offered it I took it with open hands.

Price's BBC contract guaranteed him a respectable but hardly generous $1,000 per episode, which had risen to $1,750 by the last series; but it did prevent him from appearing in any other television productions during the show's run. (Carmichael, the bigger star, was by the last show earning over $2,750 per episode.) The show's unexpected success brought Price critical plaudits and sacks of fan letters but he was as modest as ever about his achievements. When a journalist for the *Sunday Express* asked about his days as a film star, he said:

> They are behind me now, dear chap. The truth was I was inflated too high for my worth. I had some damn good parts and a very reasonable income but I don't think I could have kept going as a lead. I wasn't born with the kind of looks that last. And let's face it, there is no use being an over-aged juvenile lead. You must always look to the future.

British films had little to offer him beyond the modest little comedy *Just Like a Woman* in which he revived his smooth-talking salesman act, luring housewife Wendy Craig into parting with her money for (of all things) state of the art bathroom appliances. At the time Price was living in Curzon Street, Mayfair, a very exclusive address, and his gambling was, by his own admission, "out of control." He simply didn't have the money to support his lifestyle and, unable to curtail his spending, made the remarkably commonsense decision to relocate somewhere more affordable. Price chose to leave London once and for all and move to the remote island of Sark, a UK dependency but part of the tax haven formed by the Channel Islands. Years later he scolded a reporter who suggested he was avoiding his tax obligations:

> Quite ridiculous, my dear, and untrue; I am subject to tax as is any other British subject. I'd have gone to live in Switzerland like many others if I had other intentions.

In the same article he extolled the virtues of the tiny island which even today has no roads or airport:

> It doesn't seem strange that we have no cars on the island. You just get the buggy on the wharf to handle your baggage. Otherwise you walk. Very pleasant—but not so different from life in any other part of the country; I do what everyone else does when at home; I play some golf, go to the pub and watch television.

To take full advantage of Sark's tax status, Price had to limit the time he spent working in mainland England; over the next few years he restricted himself to cameo appearances filmed over a couple of days on the mainland or in Europe. AIP's *Those Fantastic Flying Fools*, which was filmed at Ardmore Studios in Ireland, features him in what was hailed—by the producers at least—as "the most fabulous entertainment event of the year!" Adapted from Jules Verne's science-fiction novel *De la Terre a la Lune* (*Rocket to the Moon*), the film owes its style and presentation to the success of the far better *Those Magnificent Men in Their Flying Machines*. AIP's effort features the fast action and slapstick humor, but on a far lower budget. The AIP brand, more often associated with Vincent Price horror flicks, also disguises the presence of Harry Alan Towers lurking behind "Jules Verne Films Ltd," a company specifically formed for this film. Filming in Ireland forced a location switch from Verne's Florida setting

to Victorian England, or more precisely Wales, where American showman P.T. Barnum is building a giant cannon capable of firing a capsule, piloted by the midget General Tom Thumb, to the moon. Fuelled by nationalistic pride, Price's Duke of Barset (a character lifted from an Anthony Trollope novel) forms a committee to usurp the money, grab Barnum and secure the moon for the British Empire. Their efforts are undone by the pantomimic villainy of Terry-Thomas, obligatory in this type of film, and his sidekick Lionel Jeffries, who are determined to turn the project to personal advantage. A rousing score by John Scott and assured direction from Don Sharp fail to negate a dumb script and a labored performance from leading man Troy Donahue. Even a steady parade of reliable British character actors, including Graham Stark and Edward de Souza, as well as Towers favorites Daliah Lavi and *Goldfinger* actor Gert Frobe, fail to enliven proceedings. Another Towers regular Klaus Kinski was announced but replaced by Joachim Teege. Price adds dignity to the role of the bemused and frustrated aristocrat, but one wishes the filmmakers had been more adventurous and cast him in the Terry-Thomas role.

Price enjoyed the location work in Ireland where he felt at home with the pace of life, the abundance of Guinness and good company. The British authorities, for reasons best known to themselves, chose that particular moment to present the actor with a summons for unpaid taxes. A tax officer flew from London to the film's location with a final demand for settlement of all back taxes within seven days and this time there was no question of reaching an out of court settlement. A very shaken and contrite Price was summoned back to London to attend bankruptcy hearings. The trial proved an ordeal, and he was unable to give precise answers to the questions raised by the official receiver, Mr. Norman Saddler, so the press took the view that the actor was being deliberately evasive. The following exchange between the two men was typical of the whole proceeding:

Sadler: "Do you know it is a criminal offense not to make a full disclosure of your assets?"

Price: "Yes I know that."

Sadler: "Cannot you produce any confirmation at all?"

Price: "I don't know exactly at what betting shop, which racecourse or which card table I lost it."

Sadler: "You have no friends who will come along and tell the Official Receiver in confidence that they have seen you lose those large sums of money?"

Price: "I don't think so."

The Court heard Price had two creditors, Inland Revenue ($28,900) and his accountant ($700). Price's solicitor also confirmed he had gambled away more than $8,300 and spent some $51,400 between April 1, 1965 and May 3, 1967. Also disclosed were Price's household accounts: $300 per month on entertaining and $90 per week on taxis and cars. The result was a foregone conclusion and Price returned to Sark bankrupt. He told reporters he wished only "to put my sad little house in order and avoid my most inept gambling passions."

Harry Alan Towers again came to Price's assistance by introducing him to the eccentric Spanish director Jess Franco whose work includes such delights as *The Girl from Rio* and *The Blood of Fu Manchu*. Despite a brief association with Orson Welles, Franco devoted much of his energies to flirting with extremes in both the porn and horror genres. His frantic, comic book approach to sex and violence, highly individual camera work and refusal to pander to mainstream sensibilities won him legions of fans, and at the same time isolated him both from industry colleagues and a more general audience. The quality of his work varies so dramatically that it is difficult to gauge whether he was an untalented amateur or a gifted visionary. Whatever his faults Franco developed a genuine affection for Price and an admiration for his work, and proved a loyal employer at a time when the actor's health was failing and his drinking was becoming excessive. Towers and Franco had collaborated on a script called "Black Angel" about a black jazz musician whose obsession with a mysterious white woman leads to his destruction. Franco originally envisioned a small, personal film, partly as a tribute to some of his own jazz heroes, but Towers' predilection for multinational finance deals forced a series of compromises. The biggest casualty was the premise. After snapping up the North American rights, AIP warned Towers that its audience wasn't ready for an interracial relationship.

The redraft has a white trumpeter called Jimmy Logan stumbling across a naked body washed up on a beach and recognizing her as Wanda Reed, whom he had earlier seen participating in a bizarre orgy. "Man it was a wild scene," says a bemused Logan as Wanda is tortured and whipped by lesbian dominatrix Olga and her playmates Kapp and Ahmed. "But if they wanted to go that route, it was their bag." From here the story embarks on the standard revenge plot as Wanda, now a succubus, avenges herself on her tormentors. Franco's handling of the narrative makes for a memorable if confusing film, weaving flashbacks and flash-forwards with surreal imagery, hallucinatory dreams and slow motion sequences, all intermingled with his trademark zooming camera and soft focus lensing. AIP then hit on the idea of promoting Leopold Von Sacher-Masoch's novel *Venus in Furs* as the film's source, despite the fact that the book wasn't widely read in the U.S. Franco reluctantly agreed to introduce the motif of animal furs and shot several sequences with Wanda clad in furs or dragging a fur coat behind her. AIP also insisted on the casting of television star James Darren as Jimmy and black cabaret singer Barbara McNair as his

Price as Kapp. a playmate of the orgy-loving Wanda (Maria Rohm) in *Venus in Furs*.

love interest. (Apparently it was acceptable to have a white man with a black lover but not vice versa.)

To satisfy the European backers, the role of Wanda went to Maria Rohm (aka Mrs. Harry Alan Towers), with parts for Margaret Lee (English-born but popular in trashy European exploitation) and Klaus Kinski, playing the bat-eared, blood-drinking Ahmed. Aware that Franco's movies seldom opened in the UK, Towers suggested Price as Kapp who rips the clothes from Wanda in the opening sequences and holds her down for Olga's lesbian assault. Price's main contribution, Kapp's death scene, is one of the highlights of the film. When his dirge-like piano playing is interrupted by the appearance of Wanda, complete with furs, a brunette wig and stockings, Kapp allows himself to be lured into the bedroom for some fetishistic foot kissing. Shot mainly with mirrors, Franco alternates between lingering caresses and sharp cuts as Wanda works Kapp into a frenzy of excitement until he "orgasms" with a heart attack. It's a stunning and erotically charged sequence elegantly played by Rohm and Price, who maintains his dignity throughout, never removing his jacket and tie! Surprisingly, he looks relaxed and distinguished, if slightly ruddy-cheeked. Franco thought he enjoyed his experience:

> He told me he liked the story very much and liked the way that I was approaching it; he wasn't in the least bit put off by

the subject matter. I had him for four or five days so he got to know Maria Rohm well and I think that they had a mutual respect for each other, certainly there was affection and it comes across in the death scene. Dennis is so good in that and he knew exactly what I wanted; we didn't need to discuss it or analyze it, Dennis got it right away.

Shot across Europe in Rome, Marbella and Istanbul, with Price's scenes filmed in Barcelona, the film looks wonderful but displays the very best and the very worst of Franco's work. Several sequences have a genuinely decadent and unsettling feel, but the director's penchant for soft focus and endless zooming defuses any real tension and quickly undermines the suspension of disbelief. The score by Manfred Mann and Mike Hugg is quite stunning and shows Franco's obvious love of jazz. Neither Price nor Kinski are given much to do but lend the film considerable presence and seem to convey the fetishist perversity that Franco requires. The rest of the cast is pretty disappointing, particularly James Darren who is dreadfully wooden. The dialogue is quite unfathomable. At one point Jimmy Logan asks no one in particular, "How do you run from a dead person unless you are dead yourself?" How indeed? In fairness to Franco, he may have been at the mercy of his dubbing editor, but Darren's lifeless delivery certainly doesn't help.

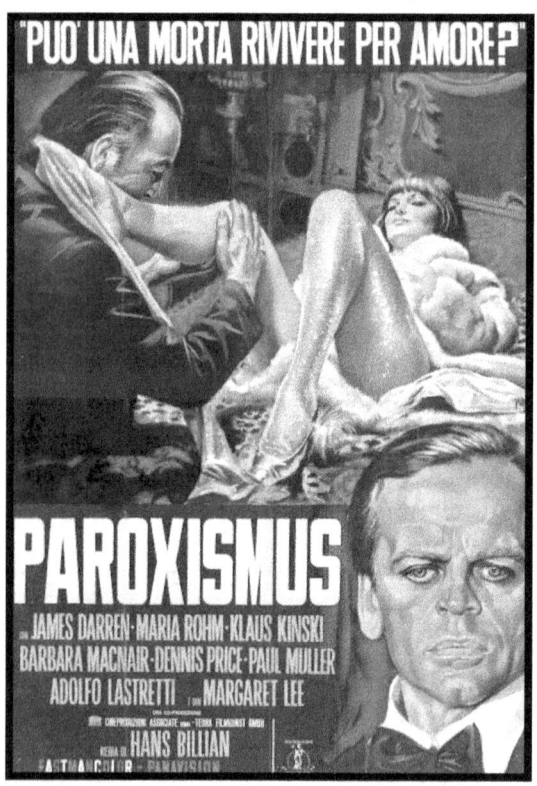

Overall it is an interesting rather than an impressive film, but one of which Franco was particularly proud; it also marked the high point in Price's collaborations with the Spaniard. In the U.S., AIP wanted nudity and didn't mind kinkiness but were shy of a possible "X" certificate which would severely restrict the audience. The film was cut accordingly, but that didn't stop them selling the film as a porno-thriller. It received some interesting notices: *Variety* noted that it was a "slickly-produced, soft-core vehicle of sex, sadism and lesser fetishes." Not quite the "masterpiece of supernatural sex" promised on the posters, the film did marginal business. In Europe, where it was cut and packaged more for the art-house circuit, the film was far better received.

Price returned to Britain briefly for a few days work on *Horror House,* a stalk and slash movie marking the inauspicious debut of Michael Armstrong, known mainly for the infamous *Mark of the Devil.* Written under the much more evocative title "The Dark," Armstrong's script is a grisly whodunit with strong psychosexual undertones set in a seemingly deserted, crumbling mansion. The original script follows the exploits of a group of teenagers spending a night in the house and discovering far more about the darker side of their personalities than anyone should know. The complex interplay between the characters and the sexual politicking made an intriguing backdrop for the "madman on the loose" front story. Tony Tenser's Tigon outfit had already produced *Witchfinder General* with AIP and optioned Armstrong's script for what they envisioned would be the next in a series of co-productions with the American company. Initially Armstrong was overwhelmed with enthusiasm for the project:

> I met with James Nicholson and Samuel Z. Arkoff at AIP and they told me how much they liked the film, then Tony introduced me to their man in London, Louis "Deke" Heyward, who also said he loved the script. Hands were shaken, contracts were signed and commitments made. I thought this was how all films were made—what a fool I was!

Still expressing total support, Heyward suggested the film needed more punch at the box-office and wanted Boris Karloff added to the mix—ignoring Armstrong's protests that there was no suitable role. To accommodate the octogenarian horror icon, Armstrong reluctantly expanded the minor part of a police inspector but still Heyward wasn't content:

> Boris needed to be seen as a red herring which was absurd; he was very ill by then and confined to a wheelchair so it was hard enough to imagine him as a police inspector, never mind a knife wielding maniac! "Deke" decided that if I wasn't going to do it he would, so he ripped up page after page of my script and inserted all these ridiculous scenes with Boris, his knife and his wheelchair. They were desperately awful.

By now the film had been cast with AIP contract player Frankie Avalon taking the lead, supported by Jill Haworth, a fragile English actress better known from Otto Preminger films. British-based actors, including Robin Stewart and Julian Barnes, make up the rest of the teenagers. After the initial upset over

Karloff, Armstrong was settling in to the mechanics of making the film, but Tenser's arrival at the Southport location added another twist to the already convoluted saga, as the producer remembered:

> By the time we came to film, Boris was just too ill to even start the picture. I contacted a few people to see who was available and the first one to call back was Dennis Price's agent who offered me Dennis at a very reasonable rate and I thought, he's a name, why not?

Tenser found that he couldn't have been more accommodating:

> We had a very low budget and we didn't do *per diems* or things like that. There wasn't the money but in Dennis' case his agent insisted that he had a crate of Guinness every day he worked for us. It was actually written into his contract.

With the residuals for *Wooster* drying up, three days work for Tenser seemed ideal, but the "above the title" billing hardly reflected the size or significance of the role. Nor not did it give any indication of just how misused Price would be. Armstrong continued:

> Even with Dennis quite able bodied they didn't change the script or at least the Heyward version of the script. The idea of Dennis in a wheelchair produced howls of laughter! But that's what they—I mean Heyward—wanted. I had nothing to do with these scenes but I still needed a policeman in my version so Dennis effectively played the part twice, once with and once without the wheelchair. It was quite ludicrous, they had the character popping up everywhere, in the nightclub, at the party—there would be a knock at the door and in wheeled Dennis Price!

Having finished shooting, the producers, who were less than satisfied with the final product, removed Armstrong from the film; additional scenes were then shot involving George Sewell and randomly edited into Armstrong's footage. The end result is a mess, a pointless and inane horror flick, with what little remained of the homoerotic subtext and tension dissipated by some sloppy rewriting and poor editing. A catchpenny title, *Haunted House of Horror*, was added by Tony Tenser shortly before the UK release, with AIP opting for the more succinct but equally tacky *Horror House*. Luckily for all concerned the wheelchair scenes were all excised from the final cut, but Price's few remaining scenes are still superfluous, arbitrarily inserted without any regard for structure or logic. Understandably Armstrong has few positive things to say about the film, but he does remember his brief association with Price with warmth:

> He was delightful, very charming but he kept to himself. I would go into his room every morning and he would have a crate of Guinness and we would sit and chat. By that time he wasn't interested in what the film was or anything. He was paid "X" for "Y" days, and then he went off and spent his money—on more Guinness I suppose.

The film opened in the U.K. on a double bill with the gangster flick *Clegg* to dismissive reviews but healthy returns for Tigon. In the U.S., where it made up a bill with *The Crimson Cult*, another Tigon-AIP co-production and one that did feature Boris Karloff, the reviews were equally poor but the film did achieve modest returns.

In February 1969 Price was briefly reunited with Peter Sellers in *The Magic Christian*, directed by Joe McGrath. Intended as a comic satire on greed and materialism, the film depicts the human condition as seen through the eyes of Sellers' Sir Guy Grand, the richest man in the world and his adopted son Youngman, played with no discernable charm or talent by Ringo Starr. Price appears early in the proceedings as chairman of

a sycophantic board whose members are summarily sacked by Sir Guy and instructed to leave their pencils and lapel flowers on the table on the way out. It is a particularly pointless appearance in a film all but sabotaged by Sellers' outrageous interference and the gimmicky casting of his chums in a series of pointless cameos. Amongst those who should have known better are Yul Brunner as a transvestite cabaret singer, Raquel Welch as an S&M bondage bitch and Christopher Lee as, naturally, a vampire. The home-movie feel extends to the narrative, which borrows liberally from Sellers' earlier work, most notably the ending of *I'm Alright Jack*, but fails to generate any identity of its own. Sellers wanders through the unfunny vignettes, exhibiting only detached boredom. Interestingly McGrath first met and befriended Sellers in London over a decade earlier at a public screening of *Your Past Is Showing*, a far better satire about the nature of greed. Any humor there may have been is lost in the self-indulgence, and the tagline "The Magic Christian is: anti-establishmentarian, antebellum, antitrust, antiseptic, antibiotic, antisocial and antipasto" is about as witty as it gets. Even a soundtrack written and performed by Paul McCartney couldn't save the film from deserved obscurity. The title incidentally refers to Sir Guy's luxury cruise ship.

Price's next film for Jess Franco was far more interesting. *Vampyros Lesbos-Erbin des Dracula* features the Spaniard overindulging in his two favorite obsessions, sex and death, wrapped for the sake of the box office in a fashionable lesbian vampire theme. In 1970 Franco and Towers hired Christopher Lee for *Count Dracula*, claiming it to be the definitive version, but the financial failure and the critical drubbing, particularly in Spain, persuaded Franco to end his professional relationship with Towers. Relocating to Paris, he took control of his own financial arrangements and began work on *Vampyros Lesbos,* nominally a Spanish-German coproduction. Franco claimed his film was inspired partly by Bram Stoker's short story "Dracula's Guest," an episode edited out of the novel *Dracula*, though the relationship between the film and Stoker is tenuous, to say the least. Filmed in Istanbul, Alicante, Barcelona and Berlin, the film again displays all the signs of cross-border compromise in the casting and its fragmented storyline. Stylistically Franco is as erratic as ever, the muddled narrative and bizarre symbolism suggesting an art film, while the full frontal lesbian couplings push it into porno territory. The trappings and presentation belong very much to the horror genre.

Price and Ewa Stroemberg in *Vampyros Lesbos*

Price plays the central role of Dr. Seward, the director of a private clinic whose obsession with the occult seems partly fueled by another patient, Linda Westinghouse (Ewa Stroemberg), an American suffering from memory loss and severe shock. We learn that Linda visited the remote island home of the sensual but melancholy Countess Nadina Corody (the hauntingly beautiful Soledad Miranda, sometimes billed as Susan Korda). It transpires that the Countess is a vampire who leisurely seduces her victims and then drains their blood. It seems Seward is already familiar with the Countess and her practices through one of his other patients, the hopelessly insane Agra. He reveals in his journal:

> The more I study the phenomenon of vampires the more I am drawn to their world. Its power stems from unknown depths, powers that are inaccessible to most of us. I can barely resist the temptation to cross over into the dark world of the supernatural.

We learn that Dracula himself saved the young Cordoy from rape by soldiers only to use her to satisfy his more bestial instincts. "Men still disgust me. I hate them all," she insists before speaking fondly of the Count: "It was wonderful how much he gave to me…" Franco's flagrant disregard for the conventions of the genre renders his vampire an interesting creation: Perfectly happy in daylight, she spends her days sunbathing nude on the patio and her evenings performing erotic cabaret in a local jazz bar. A beachfront villa replaces the Gothic castle, though Franco retains the dinner table, complete with blood-red candles. In a nice touch this vampire drinks wine, red of course, while a transparent black negligee and red scarf replaces the more traditional red-lined cape.

Seward soon emerges as an amalgamation of Stoker's Van Helsing, Seward and Quincey characters, with the nubile Agra clearly derived from Renfield. Curiously Seward never develops into the expected vampire hunter and, where Hammer films relied on the dynamic tension between Van Helsing and Dracula, Franco's hero is much more ambiguous. Price, who is mercifully remote from the more salacious scenes, is first introduced sitting in his study, musing, "The moon will be red as blood and the undead will step from the dark, looking for victims, ruthless and cruel." Seward's cunning plan is to use Linda to lure the Countess to his clinic and then demand initiation into the dark arts. Linda is a little put out by the prospect and hardly reassured when Seward announces with no real conviction that

> I'm one of the few people who know how to protect themselves. It depends on the desire to live and to free yourself. If you succeed in killing a vampire the body will vanish into nothing. The brain must receive a deadly blow. You have to split the head with an axe or pierce it with a bar.

It is unfortunate for the film's plot development that Seward hardly represents much of a threat to the Countess. Never a physical actor in his younger days, Price, at age 51 and weakened by years of drink and ill health, looks far too frail to match the athletic Corody. In the one scene where he is called into action, trying to subdue Agra, he looks awkward and fragile; later when attacked by Morpho he succumbs with barely a whimper. Contractually billed below both Miranda and Stroemberg (though in some later versions he is given top billing), Price acquits himself well, despite his physical limitations, and adds a solid and dignified presence to the core of a film that is sometimes frantic and vague. Sadly his dialogue is all dubbed into a gruff German dialect, robbing us of the melodious tones, which may just have saved such rubbish as "You have been chosen by the Spirits of the Night. I'm frightened of these powers—and yet I have to study the phenomenon." Whatever the voice, the sadness in his pale blue eyes is unmistakably Dennis Price and *Vampyros Lesbos* is arguably the highpoint of his work with Franco.

In 1970 Price made his first film for Hammer since *Watch It Sailor* but the company wasn't the force it once was. Their by-the-numbers horror movies were out of fashion and Hammer was finding it increasing difficult to adapt to a more permissive age. When *Frankenstein Must be Destroyed,* arguably the best and most intelligent of the series, had a disappointing box-office reception, James Carreras decided it was time to rethink the approach. *Horror of Frankenstein*, written by Jeremy Burham, was a straight reworking of the film that started it all, *The Curse of Frankenstein*, only this time the stalwart presence of Peter Cushing was replaced with a younger, sexier Baron (Ralph Bates). This was the first film under contract to Associated British Pictures Corporation (later EMI), which meant shooting entirely with British financing without the safety net of a pre-sell to an American distributor. After years of American finance and free access to the North American market, Hammer was returning to the dark old days when British films had to compete on their own merit; it was turning the clock back to the postwar days of Rank.

Carreras pressed on regardless but Burham's script pleased no one. The obvious person to re-work it was veteran Jimmy Sangster, now comfortably ensconced at his Los Angeles base. Sangster, having written many of Hammer's classic films, dismissed the idea out of hand, claiming, "I took one look at it and said why I would want to waste my time rewriting this? It's my own script. I wrote it 20 years ago!" As an additional sweetener Sangster was offered the role of producer which again he declined but, realizing he had the studio over a barrel, offered to return to England only if he could write, produce and direct. "A bit like being God!" he remembered, adding ominously, "Unfortunately there was no one around to tell me what would or wouldn't work." Relishing his new role(s), Sangster constructed a new approach:

> I can't say I had any burning desire to direct. It was just something I hadn't done before and the opportunity seemed too good to pass up. I didn't see the point in doing a remake of a film we had already done so I decided to do it as a send up. Hammer didn't seem bothered one way or another, they left me to it. I knew it needed to be different so I tried to make it funny and I tried to make it sexy.

Price and Joan Rice on the set of *Horror of Frankenstein*

The British censor had just redefined the "X" certificate raising the threshold age to 18 rather than 16, and this relaxation allowed filmmakers to push the boundaries on depicting sex—or at least nudity—and horror. Sangster's new Baron would make full use of both as he murders his own father to get his hands on the title, money and mistress, thereafter building a creature more to satisfy his own ego than any scientific curiosity. Along the way he makes improper use of Hammer starlets Kate O'Mara and Veronica Carlson. It is Price's obsequious "body snatcher" who gleefully furnishes the Baron with the spare parts to assemble his monster, and he is clearly having fun with a meatier than usual role. Sangster's earlier work shows what can be done with a well-delivered line but *Horror of Frankenstein* shows that he was no Robert Hamer or even Terence Fisher. Too often the director loses his way and falls back on heavy-handed slapstick rather than wit. As a straight remake the film may have worked: It has some interesting things to say about moral corruption and has a good cast, particularly Bates and Kate O'Mara. Perhaps the less said about the creature played by Dave Prowse the better. Sangster was realistic about the film's limitations:

> I have to confess I have never had such a good time on a film. I loved every minute of it but I have to say it wasn't much of a film and I guess that's my fault; I simply didn't make a very good movie. I certainly can't blame any of the cast who were all very good. Dennis was a dear man, a very sweet person and very grateful for the part, I think he was a little hard up by then. He had been a big, big star but I don't think he was working very much; Joan Rice who played his wife was in the same position. I certainly didn't write it with Dennis in mind. I didn't write it with anyone in mind but he was such a good actor, he could turn his hand to anything.

Price and Joan Rice make an appealing double act and have the deftness of touch to prove that at least some of Sangster's lines are actually quite humorous. Particularly effective is the scene where quick-witted Price sits by the graveside, singing and eating his dinner while his naive and trusting wife digs down to the coffin, motivated by Price's patronizing promise of another baby, "if every thing goes well!" Later when Price asks his wife to re-read the gruesome newspaper reports of a boating accident, his eyes are wide with manic glee as he chuckles, "I love that bit. The good Lord has been kind to us, luvvy." In his scenes opposite Ralph Bates, Sangster allows Price to mug furiously, a style of broad humor not out of place here. The constant muddling of the correct form of address—"Your Grace", "Your Lordship", "Squire"—is a running joke milked beautifully by Price, who goes on to draw a wry smile from "Would you be more interested in male or female? No offence, Squire, you meet some very strange people in my line of work." Price then gushes enthusiastically about the delivery of a batch of bodies: "Not sure about quality but you won't have any complaints about the quantity, that's for sure!" It is Price's clumsiness, in dropping the "perfect brain," which unravels the Baron's plans and the body snatcher ends up in the Baron's acid bath. It is only after Price's departure from the film that one realizes that he was carrying the humor, and the remainder of the film is leaden and lifeless. Prowse's lumbering, inarticulate creature could serve as an apt metaphor for the film itself. Sangster, openly dismissive of the film, was also ambivalent about Price:

> He came in probably for a couple of days, certainly no more than three, and we shot all his stuff at the same time, I think it was all around the castle anyway. He was a very pleasant

man, no airs and graces, certainly no suggestion of a big star slumming it. He was very professional but by then his career was more or less over, both he and Joan Rice had done so much in the past that they knew exactly what they were doing; they didn't need any input from me. Anyway this was low budget filmmaking, Price did what was asked, he said his lines and made sure he didn't trip over the furniture.

With an ending that left the way open for a sequel, Hammer felt that the gamble on a new Baron had paid off and Bates was heavily touted as their latest horror star. The distributors were less impressed and played down the humor by promising patrons that a "new young Frankenstein sheers the screen with excitement." In Britain Price was featured prominently in the trailers and advertising but, while American audiences were promised that their ticket "entitles them to be frightened out of their wits, at no extra charge," the actor wasn't mentioned at all. Sadly the film proved out of step with public tastes on both sides of the Atlantic and flopped. From now on Hammer was going to find it increasing difficult to get its films into American cinemas.

If Price was frustrated by being very good in a poor film, nearly a year later he had the consolation of a minor part in one of Hammer's superior efforts, *Twins of Evil*. After humor failed to ignite the box-office, Hammer went back to it's more straight-faced horror trademark. Hammer's relatively comfortable

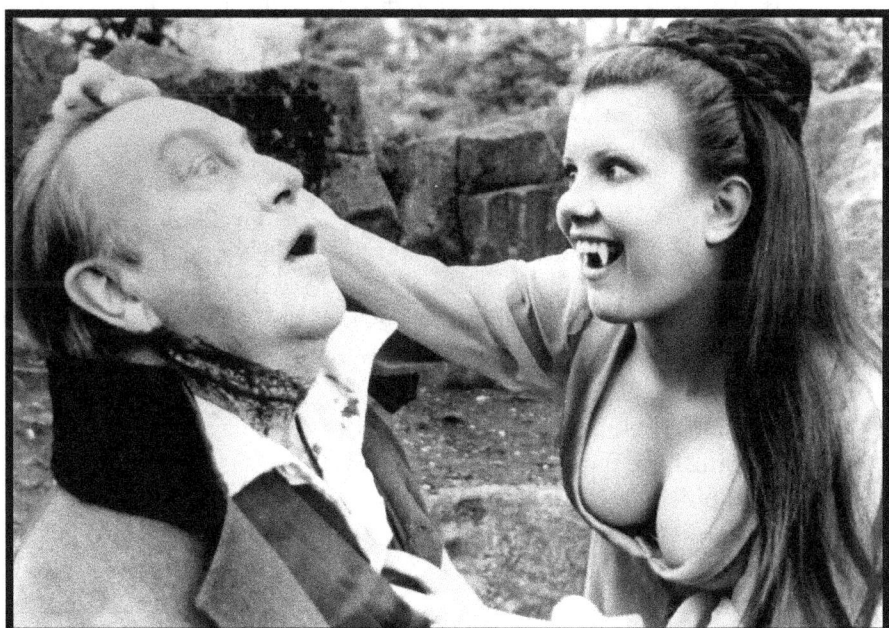

My what big...fangs you have. Price with one of the Collinson sisters in *Twins of Evil*.

financial position, albeit it precariously balanced, meant it had the relative luxury of finance at a time when the rest of the British film industry was scrambling for the last few dollars. The company became a haven for independent filmmakers keen to push the sedate British horror movie into previously uncharted territory and produced some of the most inventive horror movies for over a decade, *Countess Dracula*, *Hands of the Ripper* and *Dr Jekyll & Sister Hyde*.

Producers Harry Fine and Michael Style, together with scriptwriter Tudor Gates, had sold James Carreras on a version of Sheridan Le Fanu's 19th century novella *Carmilla*, a sedate vampire tale, which predated Bram Stoker and introduced an undercurrent of lesbianism to the genre. Setting up an independent unit, Fantale Productions, but operating under the Hammer umbrella, the three men crafted the sensual *The Vampire Lovers* directed with some style by Roy Ward Baker and featuring Peter Cushing and the voluptuous Ingrid Pitt as the predatory Carmilla Karnstein. The film proved a surprise box-office hit, due in no small part to its full-frontal nudity. A sequel, *Lust for a Vampire,* commissioned while its predecessor was still in production, with an unenthusiastic Jimmy Sangster at the helm, flopped despite an interesting cast and strong storyline. By then Gates had identified a minor character in the first two films as, in his words, a "potential Dracula in waiting, a great way of spinning out future films." With Hammer's blessing, Gates built the third film around the decadent Count Karnstein.

Using Hammer veterans to direct the previous films had been a mixed success and Fantale now turned to television director John Hough to inject style and energy into what was probably the strongest script of the three. Damien Thomas plays Karnstein, one of those aristocrats bored with womanizing and mock black magic who is on the lookout for something new — in this case, vampirism. No sooner has Karnstein started his reign of terror than he comes up against the Brotherhood, an organization of religious fanatics under the leadership of the mildly psychotic Weil (Peter Cushing). Members of the Brotherhood like nothing better than spending the long winter nights burning local wenches at the stake and are only too happy to switch their attention from witches to vampires. Weil's beautiful nieces (*Playboy* centerfolds Mary and Madeline Collinson) become pawns in the ensuing power struggle between the zealots and the vampire lord.

To retain some loose continuity with the series, Camilla reappeared (naked, of course) nominally to induct her descendant into the ways of the vampire, but the whole vampirism theme is extraneous to a plot which would have worked just as well presenting Karnstein as a sort of cross between the Marquis de Sade and Lord Byron. Gates added layers to his narrative by bringing in such incongruous (for a Hammer film, anyway) themes as religious paranoia, bigotry and class warfare. Hough's visual flair and an overwhelming air of moral corruption and sexual hypocrisy make *Twins of Evil* far better than the average

action-horror movie of the period. Cushing headlines but Price all but steals the early part of the movie as Dietrich, major domo to Karnstein and procurer of the after dinner "entertainment" usually involving young girls. Although he is killed off relatively early in the proceedings, stalked and murdered by a buxom vampire, Price was given second billing, and in many of the European territories it was only Cushing and Price who were quoted in the publicity! Tudor Gates remembered the casting of Price was a happy coincidence: "Dennis' agent was a friend of Harry Fine, so he was cast really as a favor," but conceded, "We thought we were very lucky to get him." It is a view shared by John Hough:

> First and foremost he was a name, he had been a big star earlier on; in fact that is the reason he gets major billing—he gets billed above the Collinson twins on the film. Although he was cast because he was a name he was adaptable; he had been a leading man and now he was taking cameos and things; he was a fine actor and we were really thrilled to get him to do this part for us.

Hough was impressed with his commitment to what was really a cameo:

> He was impeccably behaved, very polite, very sweet if that is the word. He came in with no airs and graces and really cared

about doing a good job; he really did it all himself, right down to thinking about how his character would be dressed. He picked the clothes himself and made sure he didn't outshine Damien which he could easily have done but instead he chose a very discreet style, relatively anonymous, so it wouldn't overpower the Karnstein character. He could easily have overdressed for the character.

Damien Thomas, who appeared in most of Price's scenes, agreed:

> Dennis was an absolute delight to work with; it was one of the highlights of my career. I got to know him very well and we had dinner several times during the making of *Twins of Evil* and despite all the trials and tribulations he had been through, he never once complained. He wasn't in the best of health during the making of the picture, he had difficulty walking, he was in constant pain from his legs but he was never less than cheerful and charming.

Shooting at Pinewood (*Horror of Frankenstein* had been shot at Elstree) meant the sets were not only bigger, but the whole film has a more sumptuous feel. To accommodate Price's frailties all but one of his scenes had to be shot on the elaborate castle set and walking kept to a minimum. Despite the difficulties Hough was impressed with Price's professionalism:

> He didn't need any direction from me, he was a "one take man," everything was just one take, and he got it so right all the time. Those marvelous little looks he had all the time really make an impact. He didn't need a lot of direction from me, one line or two and then he got it. I always thought that there were shades of Olivier in the way he played the character so introverted. Whenever Olivier played a subsidiary character he played it deep down within himself and that is what Dennis did; his sheer acting skill was marvelous.

With fine performances throughout and Hough's lively direction, the film enjoyed a reasonably successful run in the UK but flopped in the States where the distributors, uncomfortable with the juxtaposition of gore and nudity, trimmed all of the sex and dumped an edited version on the market without much care or attention. Perhaps unfortunate to be compared with the likes of *Witchfinder General* and *Mark of the Devil,* both very different films, *Twins of Evil* is a worthy effort and more than justifies its extended life as a "late night movie" favorite for a generation of adolescents. The critics were divided and most delivered the usual negative reviews reserved for Hammer films, but the respected fan magazine *Bizarre* did vote Price their "Best Cameo" award.

Price's last film for Hammer was also his least, *That's Your Funeral*, a big screen adaptation of the limp television series of the same name. Price was cast as the outrageously campy Mr. Soul, caught up in a trade war between two rival firms of undertakers. Former Benny Hill director John Robins labored the double entendres and excruciating puns for all he was worth but the leaden script defeated even such normally reliable performers as Roy Kinnear,

Bill Frazer and Richard Wattis. Price could be grateful his screen time was so slight in a film hailed by the *Monthly Film Bulletin* as "another nail in the British film industry's coffin." Perhaps it wasn't too much of a surprise that the film's publicist found Price in a reflective mood. The pressbook quotes him saying:

> One looks in the mirror and one realizes one has lines, grey hair and three chins but there is nothing worse than trying to hide one's age. When people are paying you a great deal of money it is unthinkable that one is not ready to work when required, to that one queries the boss—the director—or that one doesn't bother to learn one's line. Frankly I've always felt grateful to be allowed to work.

Richard Gordon then recalled Price from his Sark hideaway for one day's work on the enjoyable, if gory, *Horror of Snape Island*. Price plays Bakewell, a British Museum curator, who sends an unwary and mismatched team (including Bryant Haliday, Jill Haworth and Anna Palk) to the remote Snape Island.

Price sends archeologists Ben and Nora Winthrop (Derek Fowlds, Anna Palk), Adam Martin (Mark Edwards) and Rose Mason (Jill Haworth) to Snape Island.

One would think the brutal slaughter of some teenagers in an earlier sequence would be something of a dis-incentive but Bakewell still imagines that a little archaeological digging is required. Despite the soap-opera characterizations, the film works as a straightforward "monster on the loose" movie, and director Jim O'Connolly (perhaps best known for *Berserk!*) does a creditable job of creating atmosphere on the fog-bound sets. Sadly Price, seated behind a desk throughout, is given little opportunity to exercise the wit that marks his other associations with Gordon. Nevertheless, despite the constraints of the part and his own physical condition, Price's commitment to his craft was undiminished. Richard Gordon remembered:

> He was happy to be in the film and I was very happy to get him for this cameo. Dennis was one of those people—and he reminds me of Boris Karloff—in that, if he took a role he would give it his all and treat it the same way as he would a big picture or a big role. Otherwise he wouldn't have accepted the part.

Resuming his friendship with Jess Franco, Price took top billing for the first of two appearances as Baron Frankenstein in *Dracula vs. Frankenstein* (aka *Dracula Contra Frankenstein*, *Dracula Prisonnier de Frankenstein* and *The*

Screaming Dead). Franco's film features the vampire hunter Dr Seward who believes he had rid the world of the Count (Howard Vernon) in the opening reel by plunging the proverbial stake into his heart. Unbeknownst to Seward, no sooner has he left the castle than Dr. Frankenstein arrives with his mute servant Morpho (another character name left over from *Vampyros Lesbos*, this time played by Luis Barboo). The Frankenstein monster, looking vaguely like the Universal creature, is on hand to provide the requisite blood sacrifice, a far from innocent-looking cabaret singer, while the Baron reveals his scheme for world conquest. Dr. Seward teams up with a gypsy woman, Amira, to thwart the Baron—and this bizarre movie takes yet another twist when she unleashes a werewolf to battle the forces of darkness. Logic clearly wasn't high on Franco's agenda but, for anyone struggling to get a handle on all of this, the English language version has a convenient voice-over; otherwise there is surprisingly little dialogue.

Ignoring Franco's customary frenzied camera work and weird visuals, the familiarity of the principal characters make the film much more accessible to international audiences, and it is sometimes confused with the infantile Al Adamson movie *Dracula vs. Frankenstein* starring Lon Chaney, Jr. Generally taken by most viewers as an homage to the old Hollywood monster bashes, Franco's film contains at least one genuinely disturbed moment when what appears to be a live bat is drowned in synthetic blood; otherwise the comic book quality is rather endearing and Franco makes good use of the locations in Spain and Portugal (and interiors shot in Paris). For Price the role was at least a decade too late; tired and unwell he presents a feeble Frankenstein with none of the polish and wit one had come to expect. That Franco would want to use the actor despite his obvious physical deterioration can be considered proof, at least the director's mind, that Price had some marquee value. Unlike most Franco movies, *Dracula vs. Frankenstein* received a release in Britain where the censor cut it down to 87 minutes and issued an "X" certificate. This horrendously dubbed version gave British cinemagoers a taste of what the former leading man had been up to during his sojourns in Europe.

Luckily Price was committed elsewhere when Franco quite literally threw together *La Fille de Dracula*, the second of his Dracula-Frankenstein trilogy with Howard Vernon again donning the cape for a quickly shot, messily staged sequel. Exactly why Franco thought a second installment was necessary isn't clear but he delivers his usual patchwork of the bizarre, the perverse and the visually stunning, with the best moment coming when Vernon is staked through the forehead rather than the heart!

Even less necessary was a third outing, which Price wasn't lucky enough to escape. *La Maldicion de Frankenstein* (aka *Les Experiences Erotiques de Frankenstein*) presents Price's Baron pottering around a sparsely equipped laboratory in a decidedly Hispanic castle, putting the finishing touches on his latest monster (the oddly silver-colored Fernando Bilbao). Assisted by the faithful Morpho (Franco himself), the Baron has no sooner finished his work than he is attacked and bitten by Melisa, a blind half-woman/half-bird creature. A creation of the Baron's arch rival Cagliostro (a confused looking Howard Vernon), Melisa comes complete with feathers, talon and attitude. Leaving Frankenstein for dead, Melisa takes the monster to Cagliostro's villa where she tells her master he will be employed "raping beautiful virgins to satisfy your desires, and their bodies shall serve you for your experiments."

Learning the fate of her father, Frankenstein's daughter swears revenge but not before she and Dr. Seward conspire to revive the Baron, momentarily, to dispense some advice and guidance. Poor Price then has to endure the indignity of being shocked back to twitching life care of a "deep incision ray." What follows very much apes the style of the Italian erotic comic strips—*fumetti*—a style that has yet to catch on else where in the world. Franco never allowed a little thing like good taste to get in the way of his visuals, and amongst the more outlandish pleasures, he offers cannibalism, copious nudity, bondage and flagellation (all spread over several versions and, depending on which part of the world you are in, each more explicit and nonsensical than the last). Looking understandably bewildered, Price's contribution is restricted to lying supine on the laboratory slab and dispensing cryptic words, care of some very poor dubbing. Even for a reanimated corpse, Price looks in poor shape, far older than his years, puffy and overweight; and for once he can't even rely on the good fortune of being killed off early. Played with a tongue firmly in cheek, the film may have got by as an entertaining horror spoof but it would have needed a new script and decent acting. If that wasn't enough, the pitifully low budget and dreadful editing effectively killed off any ambitions the director may have had and the film was thought to be un-releasable outside of Europe.

Price took a day off from Frankenstein duties to shoot what would be his last film for Franco, appearing as Lindsay in *Los Amantes de la Isla Diablo* (aka *Quartier des Femmes* or *Devil's Island Lovers*), a confusing prison drama which, like many of Franco's films, exists in two completely different versions, one French and one Spanish. The former dispenses with most of the narrative and beefs up the running time with some prolonged torture sequences, while the latter is much more character driven (talky and surprisingly prudish). In both versions, Price appears in the opening sequence where he is summoned to hear the deathbed confession of the prison governor. Asked if he is the lawyer he answers, "Yes, but older and more alcoholic than when we first met." The story then unfolds in all its grim detail, and Price next appears at the conclusion, shuffling through the castle in a vain attempt to save the titular lovers. Patchy and amateurish even by Franco's standards the film sat on the shelf for two years before finding some late night bookings where its "women in bondage" theme attracted a less fussy audience. For those who did see it, Price's physical deterioration is hard to watch and he seems to be somewhat "distracted." Franco put it more succinctly:

> He was drunk before we started shooting; he started as soon as he arrived on set and continued all through the day. I liked Dennis but we never really discussed his personal life; he certainly didn't seem unhappy or troubled. I suppose it was his way of relieving the boredom. I have to say Dennis was never any trouble; he could always play his scenes and knew his lines. I don't know what kept him going, maybe he needed the money or maybe needed to work.

Price made five pictures in all for Franco (he was announced for a sixth, *The Bloody Judge*, but didn't appear in the final version) and by no stretch of the imagination do they represent the best of either actor or director. Unpredictable, unstructured and outright strange, Franco's films can be disturbing, stunning or bewildering but seldom boring; and while it is to the Spaniard's credit that he did try to push Price into new and interesting roles long after most of the industry had given up on him.

Around the same time as he was saying his farewells to Franco, Price told *The Sun*, "I have lived a disgraceful life but I enjoyed it, by and large, and the least I can do is devote the last years of my life to making amends." Price's idea of "amends" was to take whatever was offered irrespective of quality.

The best thing that could be said about *Go for Take* was that it gave Price the relative luxury of shooting at Pinewood, which must have been a relief after those drafty Spanish castles. Intended as a vehicle for the dubious talents of television "comedian" Reg Varney, star of *On the*

275

Buses, the film features two brainless numbskulls on the run from the Mob after running up large gambling debts. Hiding out in a film studio they attempt to earn enough as bit actors to repay the gangsters. With absolutely no magnetism between the leading duo, the film is little more than a series of predictable and unfunny episodes, with Varney grimacing through costume changes, drag acts and stunt misfires. Price, spoofing his new-found horror star image, appears as Dracula, or at least a hammy horror star playing the role, menacing the nubile Julie Ege. The actress, who had served her time with Hammer and would encounter a marginally more credible Count in *The Legend of the Seven Golden Vampires*, remembered Price as,

> Very amusing and even though we only had small parts he was very professional. He was a real English gentleman, very proper though I think he may have been a little lonely. There was an air of sadness about him but he never talked about it and kept himself to himself.

It was a depressing comedown for the once mighty Rank Organization but at least it allowed the filmmakers free access to the back lot which, along with a cast of familiar faces including Melvyn Hayes, Anouska Hemple, Sue Lloyd and Aubrey Morris, lent the film some appeal for nostalgia buffs but probably no one else. Very different was *The Adventures of Barry Mackenzie,* adapted from a comic strip in the satirical magazine *Private Eye* and directed by Bruce Beresford (who would find himself more at home making Hollywood films such as *Driving Miss Daisy*). The titular character Barry (Barry Crocker) is an unsophisticated Australian coming to the "mother country" who falls prey to a series of dishonest and conniving British stereotypes. Mackenzie reacts to each encounter with a bemused detachment and an unending stream of colorful euphemisms covering a variety of bodily functions. His attempts to find a toilet are typical: "Now listen, mate, I need to splash the boots. You know, strain the potatoes. Water the horses. You know, go where the big knobs hang out. Shake hands with the wife's best friend" and so on, seemingly interminably.

Price plays the patriarch of the distinctly odd Gort family who, mistaking Mackenzie for an eccentric millionaire, plot to marry him off to their plain daughter, Sarah. Gort's plans hinge on the couple playing "doctors and nurse" but when Mackenzie fails, despite his best efforts to consummate the affair, he is driven from the family home. Whatever the merits of the film, Price seems to be having fun. It is obvious from an early berating from Mrs. Gort who wears the trousers in the relationship, and that Gort takes some satisfaction from that situation. "You great bone-headed fool," she snaps, then seeing his obvious pleasure sneers, "you filthy old perv."

A graduate of the appropriately named Whippington Grammar school, Gort is soon outfitted in a schoolboy uniform, imploring a confused Mackenzie to instill "a touch of iron discipline." The humor here rests on the absurdity of the otherwise respectable Gort bending over his desk pleading for a flogging, a joke Beresford thought so good that it is repeated a few scenes later. No opportunity for a double entendre is missed and Gort apologizes for his excesses by saying, "I don't know what nearly came over me." With the usual targets--homosexuality, aristocracy, television and the police—lining up, there isn't a lot of subtlety in a film, which mistakes vulgarity for satire and relies almost totally on profanity for its laughs. To the disbelief of critics, *The Adventures of Barry Mackenzie* managed to earn some $1 million in its initial release, a considerable achievement for a low-budget comedy and more than enough to ensure a sequel, *Barry Mackenzie Holds His Own,* which again stars Crocker, this time around traveling to Europe and encountering Donald Pleasence as Count von Plasma.

Price was then asked to play more or less the same character in a much better film, marking his third and most memorable collaboration with Richard Gordon. The truly bizarre *Horror Hospital*, directed with unashamed gusto by Antony Balch, stars Michael Gough as the maddest of mad scientists Dr Storm who hides his fiendish activities behind the front of an innocuous country rest home. The dinner table, lined with zombie-like victims of his lobotomy experiments, betrays Storm's true purpose. Price plays Pollack, a sleazy travel agent-cum-blackmailer who uses the ad line "Storm your way back to health" to lure victims into Storm's clutches. Pollack's seedy office at "Hairy Holidays"

HORROR HOSPITAL

attracts the interest of Jason (Robin Askwith) who, as Pollack tartly points out, "could do with a few early nights." Only Price could dismiss claims that Jason can't afford an expensive holiday by ogling his crotch, winking and purring, "If you change your mind about that trip to the Bahamas, come and see me and we will work something out together." Of course Pollack can't resist a little extortion on the side. "Blackmail is such a strong word," Pollack chides the equally demented Aunt Harris. "After all, none of us are perfect, are we?"

Ever the dandy, Pollack, flower in buttonhole and hat doffed, toddles happily from Storm's mansion, clutching his envelope of ill-gotten five-pound notes, only to be brutally decapitated by a lethal limousine—a sequence that has to be seen to be believed. *Horror Hospital's* script, written by director Antony Balch and Alan Watson, manages to be both an homage and pastiche of the classic horror movies of the 30s and 40s, combining every horror staple imaginable, from creepy mansions and zombies, to lunatic scientists and homicidal dwarfs. To get his leading villain into the right frame of mind, Balch screened old Bela Lugosi movies for Gough, and the film is certainly pitched at those with a fondness for both the era of Hollywood's mad doctor movies and a healthy sense of humor. Supplementing the twisted narrative, Balch added generous twists of gore and sex, creating a movie that manages to ooze both sleaziness and riotous fun, all for less than $100,000! Previously Balch had only one credit, the equally odd *Secrets of Sex*, also with Gordon, and was better known as an independent film distributor. Although the fight scenes appear amateurish, Balch handles most of the action with surprising confidence and a great deal of humor. Gough, Price and Ellen Pollock (as Aunt Harris) all seem to be vying with each other to chew the most scenery and are given a delightfully free rein by their director. Price's drinking was causing concern as Richard Gordon notes:

> I wouldn't denigrate Dennis's memory but by this point his drinking could be a bit difficult and you had to be careful to ensure he wasn't doing it when you weren't looking. On *Horror of Snape Island* it hadn't been a problem because he was there for such a short period of time. On *Horror Hospital* we tried to shoot most of his scenes in the morning.

Robin Askwith also remembered Price's drinking:

> He was a fascinating man, incredibly interesting and utterly charming. He would arrive on the set and ask how long before he was needed, this was a little set at Battersea Town Hall and remember this was a low budget film so there weren't exactly a lot of facilities. The assistant director would say something like "10 minutes" and Dennis would disappear behind a screen, unpack this big black bag that he carried around with him and there would be a clinging of glasses and bottles followed by "glug, glug, glug." Dennis would pop out 10 minutes later, wink and say, "Just a spot of script revision, dear boy." Then he would be word perfect!

Askwith dismissed any suggestion that Price could be difficult on or off set: "He was near the end of his life really but he was very sweet and very homosexual, and of course I was young and pretty then, so we got on great." Gordon, who as a fan had watched Price in movies from his Rank days, retains only fond memories of their professional association:

> He was a fine man and I was very fond of him. When we finished filming, he wrote me a lovely letter when he got back to Sark, saying how much he enjoyed doing *Horror Hospital* and how grateful he was. It was a very sincere letter and I valued it very much.

The *Financial Times* called the film "A piece of brilliant surrealist film making…a film of genuine individuality and style." As a measure of Price's standing in Europe, the actor was billed above Gough and Vanessa Shaw in all the publicity, while Robin Askwith wasn't mentioned at all! Price's health was already failing before he finished *Horror Hospital* and, although he would complete two more films, both would be released posthumously, arguably representing the best and worst of the actor's last decade.

Price as Snipe in *Theatre of Blood*

Theatre of Blood stars Vincent Price as a homicidally bad Shakespearean actor, Edward Lionheart, murdering in graphic detail the critics who deprived him of their annual Best Actor Award. Directed with considerable pace and black humor by Douglas Hickox, the film is a thinly disguised retread of the much less satisfying *Dr. Phibes* movies, utilizing the revenge theme and structure of elaborate set-piece murders—in this case modeled after Shakespeare's plays. The film adopted the tagline, "its curtains for his critics!" for once reflecting both the tone and content.

Price was cast as Hector Snipe, the bitchiest of the critics whose sole comment on hearing that his colleague has been ripped apart by vagrants is "a headline rather than a by-line." Snipe is then lured to an abandoned theatre (shot at the derelict Putney Hippodrome) by a heavily disguised Diana Rigg and there confronts the demented actor. While Lionheart reads out some of the damning reviews, Snipe warbles away, oblivious to his imminent demise. Snipe's last "appearance" is as a lump of raw meat dragged behind some horses, a la Hector in *Titus Andronicus*. Featuring an all-star cast including Jack Hawkins, Ian Hendry, Diana Dors and Arthur Lowe, the film is witty and intelligent with energetic performances by Vincent Price and Diana Rigg. Hickox directs with flair, and if the premise starts to wear thin before the last murder, the enthusiasm of the cast never wanes. Madeline Smith, who is one of the few to appear throughout the running time, remembered that it was the same off camera:

> I think the producers had very little money; they spent it all assembling this amazing cast. But anyway they made us all work ridiculously long days, I mean really long days. That scene where we were all in Ian Hendry's flat was shot at 11 o'clock at night. No one complained, no one moaned; all these famous actors just got on with it. They were all very cheerful and charming and never for one second forgot what we were there for.

It is refreshing to see Price more than hold his own against a stellar cast and surprisingly, given the subject matter, the film found considerable favor with the public as well as the critics; more than one reviewer thought Price's performance worth a mention and many compared it favorably with his earlier work.

Sadly this could not be said for his last film, *Count Downe*, sometimes known as *Son of Dracula*, conceived and written for Ringo Starr, who was trying to launch a film career. The "story," for lack of a better term, has the offspring of Dracula traveling to England to claim his inheritance as "Overlord of the Netherworld" and pursued by Dr. Frankenstein who believes that he, not Count Downe, is the rightful heir. Downe in the meantime falls in love with a human, Amber, and decides to renounce his birthright and pursue the life of a pop singer instead. Financed by Apple Films, it is every bit as bad as it sounds despite the presence of professional actors such as Freddie Jones as Dr. Frankenstein and Suzanna Leigh as Amber. Price has the misfortune of playing a decrepit Van Helsing, while the dog's breakfast of a script also finds room for Ringo as Merlin—complete with pointed hat and wizard's beard. Noted horror film director and Oscar-winning cameraman Freddie Francis had the unenviable responsibility of directing the whole thing, a task he remembered as being more like the work of a ringmaster:

> It was one of the strangest films I was ever involved with. Ringo sent me the script, which I have to say was more than a little odd but it had David Bowie attached as the lead and he was a very, very big name then. Ringo said I could change the script as much as I needed to, so I brought in a friend of mine (Jay Fairbank, also known as actress Jennifer Jayne) who did a pretty good job. Somewhere along the line Bowie dropped out and Harry Nilsson came in and then just before we were due to start Ringo told me it was going to be a musical. This was literally the eleventh hour.

The movie was not much more than a poor excuse for pop stars to hang out together and indulge themselves. Francis endured long periods of inactivity waiting for the leading players to show up on set, but he recounted that everybody had to grin and bare it:

> It was really hard for the actors like Dennis Price who were used to a more structured way of filmmaking. Actually it was hard for us all. I can't say anyone complained about it, we all just had to put up with it. I did feel for him though…Dennis wasn't in good shape and he was older than the others so he probably felt it more.

For Suzanna Leigh, who was no stranger to B movies, the whole thing was a depressing experience and, as she recorded in her autobiography, Price was equally disheartened: "My life has taken me through some bad times recently my dear and this is my Waterloo. It will be all right for you, Suzanna, you are young enough to be able to wait for 10 years or so. But, for me, it's over." A little melodramatic perhaps, and he may have infused one too many brandies at the time, but Price's words were prophetic. Much to the relief of those involved, *Count Downe* was never properly released but it wasn't without its admirers: *Cinefantasique* described it as "fun," noting that Price "underplays Van Helsing...his performance somehow balances out the overplaying of the others." The *Hollywood Reporter* found it "a surprisingly serious, even intellectual, adaptation of horror film mythologies."

In August 1973, soon after completing his work on *Count Downe*, Price was admitted to the Princess Elizabeth Hospital in Guernsey, having broken his hip in a fall at his cottage in Sark. He had struggled on despite circulatory problems in his legs and difficulties with his liver, but weakened by years of abuse, his body was simply worn out. He was confined to bed and made as comfortable as possible but, with complications setting in, he slipped into critical condition. Dennis Price died at the Queen Elizabeth on October 6, 1973, the cause of death listed as heart failure. He was 58.

The obituary writers were, on the whole, kind. John Whitley, writing in *The Sunday Times,* said that he had shown promise but too quickly:

> Retreated behind his own mannerisms and became the natural fall-guy, the smooth talking, ever-presentable villain whose offers anyone could refuse, who never quite got his hands on the loot...Though his character studies were often beautifully observed, he never seemed to find the director who would push him into top gear for a whole film, and in later years especially, he allowed himself to coast through performances by relying on his natural charm and sense of style.

The Times identified him as "an intelligent and sensitive performer—at times too sensitive for the hurly-burly of filmmaking." A measure of how little impact British films had made on the U.S. market was evidenced by *The New York Times* obituary which was limited to one short paragraph headed up, "Dennis Price, Actor, Dies: Appeared in Many Movies." Price would probably have approved of the simplicity of that. In the 1950s he had summed up his career with characteristic modesty in an interview with the *Sunday Express*:

> That film about Lord Byron was the turning point, I suppose. The critics slated me. I still have the stories papering the walls of my bathroom. The critics really pulled the plug on me that time. It was probably just as well. You know, when you are reasonably young you have a revolting conceit of yourself—

and then suddenly you find that what you have set out to do isn't going to work. After that film I realized that I would have to get down and be a character actor playing bishops and butlers.

His memorial service, paid for by Alec Guinness, was held at St. Martins in the Fields Church, where a simple plague was mounted on the wall, quoting:

Dennis Price
"Kind hearts are more than coronets"

If you enjoyed this book write for a free catalog:
Midnight Marquee
9721 Britinay Lane
Baltimore, MD 21234

or visit our website at
WWW.midmar.com

www.ingramcontent.com/pod-product-compliance
Lightning Source LLC
Chambersburg PA
CBHW071224080526

44587CB00013BA/1491